The Coinage of the Roman World in the Late Republic

Proceedings of a colloquium held at the British Museum in September 1985

edited by

A.M. Burnett and M.H. Crawford

BAR International Series 326

1987

B.A.R.

5, Centremead, Osney Mead, Oxford OX2 0DQ, England.

B.A.R. -S326, 1987: 'The Coinage of the Roman World in the Late Republic'

ISBN 9780860544203 paperback
ISBN 9781407345970 e-book
DOI https://doi.org/10.30861/9780860544203
A catalogue record for this book is available from the British Library
This book is available at www.barpublishing.com

CONTENTS

		Page
	Introduction	iv
	Acknowledgement	vii
	Abbreviations	viii
One	Celtic Chronology in south Germany, by B.E. Overbeck	1
Two	Spain, by R.C. Knapp	19
Three	Sicily, by M.H. Crawford	43
Four	Macedonia, by I. Touratsoglou	53
Five	Thrace, by O. Picard	79
Six	Southern Greece, by M.J. Price	95
Seven	Asia Minor, by P. Kinns	105
Eight	Syria, by H.R. Baldus	121
Nine	Egitto, by A. Gara	153
Ten	Crete and Cyrenaica, by T.V. Buttrey	165
Eleven	Africa, by A.M. Burnett	175

INTRODUCTION

I

Roman conquest did not necessarily bring Roman coinage in its wake. The modern commentator may find it surprising that the growing Roman empire did not have a single integrated monetary system, and the first aim of the papers given at the colloquium was to characterise the extraordinary variety that is encountered in the different provinces during the late Republic, from the defeat of Hannibal in the west and increasing Roman involvement in the east until the beginning of the reign of Augustus. These surveys therefore include many of what have traditionally been regarded as "Greek" or "Celtic" coins, since these were in fact produced entirely in a period of Roman control.

A second aim was to define the extent of Roman influence over and intervention in these varied currencies. Roman intervention can be seen clearly, for instance, in the demonetisation of the Hannibalic War coinages in Spain and Italy, in the demonetisation of Punic gold and silver in 146, in the cessation of cistophoric minting in Asia in 66, or in the adoption of Roman types on the bronze coinage of Bithynia in the 50s. Such cases as these, however, seem to be exceptional and, generally speaking, the Romans adopted (or adapted) whatever they happened to meet, as in many other areas. The arival of Rome had no immediate effect on the coinage of Asia Minor, Cyrenaica or Egypt, and no effect at all on the bronze currencies of Africa or Cyrenaica, two areas which were left for several centuries to make do with their pre-Roman issues. Elsewhere local coinages were adapted to meet Roman needs. The Asian cistophori were only gradually Romanised in function, while the coinage of the Syrian kings was made into the Roman provincial coinage of Syria.

Against this pattern there was a gradual increase in the role of the denarius. Initially confined to Italy and Sicily, its importance spread in the second century to Spain and Africa; to Greece from the early first century; and to Asia during the civil wars and to Syria, perhaps, during the reign of Augustus, although it never attained the same monopoly in these latter areas. As far as one can tell, Roman denominations seem to have followed the adoption of Roman coinage; Roman units of reckoning are known from Sicily and Spain from an early period, and arrived elsewhere, e.g. in Asia or Syria, perhaps with the arrival of the denarius. Even so they did not completely replace the existing local systems, which might be adapted to fit in with them, as one can see from first century Tauromenium or imperial Asia and Egypt.

Thus the process of Romanisation was only gradual, and there is no trace of a concerted policy for the currency of the provinces as a whole. From time to time measures were taken to deal with particular problems, as instanced above, but these are exceptions which stand out.

The fact that the Romans did not impose their own coinage on their empire, raises an important problem of interpretation. How can we tell that a locally produced coinage was Roman in inspiration and purpose, or that it was produced by a particular city to meet its own needs? As a rule of thumb, it seems plausible to think that larger, higher value coinages were "Roman", e.g. the Aesillas tetradrachms of Macedonia or the Antioch tetradrachms of Roman Syria, but that smaller, low value coins were "local", e.g. the restricted bronze coinages of numerous small communities throughout the empire, produced to meet a variety of local expenses like the distribution of largesse. Between these two ends of the spectrum, however, it is very difficult to define the role of the different coinages. To what extent, if any, were Iberian denarii, Celtic gold and silver coins or Asian cistophori minted to meet local or Roman expenses? Who provided the bullion for them? These are, of course, not just questions of definition, but issues which affect our picture of the scale of Roman state expenditure, which might therefore be larger than just represented by "Roman" denarii.

II

To a certain extent these issues and the theme of the colloquium overlap with the contents of Michael Crawford's Coinage and Money under the Roman Republic (London, 1985), and the papers published here have a rather uneasy relationship with that book. The colloquium was held in September 1985 in the expectation that the book would have been published in the previous spring. In the event, however, publication was delayed until after the colloquium, so that the participants were able to take account of it only for the short period available for revising their papers for publication. That said, however, there are a number of disagreements between CMRR and the papers published here, which may therefore be regarded in a sense as a partial review.

The coverage of the volume is not complete. Some of the gaps are deliberate, some less so. The period, from Hannibal to Augustus, was chosen to avoid the complexities of the Second Punic War, a watershed in the currency of many areas, and to leave the Imperial currency of the provinces, where, for instance, chronology is less of a problem, on one side. Some areas are not included in this volume. Italy was excluded as having little "non-Roman" coinage, but accounts of Italian currency can be found in CMRR or in A.M. Burnett, 'The Currency of Italy from the Hannibalic War to the reign of Augustus', AIIN 29 (1982), 125-38. B. Overbeck, who was assigned the Eastern Celts, wisely decided to restrict himself to one area, given the complexities of eastern Celtic coinage; a paper was given at the colloquium by D.E.M. Nash on the Western Celts, but she was not able to publish it here. More information can be found in D.F. Allen and D.E.M. Nash, The Coins of the Ancient Celts (Edinburgh, 1980), although that book was written from a different standpoint and now suffers from the rapid changes in Celtic numismatics. Once again the relevant topics are treated in CMRR, as is the coinage of Massalia, which was discussed at the colloquium by C. Brenot.

III

To return to the two aims of the colloquium outlined above, it can be reasonably claimed that the first, the aim of characterising the diversity of coinage produced, has been substantially achieved. The second aim, to define Roman influence and intervention, has not been so successfully fulfilled, partly because of the very difficult problems of interpretation which arise. It is easy to show that the circulation of Roman denarii came to characterise an ever greater number of Mediterranean countries; but it is much harder to produce a satisfying picture of how denarii were used in the areas where they were present, for even in the East the evidence of inscriptions and literary sources is often inadequate and in the West it is almost wholly lacking. Hardest of all to demonstrate is the effect of the Roman presence on local issues.

Perhaps the most dramatic revision of accepted ideas is achieved by the paper of Overbeck; he is able to show that La Tène D1 is to be dated between the late second century and the 50s BC and in conseqeunce that in many areas north of the Alps Celtic coinage had disappeared before the Romans came to the scene.

In other areas Roman influence on local issues is clearer, for instance in Spain, Sicily, Syria, Cyrenaica and Africa, as emerges from the papers of Knapp, Crawford, Baldus, Buttrey and Burnett. In the present state of the evidence there remains much room for disagreement over the interpretation of the changes that were taking place.

But perhaps the most important feature of the colloquium is that it has defined fields where more work is urgently needed. The difference of opinion between Touratsoglou and Price over the dating of the bronze coins of the Macedonian regions and the Macedonian cities can only be resolved when the relevant hoard evidence is fully obtained. At the moment, *non liquet*. Similarly the interesting questions raised by Gara will only begin to be answered when someone has sat down and worked out the arrangement for the Augustan bronze coinage of Egypt from scratch, instead of depending on the unsatisfactory arrangement of Milne of half a century ago.

The different characters of the papers by Picard and Kinns are also instructive. The former appears to show city issues proceeding in unruffled calm under Roman rule as if nothing had happened. By way of contrast, Kinns is able to point to a variety of developments with substantial historial implications, despite the fact that much of the basic groundwork still remains to be done. Asia is undoubtedly an area where given the diversity of the source material, further work will pay rich dividends.

ACKNOWLEDGEMENTS

The colloquium was held at the British Museum, and we should like to thank the Director and Trustees of the Museum for their financial support. We should also like to thank Rozalyn Todd for her help in the preparation of this volume.

ABBREVIATIONS

ADelt	Archaiologikon Deltion
AIIN	Annali del Istituto Italiano di Numismatica
AJA	American Journal of Archaeology
AJP	American Journal of Philology
AMC	C.H.V. Sutherland and C.M. Kraay, *Catalogue of the Coins of the Roman Empire in the Ashmolean Museum* (Oxford, 1975).
ANRW	Aufstieg und Niedergang der römischen Welt
BCH	Bulletin de Correspondance Hellenique
BSFN	Bulletin de la Société Francaise de Numismatique
CAH	*Cambridge Ancient History*
CH	Coin Hoards
CPh	Classical Philology
CRAI	Comptes-Rendues de l'Academie des Inscriptions
Crawford, *CMRR*	M.H. Crawford, *Coinage and Money in the Roman Republic* (London, 1985)
Degrassi	A. Degrassi *Inscriptiones Latinae Selectae*
Essays Thompson	O. Morkholm and N.M. Waggoner (eds.), *Greek Numismatics and History. Essays in Honor of Margaret Thompson* (Wetteren, 1979)
Giovannini, *Rome*	A. Giovannini, *Rome et la Circulation Monétaire en Grèce au IIe siècle avant Jesus-Christ* (Geneva, 1978)
Grant, *FITA*	M. Grant, *From Imperium to Auctoritas* (Cambridge, 1946)
HSCP	Harvard Studies in Classical Philology
IGCH	M. Thompson, O. Morkholm and C.M. Kraay (eds.), *An Inventory of Greek Coin Hoards* (New York, 1973)
JNG	Jahrbuch für Numismatik und Geldgeschichte
JRS	Journal of Roman Studies
MMDAI	Madrider Mitteilungen (Deutsche Archaologische Institut)
NC	Numismatic Chronicle

NH	Numario Hispanico
PBSR	Papers of the British School at Rome
PrakArchEt	Praktika tes Arch. Etaireias
QT	Numismatica ed Antichità Classiche. Quaderni Ticinesi
Raddatz	K. Raddatz, *Die Schatzfunde der Iberischen Halbinsel* (Berlin, 1969)
RevPhil	Revue Philologique
RIC	Roman Imperial Coinage
RN	Revue Numismatique
RRC	M.H. Crawford, *Roman Republican Coinage* (Cambridge, 1974)
RRCH	M.H. Crawford, *Roman Republican Coin Hoards* (London, 1969)
SM	Schweizer Münzblätter
SNR	Schweizerische Numismatische Rundschau
Svoronos	I.N. Svoronos, *Ta Nomismata tou Kratous ton Ptolemaion* (Athens, 1904)
Troxell, *LL*	H.A. Troxell, *The Coinage of the Lycian League* (New York, 1983)
Walker, *Metrology*	D.R. Walker, *The Metrology of the Roman Silver Coinage.* Vol. I (Oxford, 1976)
ZfN	Zeitschrift für Numismatik
ZPE	Zeitschrift für Papyrologie und Epigrafik

CELTIC CHRONOLOGY IN SOUTH GERMANY

Bernhard Overbeck

In 1981 Rainer Christlein gave a talk on recent Celtic archaeological discoveries in south Bavaria.[1] He spoke at the numismatic colloquium at Würzburg, but almost nothing was said on Celtic coinage. Nevertheless, his thoughts were the final conclusion of about 20 years of discussion about La Tène chronology, including the coinage. Anepigraphic as Celtic coins of this region are, there is only one way of establishing a reasonably sure chronology, the exact observation of the archaeological environment. In south Germany, there is one Celtic site, which as an oppidum of an immense size and certainly a tribal capital has always been in the focus of research: Manching near Ingolstadt.[2] All scholars used to agree on the chronology of this place, as presented by Werner Krämer, the excavator.[3] For him there was, at the beginning of his research, no doubt that the end of the oppidum was directly connected with the establishment of the Roman province of Raetia in 15 BC, the conquest of this region by Drusus and Tiberius. Bones of men, evidently fallen in combat, seemed to confirm his view, even though not a single Roman weapon, or a single arrowhead, was found.[4]

For celtic numismatics the coins found in Manching dated from La Tène C to D 1 and, one had to suppose, D 1 ended in 15 BC. The hoard of silver coins found in Manching was also naturally connected with the violent end of the place. These mere suppositions became fact in the literature on La Tène chronology. The earthenware pot, which had contained the hoard, was dated late by the so-called evidence of coins.[5] There were also consequences for the chronological arrangement of coins from other sites, and of course of other archaeological objects, as pottery, brooches, belt buckles etc. But there were some open questions, which contradicted this chronology: it was odd that the Manching coin types never occurred in the early Roman currency in and outside Raetia.[6] Further, there is another level of La Tène material, the La Tène D2 stage, which is not at all represented in Manching, although it is totally "barbarous", not romanised. In Krämer's first proposal of a chronology, this stage consequently was Augustan.[7] Archaeological evidence more to the West provided a new clue to the problem. Andres Furger-Gunti and Louis Berger proved that the D2 phase at Basel Münsterhügel succeeded the D1 phase at Basel-Gasfabrik (thereby also establishing the chronological arrangement of the potin coins of the Sequani), and that after D2 at Basel-Münsterhügel the next layer is Augustan. This sequence D1, D2, Augustan can also be observed at other sites.[8]

What are the historical conclusions? For Basel Furger-Gunti established that the end of Basel-Gasfabrik reflects the migration of the Helvetii to southern Gaul in 58 BC, and the beginning of the settlement at Basel-Münsterhügel their return after their defeat by Caesar. From his work we are therfore lucky to get a date which enables us to date not only these two places, but also the whole horizon of La Tène D1 and D2 in central Europe. One of them is Manching (for D1). To that phase have to be added certainly Hüfingen, Heidengraben, Altendorf near Bamberg,[9] the very important site of Pollanten,[10] and probably also, as far as the insufficient state of research permits, Kelheim[11], Straubing and Passau.[12] there is, however, one very important difference between Basel and all these other sites: there are otherwise no oppida and no settlements in the Raetian area succeeding the D1 sites. We have in south Germany from the D2 phase a few cremation burials at different sites, the finds of which differ from the archaeological remains of the D1 phase, and even fewer settlements, probably farms, but not a single oppidum.[13]

This cremation-burial horizon, the so-called Uttenhofen-Kronwinkl-Hörgertshausen horizon,[14] is in every respect very different from the La Tène D1 horizon. The pottery is of typically wheel-made Celtic form and design, but differs from D1 ware in the composition of its clay, which lacks the otherwise typical graphite. Brooches and belt-buckles are different too, and very typical is the extensive use of iron instead of bronze. From a comparison with the finds in germanic cremation burials from east Germany and even north Bavaria archaeologists concluded that the D2 stage in Bavaria was strongly influenced by germanic habits and fashion, and even by different living habits, as there are no oppida. But one has to suppose Celtic origin, as the wheel made pottery, significant for this group, shows is probable. This sparse east Celtic group settled in just some areas in the east of Bavaria and had arrived after the withdrawal of the D1-celts, the founders of the oppidum-civilisation.[15]

Thus archaeology shows us what Caesar reports for the west: pressed by German tribes from the northeast there was a Celtic movement from east to west. The best known examples, reported by Caesar, were the migrations of the Helvetii (58 BC) and the Suebi under Ariovistus in the west, which impinged on Gaulish affairs.[16]

After 58 in central Germany the D1 Celtic element never returned; the oppida as tribal centres and mints remained abandoned, and eastern Celtic settlers occupied only parts of the empty territories. Only in the west do we have evidence of a re-establishment of D2 oppida, evidently by the returning Helvetii, and evidence of the installation of new mints.

Except Noricum,[17] which evidently did not cease striking coins under the authority of local chiefs till the installation of the Roman province under Claudius, the end of the oppida-civilisation meant the end of autonomous coinage in central Europe, that is to say that the so-called Vindelician coinage ends in about 60 BC.

So far we have only answered the question of the end of independent striking of coins in south Germany; we can now try to give a more detailed account of the chronology of Celtic coinage from south German sites. One of the most important contributions to this problem is a study of Celtic burial-inventories from central Europe containing coins.[18] The following burials gave some clues to the chronological arrangement of south German Celtic coinage:

1. Giengen, Kreis Heidenheim (southeast Württemberg)[19]. The finds from this cremation burial include a small gold 1/24 stater with janiform head on the obverse and horse to left, with a human head above, on the reverse (cf. Fig. 1). The whole find can be dated to La Tène C1 of Krämer's chronology, i.e. about 250/200 BC, and no doubt represents the oldest phase of coin striking in central Europe.[20]

2. Dühren, City of Sinsheim, Rhein-Neckar-Kreis (north Baden).[21] This

inhumation burial is typical for the La Tène C2 horizon, about 185/70 - 120/05 BC in absolute terms. It contained one 'monnaie à la croix' of the 'Tectosagi-type' (silver), cf. Fig. 2.

3. Nierstein, Kreis Mainz-Bingen (Rhine-Hesse).[22] The finds from this cremation burial are typical for late C2/early D1 phase of Krämer's La Tène chronology and therefore can be dated to approximately 120-100 BC. This gives us an excellent clue for the dating of the 'Vindelician' rainbow cup (gold) it contained, cf. Fig. 3.

Hoards and their compositions give some more evidence on the chronological arrangement of the south German Celtic coinage:

4. The Lauterach hoard, found close to Lauterach in the vicinity of the Lake of Constance, in Vorarlberg/Austria. For a long time this hoard was misinterpreted[23] as a document of the Roman conquest in 15 BC. 24 Roman Republican denarii struck between 189 and 117/16 BC, give us the rare opportunity of dating the 3 Celtic silver coins in this hoard. The two local 'monnaie à la croix' pieces of south German origin and the 'Caletedu' quinarius must have been struck not very much later than around 120/100 BC, if we suppose that the hoard was buried not very much later than 100 BC.[24] This contradicts Colbert de Beaulieu's dating of the 'Caletedu' type to about 60 BC, which I can see no reason at all to accept.[25] This hoard also contained a pair of brooches, connected by a silver chain, a silver bracelet and two small rings (one silver and one bronze) (cf. Fig. 4).

5. The Schönaich hoard[26], found in the neighbourhood of an old road between Schönaich and Rohr, Kreis Böblingen (Württemberg) consists mainly of 'monnaie à la croix' silver of the same type as in the Lauterach hoard. This link puts the hoard into the same chronological level of about 120/100 BC as the Lauterach hoard. Further there is an interesting link to other hoards, as Schönaich contained a silver coin of the 'bushel' series[27] and two gold coins, one of them a typical rainbow cup quarter stater of the 'smooth type' with a cross on its concave reverse.[28]

6. The Langenau hoard,[29] Alb-Donau Kreis, Württemberg, is another example of a mixed hoard, containing gold and silver coins and two pairs of brooches, richly decorated by gold and coral balls. Its chronology is puzzling. On the one hand the silver brooches certainly belong to the La Tène D1 period, as does the rainbow cup stater, which is of the same bird's head/torques and balls type as the Nierstein specimen.[30] The bushel silver coins, although of an advanced style, would not contradict this date of about 100 BC. On the other hand, the hoard contains one silver quinarius of th NINNO MAVC type, attributed to the Rauraci, which shows a very different style, influenced by Roman design and stylistic perception, and so has to be later. Even if one does not agree with the arguments previously used for the chronology of this coin type,[31] one has to admit that it must be dated comparatively late, i.e. into approximately the time of Caesar's Gallic war.[32]

7. The Neuses hoard from Neuses, Gemeinde Eggolsheim, Kreis Forchheim, in north Bavaria[33] is comparable to the Schönaich and Langenau hoards (cf. Fig. 5). It too contains gold and silver. Of the four rainbow cup staters, there are three in Prähistorische Staatssammlung (cf. Fig. 6a-c). Two pieces have a bird's head, another has a dragon, and the fourth is the same type as the quarter stater in the Schönaich hoard (obv.: smooth, rev.: small cross). There are, in addition more than 400 silver pieces of two sorts:

firstly, different varieties of the 'bushel' silver coins with a 'naturalistic' or abstract head on the obverse and a horse with different attributes on the reverse, representing the silver unit of an average weight of about 1.8g (cf. Fig. 6d-e). Secondly, there were small silver pieces with an average weight of exactly a quarter (0.42/0. 45g) of the bushel unit. This 'hedgehog' type ususally has a hedgehog-like head on the obverse, a horse and different additional marks on the reverse (cf. Fig. 6f-g). The pot, which contained the coins[34] belongs to the La Tène C or early D1 phase, i.e. to about 100 BC, a date fitting neatly into the chronological framework we already have from the hoards discussed above.

We have so far looked at hoards of silver alone or mixed silver and gold; now we must turn to another group of hoards, consisting of gold only.

8. The most famous hoard, never completely published was found in 1858 in Irsching,[35] Kreis Ingolstadt, Bavaria, quite close to Manching. Originally of about 1000 rainbow cup staters, this hoard was dispersed and partly melted down in the Royal Bavarian Mint. Eighty-five pieces, a selection of all types represented in this hoard, are preserved in Staatliche Münzsammlung, München. These different types contain almost every design known of the 'Vindelician' type rainbow cups, from the bird's head/torques to the completely smooth types (cf. Fig. 7a-h), all shown in excellent steel engravings in Streber's publications.

9. Geographically, and by its contents, rather close to this hoard is another Bavarian hoard from Gagers, Kreis Aichach-Friedberg,[36] the oldest hoard known and published. It was discovered in 1751, and soon afterwards published in a copperplate engraving (Fig. 8), which has allowed the identification of those staters still preserved in Staatliche Münzsammlung, München (cf. Fig. 9a-f). There are two unique rainbow cup staters[37] in the hoard, one of them with a stag's head magnificently and independently designed. Much more important is the fact that there are mussel-staters of the Boii in this hoard, showing that these Bohemian gold coins are probably approximately contemporary to the 'Vindelician' gold.

10. In some way a parallel to the Gagers hoard is the St. Louis hoard near Basel, Switzerland, discovered in 1883 and recently studied and reconstructed by Furger-Gunti.[38] This hoard, another example of a hoard containing gold jewellery (torques, bracelets, rings) and gold coins, shows the same variety of 'Vindelician' staters and Boiian mussel staters, and in addition the ball staters of western origin, attributed to the Senones in the older literature.[39]

Both the Gagers and the St. Louis hoard contain mussel staters of the Boii, connecting this western group of hoards with the Czechoslovakian group. The most famous of these Boiian hoards is the Podmokly treasure[40] of about 30/40 kg of gold, which with its mixture of jewellery and coins was compared to the St. Louis deposit by A. Furger-Gunti,[41] and most probably belongs to the same chronological period.

11. One of the most interesting hoards recently come to light is the Niederzier deposit from Niederzier, Kreis Düren (Rhineland, Germany)[42], another combination of bracelet, two torques and gold coins, twenty-six Vindelician rainbow cup staters and twenty staters of the Ambiani.[43] This hoard was found during excavations inside a settlement which belongs to the Basel-Gasfabrik (La Tène D1) period.[44]

To sum up the evidence of these Celtic hoards and burials, one can emphasise that all these finds have to belong to the D1 phase: the small gold fractions to its beginning or even to La Tène C, the 'rainbow cups' and 'mussels' to D1. There is too no doubt that the local south German 'monnaie à la croix', the Neuses bushel-silver and its quarter denominations, has to be put into this period. In absolute terms this means a date of about 100 BC, or some years later to about 80 BC, if we follow the arguments of H. Polenz.[45] Only the Langenau hoard may be later, as it contained at least one later coin of the Rauraci. The 'bushel' silver of this hoard, too, is of a different appearance and may be rather late. In spite of Allen's general study of this type[46] there is certainly a need for a further, more detailed study of the different variations of it, based upon a much larger quantity of coins. One has to point out that, whatever coin one tries to date, there is no way of making any progress by looking at the weight of one or even a few pieces of the same type. Large scale investigations on the 'Vindelician' and Boiian staters, die comparisons[47] and metrology[48] may lead to a relative and more detailed chronology. The same may be the case for the silver, the 'bushel' silver and the 'monnaie à la croix' which has not hitherto been sufficiently studied.[49]

We can now go back to the starting point of this investigation and look at the coins found in Manching, insofar as they have been published.

I have already mentioned the 1936 Manching hoard,[50] which with its composition of different bushel silver and Caletedu-quinarii fits into La Tène D1. Another hoard[51], found in 1982/83 and preserved in Prähistorische Staatssammlung, München, is very similar to the Neuses hoard, containing bushel silver and its 'hedgehog' type quarters and further 'monnaie à la croix' of the Schönaich-type (twenty-eight pieces in all). Many of the bushel silver and the 'hedgehog' types are die-linked to the Neuses hoard, which confirms that both hoards belong to the same chronological period. There are also a lot of stray finds, probably including another dispersed hoard, most of them in Prähistorische Staatssammlung, München,[52] or the Ingolstadt Museum (Fig. 10a-m). This recently discovered material[53] shows like the hoards a large spectrum of all silver denominations, some 'Vindelician' gold 'rainbow' cups and western potin coins, including the Sequani-potin coins, which confirm what has been said above about the chronology: all of them belong to the Basel-Gasfabrik period,[54] i.e. all of them were made before the exodus of the Helvetii (cf. Fig. 10n).

Comparable to Manching are the archaeological finds from the Celtic settlement of Pollanten, mentioned above,[55] which also belongs to the D1 period. The silver coins found here bear many resemblances to the Manching material. Further, there are some new types of silver coins, which are not yet known from other archaeological sites (cf. Fig. 11a-g). Other places and *oppida* of the same archaeological level have already been mentioned. This whole Celtic world must have been disturbed - abandoned or destroyed - in the same sequence of events, which led to the migration of the Helvetii and was one of the causes of Caesar's war in Gaul. When the legions of Augustus arrived in 15 BC,[56] Manching and the *oppida* civilisation of this region did not exist any more, the mints of these *oppida* had ceased to strike gold and silver and a different, rather sparse population occupied the area.[57]

NOTES

1. R. Christlein, 'Zu den jüngsten keltischen Funden Südbayerns', Bayerische Vorgeschichtsblätter 47 (1982), 175-292 (cited as: Christlein 1982).

2. For general information - including bibliographical notes - on this, probably the most important, Celtic site in central Europe see: W. Krämer, Zwanzig Jahre Ausgrabungen in Manching. Ausgrabungen in Deutschland (Catalogue of the exhibition 1975) (Mainz, 1975), 287-297. The most recent commentary by the same author on the state of research in Manching is: W. Krämer, Die Grabfunde von Manching und die latènezeitlichen Flachgräber in Südbayern. Die Ausgrabungen in Manching 9 (Wiesbaden/Stuttgart, 1985). Note especially his remarks on the absolute chronology, p. 38ff. A short report in English has been given by W. Krämer: Antiquity 34, (1960), 191-200.

3. W. Krämer, Germania 37, (1959), 147ff. and Germania 40 (1962), 293-317, especially his table 1, p. 306: cited as Krämer 1962).

4. For discussion on this evidence see: Krämer 1962, 309 ff. For the problem of explaining the human bones scattered over the oppidum: W. Krämer, Die Grabfunde von Manching und die latènezeitlichen Flachgraber in Südbayern. Die Ausgrabungen von Manching 9 (Wiesbaden/Stuttgart, 1985), 36ff.

5. Numismatic report on the coin hoard: G. Behrens,'Kelten-Münzen von Manching', Berliner Numismatische Zeitschrift 1951, 217-222. There Behrens connects the hoard with the occupation of Manching by the Romans: "... Einnahme der Manchinger Festung im Jahre 15 v.Chr."

6. From the Augustan military site of Augsburg-Oberhausen there is not a single 'Vindelician' coin known, but only those coin types - as far as one can tell - which are typcial for the currency of the western provinces under Augustus: one bronze coin of the Bochum rainbow cup type, and bronzes of the Aduatuca type and of Germanus Indutilli L. Cf. H.-J. Kellner, 'Die keltischen Münzen von Augsburg - Oberhausen', JNG 27 (1977), 21-27.,

7. The discussion of this fact, the differences between La Tène and D1 and D2, is one of the main topics of Christlein. Cf. Christlein 1982, 279ff.

8. Report on the excavations by A. Furger-Gunti, 'Die Ausgrabungen im Basler Münster I. Die spätkeltische und augusteische Zeit', Basler Beiträge zur Ur- und Frühgeschichte, Bd. 6, (Derendingen-Solothurn, 1979). On the late La Tène layers, cf. especially p. 120-136. On the chronology of the Sequani potin: A. Furger-Gunti, 'Oppidum Basel-Münsterhügel', Jahrbuch der Schweizerischen Gesellschaft fur Ur- und Frühgeschichte 58, (1974/75), 106-109; A. Furger-Gunti, H.M. von Kaenel, 'Die keltischen Fundmünzen aus Basel' SNR 55, (1976), 35-76.

9. Cf. Christlein 1982, 277f.

10. Preliminary report by Th. Fischer, K. Spindler, 'Die spätkeltische Siedlung von Berching-Pollanten', Das archäologische Jahr in Bayern 1981 (Stuttgart, 1982), 128; on the coins: H. J. Kellner, 'Die keltischen Münzen von Pollanten, Gemeinde Berching', Das archäologische Jahr in

Bayern 1982, Stuttgart 1983), 80-83.

11. Cf. Christlein 1982, 278; further on new coin finds of Kelheim-Mitterfeld, the oppidum Alkimoennis, and this site as Celtic mint: B. Overbeck, 'Eine keltische Kleinsilbermünze von Kelheim-Mitterfeld', Das archäologische Jahr in Bayern 1984, (Stuttgart, 1985), 85f; B. Overbeck, Das archäologische Jahr in Bayern 9185, (Stuttgart, 1986, in preparation): Alkimoennis as Celtic mint.

12. Cf. Christlein 1982, 278.

13. Cf. Christlein 1982, 281 ff. The differentiation between the D1 oppida-civilization and the D2 period is one of Christlein's main points in this article.

14. So called from the main sites; cf. Christlein 1982, 281, further R. Christlein, 'Ein spätkeltischer Friedhof von Hörgertshausen, 'Das archäologische Jahr in Bayern 1980, (Stuttgart, 1981), 108f.

15. Cf. Christlein 1982, 285f and fig. 5.

16. For the sequence of historical events cf. CAH. IX, 545-554. On Caesar and the archaeological evidence, see the short survey of Christlein 1982, 277f.

17. That Noricum was not totally undisturbed by the raids of Suebi in the middle of the first century BC may be indicated by Caesar, BG I, 53, 4. He mentions Ariovistus's second wife "... Norica, regis Voccionis soror, quam in Gallia duxerat a fratre missam..." Could this mean that Voccio was urged to seek a good relationship to the Suebian king? On the chronology of its coinage, R. Göbl has given an excellent account, showing that the Roman military occupation of 16/15 BC did not mean the end of a local currency: R. Göbl, Typologie und Chronologie der keltischen Münzprägung in Noricum (Vienna, 1973), 53-66.

18. H. Polenz, 'Münzen in latènezeitlichen Gräbern Mitteleuropas aus der Zeit zwischen 300 and 50 v.Chr. Geburt,' Bayerische Vorgeschichtsblätter 47 (1982), 28-222 (cited as Polenz).

19. Polenz 65-69.

20. The most recent contribution on this early group of small gold mints: B. Overbeck, 'Der Neufund einer keltischen Goldmünze am Dürrnberg bei Hallein, Land Salzburg/Osterreich', Germania 61 (1983), 589-592. This group of small denominations too is known from Manching.

21. Polenz, 58-65.

22. Polenz, 78-81.

23. One can only emphasize what Crawford writes about this hoard: "K. Castelin ... dates the fibulae (and the find) to about 15 BC; the argument is based on a bizarre view of the relevance of the Roman conquest of the area ..." See Crawford, CMRR 333.

24. For an inventory and general discussion of the hoard: B. Overbeck, Das Alpenrheintal in römischer Zeit, I (Munich, 1982), 178-181, 260f.

25. J.-B. Colbert de Beaulieu, 'Les monnaies de Caletedu et le système du denier en Gaule', Cahiers Numismatiques 2 (1965), 167f. As some of these quinarii bear the name SVLA, he argues that this name appears in honour of the dictator Sulla, a rather odd idea, as there is no other honorary or commemorative issue known in the Celtic world, and as there was no reason for any tribe in Gaul to honour just Sulla in that way. Undoubtedly this coin type is a derivative of the denarius struck in 151 BC by the moneyer P. Cornelius Sulla, RRC 205/1.

26. Short publication refering to the older reports of the nineteenth century by K. Christ, Die Fundmünzen der römischen Zeit in Deutschland, II, 4 (Nordwürttemberg, Berlin, 1964), nr. 4089; F. Hertlein, 'Die geschichtliche Bedeutung der in Württemberg gefundenen Keltenmünzen', Fundberichte aus Schwaben 12, 1904, (Stuttgart, 1905), 70-72; K. Bittel, W. Kimmig, S. Schiek (ed.), Die Kelten in Baden-Württemberg, (Stuttgart, 1981), 233, 238, 244f. (contribution on the coinage by D. Mannsberger).

27. Cf. D.F. Allen, 'The Coins from the Oppidum of Altenburg and the Bushel Series,' Germania 56 (1978), pl. 33, 36, the first modern illustration of this only bushel silver of Schönaich, which will be discussed below, when referring to the Neuses hoard.

28. For the inventory see note 26, especially Christ's list of coins, further F. Hertlein (cf. note 26), p. 88, nr. i (1). In spite of the fact that the hoard association of this piece with different silver types evidently gives an excellent clue to its chronology, it has been omitted from Castelin/Kellner's list of this particular type of quarter staters: cf. K. Castelin, H.-J. Kellner, 'Die glatten Regenbogenschüsselchen', JNG 13 (1963), 123f.

29. First published: H. Reim, 'Ein Versteckfund von Münzen und Fibeln aus der Spätlatènezeit bei Langenau, Alb-Donau Kreis', Archäologische Ausgrabungen 1979. Bodendenkmalpflege in den Regierungsbezirken Stuttgart und Tübingen, (Stuttgart, 1980), 50ff. Discussion of the burial date: Polenz, 155ff.

30. Cf. Polenz, 155, pl. 6, 3.

31. The design of this coin type is only possible in a time of strong Roman influence, as there are coins of this design known which do not bear any trace of non Roman, Celtic style. Cf. the pieces of the Schweizerisches Landesmuseum Zürich: K. Castelin, Keltische Münzen. Katalog der Sammlung im Schweizerischen Landesmuseum Zürich, Vol. I (Stäfa, 1978), nr. 960-972. I do not see any good reason to connect this coin with the denarius of L Cossutius Sabula, RRC 395/1. Numismatists generally deny that die engravers of the Celtic world had any imagination of their own, and that they slavishly kept copying prototypes. A mere glance at the strange designs of the rainbow cups, however, shows that this is not the case. The Rauraci type is not particularly Celtic in style, but looks more like the product of a Roman or Roman-influenced artist, considering what one expects a Celtic coin of this area to look like. One can only conclude that this artist was able to use his own imagination and his own knowledge of motifs and mythology, and that he did not just copy some Roman coin which he happened to have in his pocket or kept in a special collection of "prototypes".

32. This means that I come to the same dates as those proposed in K. Bittel et al. (cf. note 26), 247 (where the community name of Wasseralfingen is used instead of Langenau for this hoard), but by a different route.

33. B.-U. Abels, B. Overbeck, 'Ein Schatzfund keltischer Münzen aus Neuses', Das archäologishe Jahr in Bayern 1981 (Stuttgart, 1982), 126f. (preliminary report). B. Overbeck, Untersuchungen zu den keltishchen Münzen des Büscheltyps. Ein Beitrag zur Geldgeschichte der Spätlatènezeit in Bayern. (University of Augsburg, 1981: type-written habilitation thesis). The final publication is in preparation, twice delayed by the discovery of more coins of this hoard, which had been dispersed into private collections. All that is known of this hoard is preserved in Prähistorische Staatssammlung, München.

34. I am indebted to Ferdinand Maier, First Director of Römisch-Germanische Kommission des Deutschen Archäologischen Instituts, Frankfurt/Main for his detailed study of the hoard's container.

35. Still the most complete publication is the first report on the hoard and other comparable Bavarian hoards by F. Streber, Ueber die sogenannten Regenbogen-Schüsselchen. Erste Abtheilung. Von der Heimath und dem Alter der sogenannten Regenbogen-Schüsselchen (Abhandlungen der K. Bayerischen Akademie der Wissenschaften, I. Classe, 9. Band, I. Abtheilung, Munich, 1860); for a general survey on the hoard, more easily accessible: B. Overbeck, in Die Kelten in Mitteleuropa (exibition catalogue: Salzburg, 1980), 322f.

36. This hoard too is considered by F. Streber in his contribution (note 35); see further R. Paulsen, Die Münzpräungen der Boier (Vienna, 1974), pl. D: B. Overbeck in Die Kelten in Mitteleuropa (exhibition catalogue: Salzburg, 1980), 319-321.

37. See B. Overbeck in Die Kelten in Mitteleuropa (Salzburg, 1980), 320, M87 and 88, photographic illustration of M88, steel engravings of both types after Streber (cf. note 35).

38. A. Furger-Gunti, 'Der "Goldfund von Saint Louis" bei Basel und ähnliche Keltische Schatzfunde', Zeitschrift für Schweizerische Archäologie und Kunstgeschichte 39 (1982), 2-47.

39. Cf. S. Scheers, Traité de numismatique celtique II, La Gaule Belgique (Paris, 1977), 55-57, 308-313.

40. R. Paulsen, Die Münzprägungen der Boier (Vienna, 1974), 62f.

41. A. Furger-Gunti (note 38), 26. He explains both hoards as offerings to Celtic deities, an interpretation one cannot exclude, for these two or for other Celtic hoards, and which is not of any chronological consequence.

42. M.E. Joachim, 'Ein bedeutender urgeschichtlicher Fund aus dem Hambacher Forst', Ausgrabungen im Rheinland '78, Sonderheft (Bonn, 1979), 56-59; V. Zedelius, 'Die Goldmünzen aus dem Goldring-Depot vom Hambacher Forst', op.cit. 59-62.

43. S. Scheers, Traité de numismatique celtique II, La Gaule Belgique, (Paris, 1977), 60-65, 269-280: staters of the "type biface".

44. A. Furger-Gunti (note 38), 28, giving a short report on the evidence of the excavation, which is not yet published in its entirety. I cannot agree with Crawford, who sees in this hoard "a nice piece of evidence of the spread of Roman monetary practices", a view which would imply a much lower date. The total weight of the hoard (close to the Roman pound of 324g) may just be accidental. Cf. Crawford, CMRR 218.

45. See Polenz 127, table 1, and 159, table 4.

46. Cf. note 27.

47. Certainly the best, programmatic, article on Celtic numismatics: R. Göbl, 'Technisch-organisatorische Grundlagen der keltischen Münzchronologie', Keltische Numismatik und Archäologie, Part I (Oxford, 1984), 54-68.

48. Die-linked coins of the Neuses bushel type vary in weight between 1.54 and 2.01g, a warning against using loss of weight as a criterion of later date. For Celtic gold coinage A. Hartmann has pointed out that the evidence of weight and fineness is not totally reliable for chronological deductions: 'Ergebnisse spectralanalytischer Untersuchungen an keltischen Goldmünzen aus Hessen und Süddeutschland', Germania 54 (1976), 102ff. He especially criticises K. Castelin, who was not aware that there is a logical relation between fineness and weight, caused by the high specific gravity of gold (a gold coin of a certain volume and of a low gold content weighs less than a gold coin of the same volume, but higher gold content). Cf., too, A. Hartmann, 'Zur Materialzusammensetzung keltischer Goldmünzen - einige Ergebnisse und deren Deutung', Keltische Numismatik und Archäologie Part I (Oxford, 1984), 88-97.

49. There are two contributions by K. Castelin on the "monnaie à la croix" of South Germany, which methodologically are insufficient: K. Castelin, 'Die Kreuzmünzen bei den Rätern und Alaunen' SNR 50 (1971), 92-124; K. Castelin, 'Die Kreuzmünzen in Süddeutschland', SNR 49 (1970), 77-108f. I have commented on this article in B. Overbeck, 'Zu den keltischen Fundmünzen und der "Tüpfelplatte" vom Dürrnberg bei Hallein', Die Kelten in Mitteleuropa (exhibition catalogue: Salzburg, 1980), 106-110.

50. Cf. note 5.

51. M. Egger, 'Ein neuer Fund keltischer Münzen aus Manching', Bayerische Vorgeschichtsblätter 49 (1984) 69-78, pl. 15-18.

52. The Munich material is published by M. Egger, 'Keltische Münzfunde aus Manching II', Bayerische Vorgeschichtsblätter 50 (1985), 219-238, (pl. 13-22); M. Egger, 'Keltische Münzfunde aus Manching III', JNG 34 (1984), 135-161, pl. 16-31.

53. I am indebted to M. Egger and M. Eberlein for the photographs of the Manching coins.

54. Cf. note 8. For the Sequani potin in Manching: M. Egger, 'Manching III' (note 52), nr. 87-92.

55. Cf. note 10.

56. For a cautious and detailed study of the historical situation of this time, pointing out too some of the problems of R. Christlein's deductions (which cannot change the facts of the La Tène chronology and cannot affect the date of the end of Manching), see S. von Schnurbein, 'Die Besetzung des Alpenvorlandes durch die Römer', _Die Römer in Schwaben. Arbeitshefte des Bayerischen Landesamts für Denkmalpflege 27_, (Munich, 1985), 17-23.

57. It is on the basis of this study that I cannot agree with the historical interpretation given by M. Crawford of the conquest of Raetia and the date of the Regenbogenschüsselchen: Crawford, _CMRR_ 278.

KEY TO PLATES

Fig. 1. Giengen burial, 1/24 stater, gold. After K. Bittel _et al._, _Die Kelten in Baden-Württemberg_ (note 26), fig. 140b/1: enlarged, actual diameter c. 8mm.

Fig. 2. Dühren burial, "monnaie à la croix" silver. After F. Wielandt, _JNG_ 14 (1964), pl. 6, 9: natural size.

Fig. 3. Nierstein burial, rainbow cup stater, gold. After Polenz (note 18), plate 1, 23: natural size.

Fig. 4. The Lauterach hoard (ensemble). After _Die Kelten in Mitteleuropa_ (exhibition catalogue: Salzburg, 1980), 289.

Fig. 5. The Neuses hoard (ensemble). Photograph by Prähistorische Staatssammlung, Munich.

Fig. 6. Selected coins from the Neuses hoard, all natural size. a-c: rainbow cup staters, gold; d: bushel silver, 'naturalistic' variety; e: bushel silver, abstract variety; f-g: two varieties of the Neuses 'hedgehog' silver as quarters of the 'bushel' unit. Photograph by Staatliche Münzsammlung, Munich.

Fig. 7. Selection from the Irsching hoard, all rainbow cup staters of different design; natural size. Photograph by Chr. Zocher, Garching.

Fig. 8. The 1751 Gagers hoard, contemporary copperplate engraving by J.S. and J.B. Klauber, Augsburg. Original engraving in Staatliche Münzsammlung, Munich: natural size.

Fig. 9. Selected gold coins from the Gagers hoard, all natural size; a-d: 'Vindelician' staters of different designs; e-f: mussel staters of the Boii. Photographs by Chr. Zocher, Garching.

Fig. 10. Recently discovered strayfinds from Manching, Kreis Pfaffenhofen, all (except n, which is enlarged 2:1) natural size, after M. Egger, 'Keltische Münzfunde aus Manching III' (note 52); a: contemporary forgery of a 'Vindelician' stater, aes/gold, Egger nr. 1; b: quarter stater of the 'smooth' type, gold, Egger nr. 2; c: contemporary forgery of a 'Vindelician' quarter stater, aes/gold, Egger nr. 3; d: 'monnaie à la croix' of the Schönaich type, silver, Egger nr. 5; e: bushel silver of the 'naturalistic' Neuses type, Egger nr. 18; f: bushel silver of the 'naturalistic' Neuses type, Egger nr. 24; g: bushel silver of abstract type, Egger nr. 34; h: small silver denomination of the 'monnaie à le croix' type, Egger nr. 85; i: small silver denomination, similar to Paulsen (note 36) nr. 569, Egger nr. 78; k: small silver denomination of unpublished type, Egger nr. 75; l: small silver denomination, similar to Paulsen (note 36) nr. 580, Egger nr. 79; m: small silver denomination of the Neuses 'hedgehog' type, Egger nr. 54; n: Sequani potin of the Basel-Gasfabrik type, Egger nr. 87.

Fig. 11. Selected coins from Pollanten, after Das Archäologische Jahr in Bayern 1982 (Stuttgart, 1983), 81 (a - g: correspond to nrs. 1, 2, 5, 11, 15 and 18 of that publication); a - c: natural size, d - g: size 2: 1; a: bushel silver of the 'naturalistic' Neuses type; b: silver of new, hitherto unknown type; c: small silver denomination of the Neuses 'hedgehog' type; d - f: small silver denominations of hitherto unknown types; g: small silver denomination of the 'monnaie à le croix' type.

Plate 1.

5

6

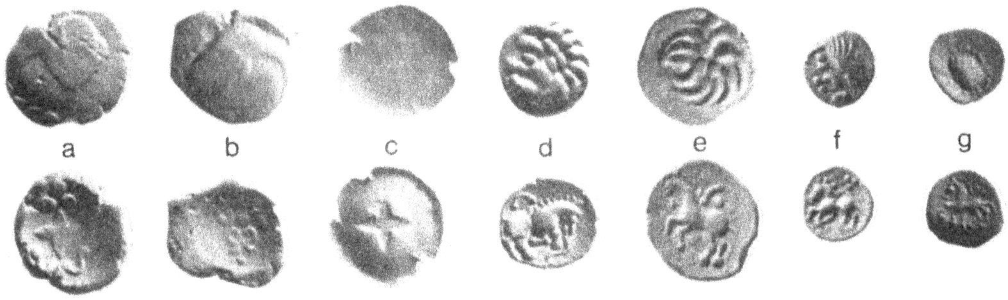

Plate 2.

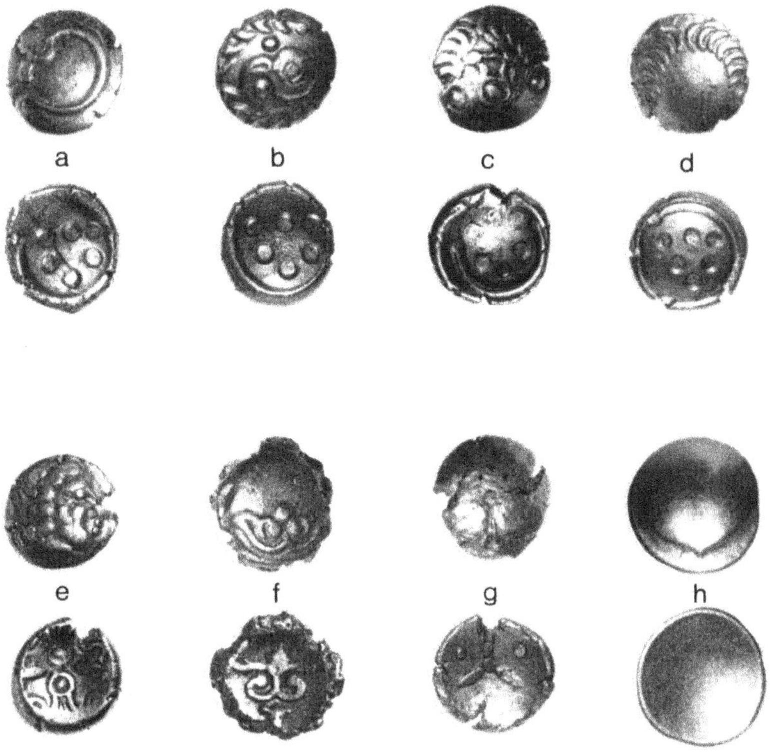

7

Plate 3.

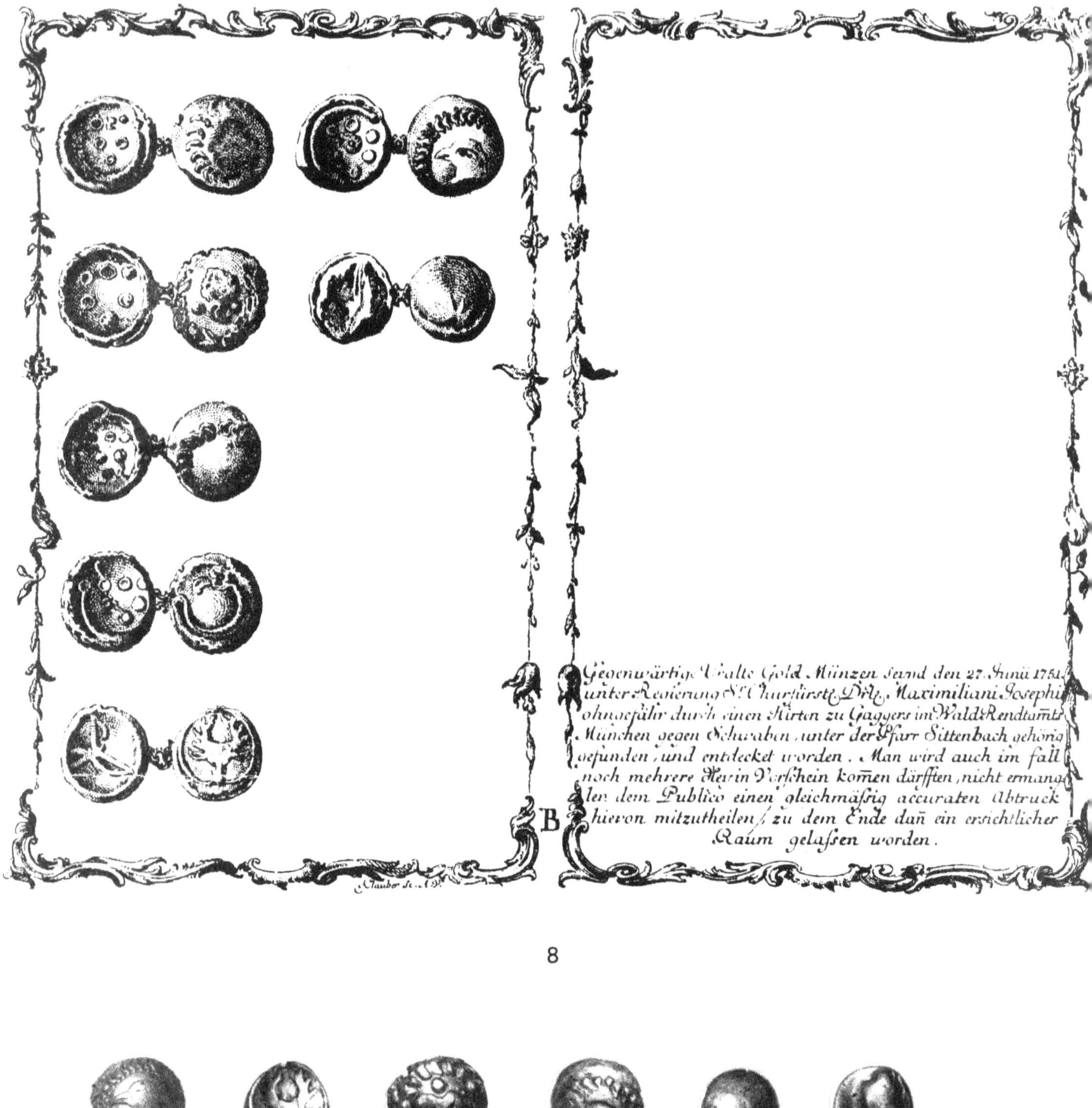

8

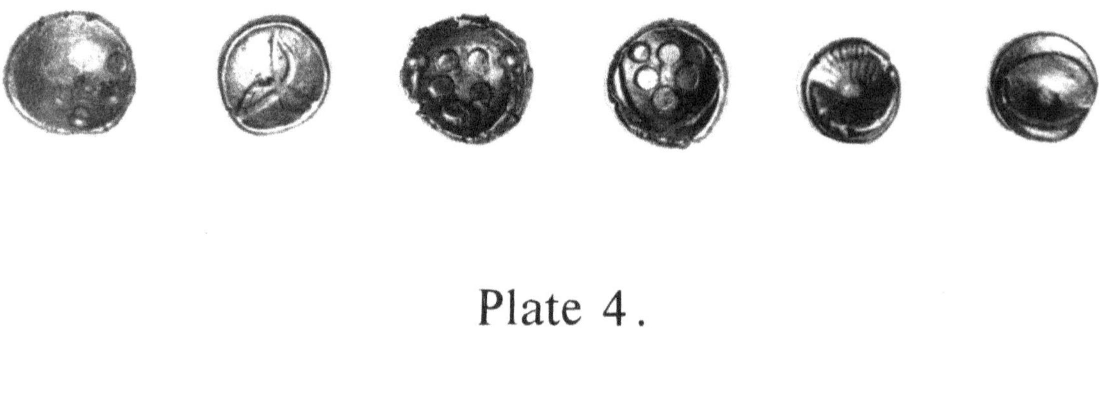

9 a b c d e f

Plate 4.

10

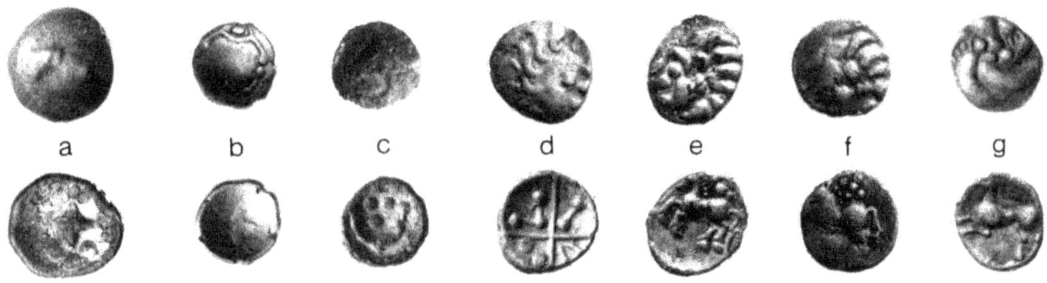

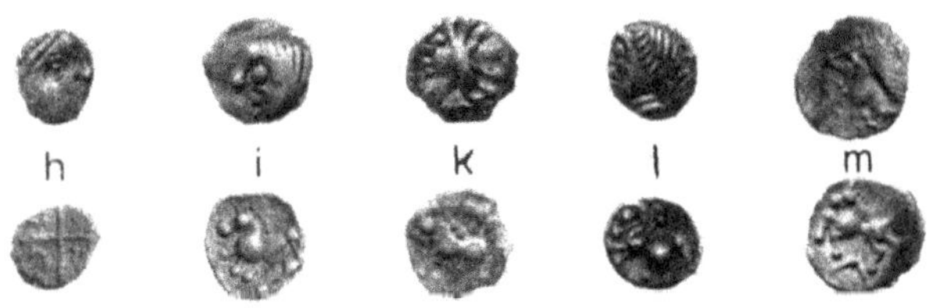

11

Plate 5.

SPAIN

Robert C Knapp

General Observations

I introduce my topic by setting out explicitly and justifying certain hypotheses that I have worked by in formulating a summary of the coinage of Spain during the late Republic. I am considering here the post-Hannibalic period to 45 BC. To limit the scope of the study more would produce artificial and unhelpful restrictions on our understanding of the coinage.

(1) Chronology. The tendency now is to date Spanish material by a combination of metrological and historical considerations. The assumption is made that silver and bronze were minted locally in accordance with the weights of their Roman counterparts from Italy and that both Roman and native weights gradually decreased in the course of the second and first centuries BC.[1] Although native issues are clearly intended to complement and circulate with Roman issues, chronological arguments based on declining weights are unreliable. Weights are, indeed, generally less in 45 BC than in 200 BC; the decrease, however, is not smooth even with the Roman coinage,[2] and the native coinage can hardly be expected to be any better.[3] In addition, the fiduciary nature of the bronze coinage is evident. If there were no other evidence, the conglomeration of bronze found at Castra Caecilia would prove this. The mixture found there of bronze going back to the first half of the second century should not be surprising; the massive bronze issues by Roman during those years and the fiduciary nature of the coinage meant that even in Augustus's day the bulk of bronze in circulation was from that early period.[4] A study of the numerous coins of Carmo, Obulco and Castulo shows that size, not weights was the factor in determining whether a coin was seen as an as, dupondius, semis or whatever;[5] this situation can usefully be compared to Italy after the Second Punic War when non-Roman coins probably circulated as the nearest-in-size Roman bronze.[6]

Metrological arguments often accompany 'historical' ones. There are two major hooks upon which coinage organisation is hung: the original division of the peninsula into two provinces in 197 BC[7] and a reorganisation after the Numantine war in 133 or thereabouts. Two points must be made. First, even if organisation in 197 and 133 went beyond the simplest arrangements, there is no reason to suppose that coinage would reflect the measure.[8] Second, Appian Iber. 99 is explicit when he refers the commission of ten senators and its work in Spain after 133 only to the territory conquered by Brutus or Scipio in 138-133; it was not a sweeping reorganisation of all of Spain as is too often assumed.[9] So, both the reorganisations themselves and their impact on native coinage are problematic.[10] A final historical fallacy also causes error. The assumption is made that a town would mint only with the permission of Rome;[11] from this assumption follow chronological systems based on when such permission most likely was granted. As far as we know, however, Rome, cared little for controlling even the silver minting of distant towns. When it came to bronze there was apparently no attempt at all to control or oversee it:[13] indeed, local bronze took pressure off the Roman state's minting activities. So, chronological arguments depending on when Rome was likely to grant permission to coin fail.

(2) Circulation. The basic principle is that bronze circulates locally and silver more widely. Although casual finds are good evidence for normal circulation,[14] all too often extensive circulation structures and accompanying networks of commerce and trade have been built on the basis of a few finds of bronze coins;[15] talk of 'wide circulation' based upon a handful of such coins found outside the minting area is common when dealing with the larger mintings such as those Castulo, Obulco and Carteia. The bronze coins were occasionally carried far afield - a coin of Corduba appears on the Danube, for example[16] - but when adequate information is available about finds, such as is available for some of the mints in the north-east, the vast majority circulates within about 80 - 100 km. of the minting site.[17] This phenomenon agrees with the behaviour of bronze in other areas of the ancient world.[18] The silver coins circulate more widely within the peninsula[19] but, once away from the area where they were recognised, they were apparently melted down, for very few are found in casual finds outside of the peninsula - indeed, few are found outside nearer Spain and the immediately contiguous mining areas.

(3) Purposes of the coinage. 'Fiscal', financial or social reasons could generate coinage. 'Fiscal' needs typically require gold (of which there are no issues in Spain), silver and large bronze (asses, dupondii) issues; 'financial' needs require smaller denominations of silver (widespread in Gaul, for example) or bronze (semisses, quadrantes, etc.).[20] 'Fiscal' reasons - reasons of state, usually expenditure for public works or military needs[21] - caused the major issues of the Roman Republic; in Spain fiscal needs of local units would be, for example, payment of tribute/taxes, or payment of soldiers required to serve as auxiliaries in the Roman army. 'Financial' reasons include the need to supply a local population with small change in order to expedite market transactions, as well as the desire to make a small profit on the minting of coins. Silver is seldom issued for financial reasons outside Spain and we should assume that native silver issues had either a fiscal or a social purpose. Bronze could have been fiscal, especially in the early second century, when Rome was herself paying her troops with bronze[22] but probably when the troops began to be paid in silver from the middle of the century bronze was not then needed to pay them, but to allow them to spend the silver efficiently; hence most later bronze issues will have been for financial reasons. It is not impossible, however, that some were issued for 'social' reasons. Note that at Paestum local issues were made simply so that a wealthy patron could distribute his largess to the town;[23] similar motives may be behind some of the small issues in Spain.

I would like to turn now to a discussion of the coinage of Spain in detail. These coinages of Spain after the Second Punic war are concentrated in three areas: the northeastern coast, roughly modern Cataluña; the upper Ebro valley; and the Guadalquivir (Baetis) valley. At first glance these areas would seem to have something in common, namely, early penetration by Rome and early beginnings of Romanization. However, the patterns of coinage are basically different in all three.

Cataluña

The Greek colonies of Emporion (Ampurias) and Rhode (Rosas) had minted for many years before the Romans came; native towns in the vicinity had copied these issues extensively. The issues had mostly been in silver, although some bronze denominations existed as well. Other coinages, notably Carthaginian issues from the peninsula and Greek coins from Massalia, circulated too, especially during and immediately after the Second Punic War. These silver coinages were generated by the needs of that war, and came into local hands through mercenary activity and the supply of military needs by the local peoples. To judge by the hoard and casual finds of the later periods, most of the pre-second century coinages were taken out of circulation either through booty or creation of bullion early in the second century. At Emporion, for example, 7% of the finds are from the earlier period while 82% are from the later Republic (195-27 BC).[24] This could be attributed to the fact that quantities of later coinage simply swamped the earlier coinages, but the rarity of pre-second century coins at sites where coins appear only later than the Second Punic War and the lack of pre-second century coins in hoards of the second and first centuries, even in areas which once were rich in such early coins, indicate that these coins were removed from circulation rapidly. This agrees with the account of Livy in which huge amounts of silver were brought back to Rome in coin and bullion during the first twenty years of the second century.

The later casual finds are mostly of native bronze, right down to the end of the Republic. For example, at Ilturo the casual finds for the period of the second and first centuries show 130 coins, 3 silver Roman coins and 127 non-Roman coins of which 76% (96) are from mints within 80-100 km. of the site.[25] At the major centre of Tarraco only one Roman coin has been found casually, while 50 native Spanish coins appear, 88% (44) from mints within 80-100 km. and 82% (41) from the local mint of Kese; almost all of these coins are bronze. Even in the collection of the Provincial Museum at Tarraco, where one would expect a higher percentage of silver and Roman coins, just because of their greater intrinsic interest, the Roman material is only 18% of the total, while Kese and Catalan mints account for 37%. This pattern is repeated at such sites as Iluro (4 Roman silver coins, 48 native bronze coins, 56% from within 80-100 km.),[26] and Serra de L'Espasa (1 Roman silver coin, 2 native silver coins, 41 native bronzes, 78% from within 80-100 km.).[27] There is no question that silver was circulating, as the hoards from the area show, but the frequency of the bronze coins indicates that they were being used in financial transactions and that the area enjoyed as close to a market economy as most areas in the Roman world ever approached.

The chronology of the Catalan issues in detail remains obscure. Mixed hoards from the Hannibalic War give secure dating to the late third century coins of Emporion, but such hoards do not occur after that war and reoccur only in the late second century. Excavations have yielded no persuasive data except the work carried out since 1947 at Ullastret, near Emporion. Here the coins stop before non-Emporitan native coins become a typical part of the casual finds.[28] Although the sample of coins is small, these, combined with other archaeological evidence, strongly indicate a destruction of the native town in the early second century, probably by Cato.[29] It is important to note that no coins from Kese/Tarraco appear at Ullastret. Nearby sites which continued to be inhabited show a good number of such coins in casual finds.[30] I would hazard that an absence of Kese's coins at Ullastret means that the coins of Kese were not being issued by 195 BC.[31]

A silver hoard from the destruction period was composed entirely of Emporitan silver;[32] the proximity of Emporion might seem to explain the presence of this mint and the absence of Kese/Tarraco but the latter's silver and bronze elsewhere circulate extensively in Cataluna and would be expected at Ullastret if it had been in circulation at the time of the destruction.[33] Tentatively, then, the excavations at Ullastret indicate that 'horseman' coinages, of which Kese is one of the earliest, and most native issues come after 195. This has serious implications for the identification of argentum oscense, as will be seen.

Other chronological indicators are lacking until the late second century BC. By this time finds such as the Segaro and La Barroca hoards[34] have horseman silver from Kese and elsewhere although the vast majority of coins comes from Emporion. The date within the second century when Kese and similar mints began their emissions remains problematic. The issues, both silver and bronze, continue into the first century as hoards confirm.[35]

The relationship of the coinages of the Catalan area to political or judicial arrangements is difficult to determine. There is one clear example of an allied people, the Tarracenses - presumably the people of Kese and environs;[36] Emporion must also have been allied, given its help to Rome in the early stages of the conquest. Slightly south of the area, at Saguntum, we probably have another allied town.[37] All of these towns minted silver in small quantities during the second and early first centuries. Whether resources or some other factor kept the silver emissions miniscule is uncertain; bronze was certainly issued in large enough quantities to be useful in the daily life of the area. Any correlation of allied towns and silver-minting centres runs the risk of circular argument, given the dearth of information about such silver mints as Ausescen.

I have elsewhere[38] attempted with only limited success to identify regiones in nearer Spain as administrative areas, each with a silver minting centre. This image of Roman organisation in Spain may still be true, but certainly the very small silver issues can have been no more than symbolic of the importance of the issuing towns. In sum, the coinages of the Catalan area give us little information about the political or judicial history of the area.

The Ebro valley

The Ebro valley was conquered by Rome during the second century. Cato must have marched up much of it, for he at one point reached Numantia and earlier had ordered the towns along its banks to tear down defensive walls.[39] There were a few issues of coins in imitation of those of Emporion (and so prior to or early in the second century), but in general, unlike in Cataluna, coinage came only with the Roman conquest and took the form of horseman denarii and bronzes.

The date of the beginning of these coinages is much debated. Briefly stated, the problem is that Livy notes that in 195, 194 and 180 BC argentum oscense was carried back to Rome as booty from Spain. The largest issuer of silver coins in the peninsula is Bolskan, modern Huesca - a name easily corrupted to 'Osca', although all are not convinced of this equation.[40] In addition, the script of the Iberian denarii has a superficial resemblance to Oscan characters of Italy. Unfortunately the hoard evidence, the only really reliable source, is unhelpful. If the core of a plated Bolskan coin appeared in the Roman camps at Numantia[41] this would provide a terminus ante quem. (However Hildebrandt, after examining the piece in Mainz, denies it is anything but a regular bronze coin, so its evidential value remains in doubt).[42] No 'horseman' turned up at Ullastret, destroyed, probably, in 195 BC this may be considered a terminus post quem. The hoards of mixed Roman and Iberian denarii from the end of the second century have been used to push the native coins back into the early second century, but only be relying on debatable assessments of relative coin wear. I have previously defended an early second century date,[43] such as was once supported by Crawford as well.[44] Crawford has most recently defended a mid-second century date correlating it with the switch in the medium of payment of Roman soldiers from bronze to silver. J.S. Richardson[45] has defended a date of 180-179 on the basis of the tribute demanded according to treaties struck then with Celtiberian tribes by Tiberius Gracchus. Villaronga has made a case for the coinages of Bolskan and other interior mints starting after a putative reorganisation of Spain in 133 BC.[46] He tries to avoid the problem of Livy's mentions of argentum oscense by arguing that it has nothing to do with Osca or the Bolskan coins, rather the argentum refers to coins of Emporion, its imitators and the horseman denarii of Kese, alleged to have begun early in the second century.[47] The reason these silver coins are relatively sparse in later hoards is that they were collected as booty in large numbers by the Romans and melted down or shipped off to Rome. Indeed, the large number of dies in relation to the number of surviving coins of Kese might seem to confirm this.[48]

On balance, I would incline toward an early second century rather than a mid or late second century date for the beginning of the native denarii simply because I think the hoard evidence and the purpose of the coinage supports this best. With regard to the meaning of argentum oscense we shall have to be content with the rival hypotheses until hoard evidence provides more definitive information.

The pattern of native coinage in the Celtiberian area of Spain is paralleled by the experience of other Celtic areas. In the Po Valley Celtic coinages began c. 225 BC in response to Roman wars there; the Romans continued a coinage system there after the conquest based on a quinarius-size silver coin, but without bronze denominations. These 'quinarii' were minted by natives until the late second century, when Roman again minted her own quinarii for use in the area.[49] In Gaul too a similar situation existed. Although the native gold coinage was eliminated after the conquest, local silver issues continued until about 30 BC.[50] The Spanish situation was similar. Natives began minting bronze and perhaps silver in the earlier second century. With the Roman conquest the mints went on, serving fiscal purposes principally, but ended c. 50 BC as Roman silver became sufficient, the interior more Romanised, and the native units ceased to be fiscally independent.[51]

I would like to turn my attention to some of the other aspects of the Ebro coinages. A clear distinction must be made between those mints which produced mainly silver, and so had a 'fiscal' reason for doing so, and those which produced mainly bronze, presumably for 'financial' reasons. The mints of the valley divide themselves quite neatly. Along the river itself, going upstream, we find Seteisken, Kelse (later the colony of Lepida), Saltuie (later the colony of Caesaraugusta), Karaues, Lakine, Kaiskata and Kalakorikos; at a little distance from the river add Nertobis, Terkakom, and Bursau. All of these mint only bronze, all asses, some with semisses and a few with quadrantes. In outlying areas we find in the area of Pamplona Baskunes, Arsaos and Arsakos; in the area of Huesca Sekia, Bolskan and Sesars. To the south of the river is Turiasu and further inland Areikoratikos and Sekobirikes. All of these issue almost exclusively silver: the finds of Bolskan are 98.5% silver, of Turiasu 99.9%, of Sekobirikes 99%, Baskunes 98%, Areikoraticos 95% and Arsaos 96%.[52] Even if the finds from hoards are eliminated, the minting is still about 75% silver for Bolskan,[53] 86% for Turiasu, and so on. Indeed, there are only two mints which are not either exclusively or very preponderantly dedicated to either bronze or silver: Beligio and Sekaisa, both in the lower Ebro valley. The finds from these mints show about 12% silver and 88% bronze;[54] they fit more nearly the category of 'bronze only mints' both in location and in output. The areas along the Ebro were evidently in need of small change, while the interior was not.

In addition, be it noted that Roman coins did not find their way into the interior. In casual finds near Pamplona, no Roman coins have been found from the later Republic; 251 coins from native mints, 40% of them silver, have been found.[55] From the area of Logrono, on the upper Ebro, there are 12 Roman denarii in the museum, along with 43 native coins, two of them silver. From Calagurris come no Roman coins,[56] from Arcobriga only one or two.[57] From Botorrita, where a recently discovered plaque attests Roman involvement in the solution of a water-use dispute between two native towns in the early first century BC, come no Roman coins, but 34 bronze native coins. This fits the picture of the excavation at Azaila, on the lower Ebro: here coins down to, probably, the Sertorian war are exclusively native and 97% bronze. There were Roman coins in circulation, but in the Ebro valley whatever needs coins were put to, they were native, not Roman coins.

Why this heavily native pattern should be so is not entirely clear. It would seem that both commerce and storage of wealth were conducted in native currency. Only at Emporion does Roman currency reach even a moderate level of 15-20% of the finds. It is clear that actual coin was sent out to the legions.[58] The question remains of what happened to the Roman coins which must have been shipped in large numbers from Rome during the early second century to pay the troops; it seems to have been the exception not the rule that local exactions met the cost of war.[59] Some were undoubtedly melted down by natives and recoined[60] while some were carried to Rome as booty.[61] The bronze continued to circulate over the next two hundred years. The coin sample from camp III at Renieblas, near Numantia, where Roman coins form 67% of the casual finds, would perhaps serve as a model for coin distribution in heavily Romanised places such as the provincial capital at Tarraco.[62] The very used condition of the Roman bronze from Castra Caecilia indicates heavy circulation; why do these coins not show up in the casual finds of the town where bronze obviously circulated well? A hint at the answer may be found in the fact that in the Balearic islands the Roman coins form a much higher percentage of the circulating medium. On Menorca Roman coins total 58%;[63] at Pollentia, on Mallorca, 67%.[64] However, on Ebusus Roman coins stand at only 6%. The difference is that a native mint existed for much of the later Republic on Ebusus producing many coins which had quite a wide dispersion.[65] These represent 81% of the finds on the island. The conclusion is clear; when a town had local coinage, it was the preferred medium; when it did not, other native coins of the area were used; only when these were not readily available because of distance did Roman coins come into heavy use. Kese is another good example of this principle. There 77% of the casual finds are of the local mint,[66] native mints supply virtually all the rest. Ebusus and Kese made large issues of their own; at smaller mints a higher proportion of necessary currency was supplied from neighbours (e.g. Illturo, with 44% coming from the local mint[67]). Evidently needs for bronze were supplied, when possible, locally. Silver is another matter. Even in places with their own mint the percentage of one mint seldom exceeds 40% (e.g. Bolskan at Huesca, about 45%;[68] Iltirta at Lérida, 40%;[69] Baskunes and Arsaos in the area of Pamplona, 40%.[70] The general principle that silver travels further than bronze is thus borne out by the Spanish evidence. However, like Roman bronze, Roman silver did not circulate extensively in the interior. What uses natives there had for silver were met by native issues.

The issue and use of the Iberian denarii has recently been related to the pay of Roman soldiers in Iberia. A comparison can be made with the Roman experience in Greece, where Rome apparently used native coinages to carry on all transactions.[71] Crawford holds that the Iberian denarii were willed by Rome after her experience in Greece; she did not impose her coinage on Greece and worked through native coinage because of the 'need outwardly to respect Greek aspirations and of the need to achieve a modus vivendi'.[72] The same sensibility, the reasoning goes, caused her to work through Iberian issues rather than her own. If Rome did create the local issues as a tool for her own needs, this would be interesting evidence of Roman control over subject peoples. Indeed the theme is taken up by Villaronga who goes so far as to describe the Roman military advance into the interior of the peninsula in terms of the mints used to supply the money: first, along the coast, Emporion, Ausesken, Iltirta and Kese; the inland mints later: 'Les ateliers ibériques que frappent de l'argent marquent le chemin de la pénétration de l'armée romaine'.[73] Villaronga, like Crawford, is inspired by the Greek example. But, it can be objected, how were Iberia and Greece similar? There was no tradition of silver coinage in the interior before the coming of Rome and so no 'aspirations' to respect; she could have used her own coinage without causing any offence, real or imagined. In Greece presumably and certainly in Asia Minor, where cistophori were used as the standard currency, the Romans had to pay bankers' commissions to exchange Roman for local currency.[74] Villaronga notes the presence of nummularii in Spain, as attested by coins (of between 72/68 and 43 BC) from a hoard from Albacete.[75] Is such a system to be assumed in Spain as well? Probably not as Roman and native coins are found together and seem to have circulated together. So, another point of comparison between the situation in Greece and Asia Minor and in Spain breaks down.

Aside from a priori suspicions about the validity of a comparison between one area (Greece) with a highly developed banking system and tradition of coinage as a symbol of local freedom and independence, and another, with the outlandish, only slightly monetised tribes of the Spanish interior, it must be added that the evidence of the hoards does not support such a comparison.

I have noted eighteen hoards with datable Roman coins and native coins together. Of these eighteen, ten close by 89 BC, another four by 70 BC and four more by 45 BC. Of the ten between 112 and 89, five are from the mining areas of the south; three are from the levantine coast, and two from the interior. However, levantine finds include only coastal silver issues (Ikalkusken, Kese); it is the finds from the south and interior that are of most interest. Why do native silver coins concentrate in the interior and upper Guadalquivir hoards? Surely this cannot be because of Roman use of the coins for, even if the coin were used to pay Roman troops, circulation would be expected where the coins could buy something, i.e., the monetised areas of the levant and lower Guadalquivir. The few silver coins that do appear in chance finds and hoards in those areas are almost exclusively Roman or at any rate non-Celtiberian. The connection between the silver hoards and chance finds in the Celtiberian interior and the mining areas of Castulo could be at least partially explained by the demands of the silver mines for slaves. Diodorus 5.36-38 indicates that the labour in these mines was slave. Strabo (C147), following Polybius, indicates that 40,000 men worked the Carthago Nova mines in mid-second century; a similar number must have been required in the Castulo mines. The lifespan of a slave in the mines was notoriously short. Replenishment was always necessary. For example, slaves were a major product of Gaul, often supplied by native chieftains from raids. Payment to local chiefs doing the same thing in Spain would most naturally be in silver from the mines.

If the Celtiberian coinage was financed in some part by slaving,[76] one would expect the hoards to concentrate in the interior, near areas where slaves were readily acquirable. This is indeed the case. In fact, with time the hoards move westward; the main mints are at Bolskan and Baskunes, well situated to acquire slaves from the Pyrenean and/or Vasconian areas, and from Turiasu, on the upper Ebro, on the highway into Cantabria. If slaving is a motivating factor in the coinage - and the hoards point in this direction - then this is one indication that Rome did not use the native mints in a way similar to her use of local mints in Greece. The question of why the coinages existed is much more complicated than that.

The purpose of the coinages, especially the silver ones, therefore, is complex.[77] The Celtic tendency to mint which is seen throughout Celtic Europe is continued in the Ebro valley issues. Likewise, Celtic coinages tend to be copies of already existing types and/or weights from nearby areas.[78] Thus it is no surprise that the Celtiberian coinages, once begun, copy each other and provide such a consistency of basic type - horseman/male head[79] - that some have supposed such uniformity could come only from Roman control or at least encouragement.[80] The <u>uses</u> the coins were put to are the normal ones - social display, storage of wealth, even, to a limited extent, perhaps commerce. But the <u>purpose</u> of the issues was surely fiscal - the mints needed bronze and/or silver coin to meet obligations. At least three possibilities come to mind - the need to pay native troops, the need to pay Roman troops (i.e., the issues would be taxes/tribute which Rome would then use to pay the army), and the need to deal with hostile tribes and/or distribute booty.[81]

If the coinages were intended to pay native auxiliaries in the Roman army - and we can suppose that, as in Italy, the native town supplying auxiliaries had to pay them[82] - one would expect that the army would muster for campaigns, fight for a season and disband, for presumably auxiliaries did not winter with the legions. This means that the natives would be paid on campaign, which almost always, in the second and first centuries, meant in the interior of the peninsula. They would then return home to towns which, again, were in the interior, for Celtiberians made the best soldiers and were heavily recruited. On this model one would expect the native silver to concentrate in the interior, where it was earned and where the recipients made their homes. Likewise men recruited for service probably buried their resources; some were killed and never retrieved the hoards.[83] This, too, would help explain the concentration of native silver in the interior.[84]

A partial analogue to this situation exists in third century Italy. There Italian allies of Rome began to mint coinages to pay troops required by Rome since Rome had begun to pay *her* troops in coin. The result is a *mixed* assemblage of coins in the finds from these towns - Roman coins, which were run into on campaign and local coins, which the allies were paid with.[85] In Spain the coin used for pay would be the only one brought back because where the troops campaigned there was scant opportunity to acquire other coins, but the principle would be the same.

Richardson has presented a very interesting scenario illustrating the use of money by natives to meet obligations to Rome. From the examples of the Scipios (father, uncle and famous son) exacting *stipendium* on campaign, notices in Livy of Ilergetes in Cataluña supplying *stipendium* to the army in the early second century, and Cato and Flaccus boasting that they needed no financial support from the home government,[86] it is clear that natives paid - and paid presumably in cash. As Africanus sent *exactores* around to collect funds to pay his troops in an emergency (Livy 28.25.9), he surely wanted cash he could disburse immediately. In 171 BC the governors of the Spains were forbidden to send prefects around to native town *ad pecunias cogendas*. Such exactions had obviously been normal; *pecuniae* certainly means coins. Since the finds indicate a dearth of Roman coins both the evidence and logic presuppose that native issues were the medium for such transactions.

If the native coinages were meant to pay the Roman troops we would have to suppose that tribute was levied on the natives, they paid in their own coin, this coin was distributed as pay to troops in the field (for the dearth of native coins in finds along the coast makes distribution in coastal billets, or the transport of much native coin back to coastal areas, unlikely) who then spent it there.[87] Since the example from Italy cited above and, indeed, common sense, leads to the supposition that soldiers do not spend all their pay while actually on campaign, and since the troops usually wintered in coastal areas - and we hear of only one case when a Roman army wintered in Celtiberia[88] - it seems unlikely that the native coins were used to pay Roman troops although some may have been used to buy supplies locally in the interior.[89]

In summary, then, the native coins were surely used for 'local' fiscal needs of the tribes - pay for local soldiers operating against other native enemies (as elsewhere in the Celtic world), payment of bribes to enemies, distribution of booty and so on.[90] The distribution of hoards rather indicates that the native coins were not extensively used by Romans. Interior hoards are heavily native while coastal hoards, except in the area of Emporion, and a few from the south, are heavily Roman. This is not what one would expect if the legions were being paid in native silver.

Within the context of the circulation pattern of the silver coinage (for the bronze circulates beyond local areas in such a haphazard way that it provides no point for discussion) it is striking that the hoards are concentrated chronologically in three .periods and geographically in three areas. The eighteen finds with native coins along with datable, that is, Roman, coins concentrate in the time periods 112-98, 79-70 and 49-45. The reason is plain to see: there was unrest, especially in the south, during the last years of the first century BC; Servilius Caepio triumphed in 107 from Ulterior;[91] Sertorius began his fame as a *tribunus militum* involved in an uprising at Castulo in the mid to late 90s, for example. The Sertorian war provides the cause for burial of hoards in the 70s while the civil war's traumas created the hoards of the 40s. The geographical areas are also explicable. The hoards in the south are in the mining areas, long recognised as 'monetised' and a target for any anti-Roman military action; the Celtiberian area was awash in native coins hoarded in the uncertainties of the Sertorian crisis; along the levantine coast where money had circulated widely for hundreds of years hoards are to be expected.

There is little administrative or political information to be gleaned from the coinage of the Ebro valley. The historical information is too spotty to be able to say, for example, if Osca had any special status such as being an ally; likewise the status of Pompaelo before Pompey made it a Roman-sponsored settlement is unknown - and it was in the 'pre-Roman' period that the denarii of Baskunes were issued. Turiasu is a complete mystery; no historical information at all is available except that it, along with Bilbilis, produced good iron products.[92] Sekobirikes, very unlikely to be located at the traditionally accepted spot of Cabeza del Griego/Segobriga in Carpetania because of the pattern of coin finds,[93] also remains an enigma.

The Guadalquivir valley

A thorough study of the coinages of further Spain is still wanting, although investigations of individual mints have been carried out.[94] The pattern of coinage has fundamental differences from that of the coinage of nearer Spain. Most basically, silver issues were never prolific in the south; indeed, except for small issues of Gades before the end of the Second Punic War,[95] no mint, not even Gades, issued silver; only six pre-Second Punic War hoards of silver have been published, most very small;[96] a study of the finds of this period is promised by Chaves.[97] The prolific mints of Castulo, Obulco and Carteia issued only bronze. During the time after the Second Punic War no mint issued silver. Sometimes the silver issuer Ikalkusken has been located in the further province - for no good reason; the finds indicate a location inland from Carthago Nova, perhaps even near Cuenca.[98] A colony is later put down in Acci. Might this be the site of the native mint? Kelin likewise issues some silver, but it is probably also to be classified with the native coinages of the north and east,[99] not with the issues of southern Spain. In sum, silver is not issued in the south. Likewise, we are lacking the hoard evidence for circulation of silver that we have in the north. Three small hoards near Cordoba (Cordoba itself, Marrubiales de Cordoba, Molino de Marrubial[100] and two at Granada[101] are all besides the numerous hoards in the mining regions of the Guadalquivir valley. Casual finds of silver are unusual, as would be expected.

On the other hand, mints of bronze are common and mint a high volume of material possibly from late in the third century in some cases, such as Castulo,[102] but most likely from the late second century.[103] While in the north the bronze is rather similar from town to town, the issues of the south have a very great variety of types, metrology and alphabets.[104] All this variety indicates issuing circumstances fundamentally different from those in the north. The native mints of the upper Guadalquivir typically begin with issues signed in native script, then shift to Latin letters. Other native mints simply begin with Latin inscriptions. Unfortunately, no study of circulation exists of the type Martin Valls and Ripollés have done for the nearer province.[105] Coins of Castulo, Obulco and Carteia circulate in the southern part of the peninsula and even beyond; other, smaller mints are restricted to small areas.

Whereas in the north, especially in the interior, fiscal demands produced the minting of silver, Ulterior's needs were more financial - the need to supply small change to an area which, like the lower Ebro valley and the east coast, became increasingly monetised from the late second century on. The most important factor was of course the army of occupation, but the needs of an influx of Italian settlers increasingly used to a monetised economy in their homeland[106] were contributors.[107] The area of the mines seems to have been highly monetised; the hoards of silver attest this and perhaps the bronze of Castulo was issued partly in response to this.[108]

A few mints deserve special attention. First of all, it should be noted that from the standpoint of coinage the mints and the finds of the upper Guadalquivir (i.e. the mining district of the Sierra Morena) have more in common with the coinage patterns of the nearer province than of the further. Native scripts are used, at least initially, and silver is found circulating and hoarded. Although this area was detached from further Spain and attached to nearer Spain by Augustus, presumably to keep the mines in an imperial province, numismatically it belonged there all along.

In the south, the mint at Carteia stands out. This Latin colony, the first outside Italy, was founded in 171 BC. Subsequently, at an uncertain time in the later second century, it began to issue extensive series of bronze coins in all denominations and with distinctive types and magistrates' names.[109] These coins turn up all over Spain. Carteia was a naval base for the natives before, and continued to be such during the later Republic.[110] The financial needs of a town with a large military establishment attached helps explain the issue of so much bronze coinage; note that in Italy, too, during the second century local bronzes are confined to harbour towns, and should be related to naval activities.[111] The town was also active commercially, being a major production and export point for garum fish-sauce. Outside the mining areas, where financial needs again may have prompted towns to profit by minting small change, response to the needs of a salaried army for bronze change probably prompted other larger issues such as those of quadrantes at Cordoba.[112]

The lack of hoard evidence makes dating the bronze of Ulterior very difficult except in the most general way. There are no excavations which have produced coins in closely datable contexts - just a few coins in second century contexts which indicate that Carmo and Castulo were minting at that time, a date anyway deducible from general considerations.[113] Carteia's and Italica's excavations, the most extensive in towns important during the Republic, have so far yielded disappointingly little in the way of new data on coins.[114] The main hoard with some southern types, from Azaila, has been dated to both the Sertorian and Caesarian period and so is of limited help. But the Castra Caecilia finds do indicate that coins from a number of towns were circulating in the early first century and it would be reasonable to suppose that the Sertorian war generated many of the small bronzes as a response to the need for change generated by a large influx of money from the war effort of both sides.[115] There are no southern coins in the finds at Numantia, but so far afield that is perhaps not relevant.

This lack of hoard evidence has reduced scholars to theories. Chaves, for example, building on her view that Rome granted permission to mints as a reward for loyal service, dates the coins according to 'politically opportune moments' in the area's relations with Rome.[116] Yet even if 'permission' was the key to the issues, 133 BC provides no reason for 'permission' in Ulterior other than a canonical faith in that date as a general political watershed.

Periods of fiscal activity most likely generated the bronze coins. The wars of the 140s against Viriathus, the unrest around the turn of the century,[117] the Caesarian civil wars - the armies of these periods generated special needs and probably produced special local issues. The Castra Caecilia finds indicate that native issues especially filled the need for bronze small denominations of the as: of 52 Roman bronzes, 48 are asses while of 160 native bronzes only 29 are asses, and the rest are small denominations. The coins of Obulco and Castulo, near the mining areas, may go back well into the second century; most issues probably have their origins in the Sertorian or Caesarian period, and perhaps met needs peculiar to the mining areas.[118]

Taken as a whole, the coinage situation of Ulterior is strikingly like that of Italy after the Hannibalic war. Roman coin is clearly the major circulating silver currency, but, in the Roman state's disinterest in supplying bronze after it was no longer used to pay troops in about mid-second century, the Roman world was left on its own to meet the needs of small change by continuing to circulate old bronze and mint local or imitate official bronze. In Italy about a dozen local coinages continue to 89 BC and beyond - all in small denominations, as was usual in Ulterior;[119] for example at Velia and Caelia only quadrantes were struck, as at Corduba and elsewhere in Spain. Imitations of Roman coins, almost all semisses and quadrantes, concentrate in southern Spanish finds, and also are common in Italy away from Rome herself.[120] These imitations date from c. 100-25 BC[121] - just the heyday of Ulterior bronze, in all probability. The need for local bronze was exacerbated by distance from Rome, so issues were more prolific in Ulterior - but in substance the coining needs and habits are very 'Italian', a not unexpected situation given the influx of settlers and the natural wealth and Italian-like climate of much of the Guadalquivir valley.

In short, the coinage of the south can tell disappointingly little about juridical and political arrangements. As in the north, any correlation between minting bodies and political status would be very hazardous. For example, of the two known federated towns, Gades and Epora, Gades mints bronze throughout the later Republic while Epora issues none. Carteia as a Latin colony has extensive issues while Corduba, in all probability another Latin establishment, issues only one denomination. Italica issues no coinage before the Augustan period.[122] Surely Rome cared not at all who issued small, local mintings; thoughts of 'permission' or 'consent' to mint as a reward for loyalty are off the mark,[123] as are uproven theories of coins marking a change of status.[124] The rhyme and reason must be mainly local, fiscal or financial, and often idiosyncratic - and hence in detail unknowable.

NOTES

1. L. Villaronga, Numismatica antiqua de Hispania (Barcelona, 1979), at, e.g., p. 143 where the chronology of southern coins is determined on these principles. H.J. Hildebrandt, 'Die Roemerlager von Numantia: Datierung anhand der Münzfunde', MMDAI 20 (1979), 258 also proceeds in this manner.

2. Crawford, RRC 595-97. Villaronga recognises these fluctuations but supposes that native coins fluctuated along with the Roman.

3. Compare the case of Italy, where local bronze after the Hannibalic War cannot be dated through a correlation of 'non-Roman weight standards to Roman sextantial, uncial or semuncial (or whatever) standards': A. Burnett, 'The currency of Italy from the Hannibalic War to the Reign of Augustus', AIIN 29 (1982), 126.

4. Bahrfeldt in A. Schulten Numantia IV (Munich, 1929) 13-14: M. Beltran Lloris, 'Problemas de la arqueologa cacereña: El campamento romano de Caceres. Estudio Numismatico,' Cronica IV Congreso Arqueologico del Sudeste Espanol (Elche, 1949) (Cartagena, 1949), 223-27; Crawford CMRR 260.

5. R.C. Knapp, Aspects of the Roman Experience in Iberia (Valladolid, 1977), 81. This is one result of minting al marco, a process acutely discussed, with chronological conclusions which remain dubious, by H.J. Hildebrandt, 'Beitrage zum roemisch-republikanischen Münzumlauf in Spanien', Chiron 9 (1979), 113-135.

6. Crawford, CMRR 71.

7. Livy 32.28.11.

8. Note that even an organisational measure so sweeping as the Lex Iulia of 89 BC did not terminate local bronze coinage in Italy (Burnett, op. cit. 126).

9. E.g., Villaronga, op. cit. 132; F. Chaves Tristan, Las monedas Hispano-Romanas de Carteia (Barcelona, 1979).

10. A third fundamental reorganization is sometimes noted - that after the Caesarian civil wars of 49-44 BC (M. Beltran Lloris, Las anforas romanas en España (Zaragoza, 1970), 22). This supposedly resulted in the Iberian coinages being replaced by 'Hispanoroman' issues. While some issues, especially in the south, may date from this period, there is no way to relate any specific coinage to an administrative, organisational change at this time.

11. E.g. F. Chaves Tristan, 'Numismatica antigua de la Ulterior,' Numisma 162-64. (1980), 99-122.

12. Silver in Italy south of the Po is another matter. Here Rome did evidently demonetise previous silver coinages after the Hannibalic War and with this began 'an agressive policy of dominating all monetary transactions with Roman coins' (Burnett, op. cit. 126). However outside

Italy there is no evidence that Rome attempted to control silver issues in subject towns although such issues do often cease since the reason and resources for such coinage disappear after the conquest.

13. Crawford, CMRR 185: "One is left with an image of a state which did not give a damn for the provision of small change".

14. M.H. Crawford, 'Money and exchange in the Roman World', JRS 1970, 40-48.

15. R. Martin Valls, La circulacion monetaria iberica (Valladolid, 1966); Chaves, op. cit. (n. 11), 118 is typical of some current thought when she indicates that the circulation of bronze can show commercial routes.

16. R.C. Knapp, 'The coinage of Corduba, Colonia Patricia', AIIN 29 (1982), 200.

17. P.P. Ripollés Alegre, La Circulacion monetaria en la Tarraconense mediterranea (Valencia, 1982), 331-512.

18. Crawford, CMRR 25.

19. Martin Valls, op. cit. (n. 15).

20. Crawford, op. cit. (n. 14), 44.

21. Crawford, RRC 633.

22. Crawford, CMRR 72.

23. Crawford, CMRR 72.

24. Ripollés, op. cit. 333-52.

25. Ripollés, op. cit. 362.

26. Ripollés, op. cit. 354.

27. Ripollés, op. cit. 382.

28. Ripollés, op. cit. 352-57.

29. R.C. Knapp, 'Cato in Spain, 195/195 BC.: Chronology and Geography', Studies in Latin Literature and Roman History II, ed. C. Deroux (Bruxelles, 1980), 33.

30. Ilturo has 11% such coins (Ripollés, op. cit. 362); Iluro a few at least (Ripollés, op. cit. 354).

31. Villaronga, op. cit. (n. 1), 119-120 dates the beginning of Kese's coinage to the late third century BC.

32. IGCH 2339; J. Maluquer de Motes, M. Oliva, Hallazgo de dracmas y divisores ampuritanos en las excavaciones de Ullastret (Instituto de Arquelogia y Prehistoria, Universidad de Barcelona: Publicaciones eventuales 10. 1965), 27.

33. Ripollés, op. cit. 377; this distribution map shows a single Kese coin from Ullastret but none is listed among the casual finds, pp. 352-357.

34. RRCH 180, 175; Ripollés, op. cit. 49-51, 27-29.

35. A.M. de Guadan, Numismatica iberica e ibero-romana (Madrid, 1969), 134-147 with maps facing p. 164, 170.

36. R.C. Knapp, 'The date and purpose of the Iberian denarii', NC 1977, 75. Tarracenses, not Tarraconenses, is the reading at Pliny HN 3.24.

37. Cf. Livy 28.39.

38. Knapp, op. cit. (n. 36), 66-79.

39. Knapp, op. cit. (n. 29), 36-38.

40. Cf. K. Baldinger, La formacion de los dominios lingüisticos en la Peninsula iberica (Madrid, 1972).

41. Schulten (n. 4).

42. G.K. Jenkins, 'Notes on Iberian denarii from the Cordova hoard', ANSMN 1958, 137 and plate 1.8 identifies it as a core; cf. Haeberlin in Schulten (n. 4), 245 No. 177. Hildebrandt, op. cit. (n. 1), 248 denies it is a core, but on p. 252 he says that it is a core and is the earliest evidence for the native denarius in Spain. The weight (3.72g) is certainly appropriate for a native denarius.

43. Knapp, op. cit. (n. 36).

44. 'The financial organisation of Republican Spain', NC 1969, 79-93.

45. 'The Spanish mines and the development of provincial taxation in the second century BC', JRS 1976, 149.

46. Op. cit. (n. 1), 167.

47. Op. cit. (n. 1), 114. The term oscense would derive from a Roman misidentification of the native script on the coins as "Oscan".

48. Jenkins, op. cit. 60.

49. Crawford, CMRR 80-81.

50. D.F. Allen, The Coins of the Ancient Celts (Edinburgh, 1980), 93.

51. Cf. Crawford, CMRR 270. Most native issues in Spain ended about 45 BC. Probably some of the last were those with Iberian types but Latin legends (Segobriga, Segovia, Toleto and Clounioq - Villaronga, op. cit. (n. 1), 240-242), although to speak of any Roman policy which forbade native legends after this date is unnecessary (Villaronga, 228). The civil war was over, the need for bronze decreased. Some towns continued to mint either to provide needed currency or to commemorate events. These issues were not as widespread as before. Some were continuations of earlier issues (Grant, FITA 472-474); a number Grant interprets as foundation issues (Dertosa, Turiaso, Bilbilis, Calagurris, Osca - pp.

158-170). These issues, all with Latin legends, in turn shade off into Augustan and later coinages which continue well beyond the limits of this investigation (Villaronga, 243-252, for the issues). The issues from c. 45 to 27 BC represent a group of issues very much in need of detailed study; they may contain important historical and administrative information, but the present lack of careful research makes conclusions difficult to sustain.

52. Table in Martin Valls op. cit.

53. Martin Valls, op. cit. 321-324.

54. Martin Valls, op. cit.

55. Ripollés, op. cit. 469-72.

56. Ripollés, op. cit. 479.

57. Ripollés, op. cit. 482-83.

58. See, for example, Sallust BJ 27.5; 36.1 and Plutarch Pomp. 11. If the analysis of Roman coins found in Sardinia is sound then it indicates shipments of denarii to the troops on the island during periods of unrest: J.R. Rowland, 'Numismatics and the military history of Sardinia', Limes. Akten des XI internationalen Limeskongresses (Budapest, 1976) (Budapest, 1977), 87-112.

59. Richardson, op. cit. 144-47.

60. Cf. L. Villaronga, AIIN 1982, 220; Allen, op. cit. 35 notes the Celtic coins in general often were minted from melted down Roman issues. Coins of Kaletedou in East Gaul have exactly the same metal as contemporary Roman denarii.

61. See Livian booty lists given, e.g., in Knapp, op. cit. (n. 36), 167-69.

62. Haeberlin, op. cit. (n. 42), 236-243 lists 12 silver and 28 bronze Roman pieces plus 20 native bronze coins. Crawford, op. cit. (n. 14), 45 states: "... the coinage of the army camps hardly included denominations smaller than the as and the production of the semis and the quadrans has therefore still to be explained". The finds from Numantia support this but at Castra Caecilia many native small denominations were found: Beltran Lloris, op. cit. (n. 4).

63. Ripollés, op. cit. 448-450.

64. Ripollés, op. cit. 454.

65. M. Campo, Las monedas de Ebusus (Barcelona, 1976).

66. Ripollés, op. cit. 375.

67. Ripollés, op. cit. 362.

68. Ripollés, op. cit. 449.

69. Ripollés, op. cit. 509.

70. Ripollés, op. cit. 471.

71. A. Giovannini, 'La circulation monétaire en Grèce sous le protectorat de Rome', AIIN 29 (1982), 165-82.

72. CMRR 132.

73. AIIN 29 (1982), 227, more fully set out in op. cit. (n.1) 130-37.

74. Crawford, CMRR 160.

75. L. Villaronga, Ampurias 1971-72, 305-320, AIIN 1982, 221. But this closes in Tiberius's reign and so, even if nummularii existed then, it is no proof that they existed during the late Republic.

76. Of course other sources existed as well - booty, mercenary pay, transport charges etc.

77. Knapp, op. cit. (n. 36).

78. Allen, op. cit. (n. 50) 2.

79. The horseman/male head is very typical of Celtic coinages in general (Allen, 38-39). It is rather startling nonetheless to notice that the Biatec silver tetradrachm from Bohemia and south Slovakia is very similar to Celtiberian coins. In Celtic areas homogeneity of types in a large area of different tribes or towns was common. A propos of Spain, comparison with the Celtic coinages of the transpadane area in Italy and with the Rhone coinage can be made. In both areas - in the case of the Po a conquered area - a quite homogeneous type was minted at different sites. No Roman control seems to have been involved (Allen, 89).

80. Crawford, CMRR 94-95. In Gaul native issues of the Rhone area hold to a common type and standard without Roman control, so uniformity need not indicate a direct Roman hand in overseeing the mintings (Allen, op. cit. (n. 50), 31).

81. Crawford, CMRR 51 - some coins of the third century were issued to distribute booty.

82. Cic. Verr. 2.5.60 indicates this. Although the Iberian coinages begin after the initial conquests the coins were probably also used to finance continuing warfare in the interior. Certainly in Gaul the native silver paid native troops to fight each other - but there, of course, Roman domination was avoided much longer than in Spain. (Allen, op. cit. 15.) Villaronga, op. cit. (n.1) 167 supposes that Rome used native coin to pay her native troops. There is no evidence or probability that native troops would have been paid in this way unless as pure mercenaries - a status seldom attested for natives in the Roman army in Spain.

83. Crawford, 'Coin hoards and patterns of violence in the late Republic', PBSR 37 (1969), 80.

84. Cf. Crawford, CMRR 193.

85. Crawford, *CMRR* 26-27.

86. Cato: Fr. $35M^3$; Flaccus: Livy 40.35.4.

87. H.B. Mattingly, *AIIN* 1982, 239 notes, citing A Alföldi, that certain dies of the last Massaliot drachmas are very like the coins struck by Flaccus there in 82/81 to pay his troops, and speculates that a special Massaliot issue helped pay those troops. Villaronga, *op. cit.* (n. 1) 137 seems to hold that native issues were used to pay Roman troops.

88. Fulvius Nobilior in 153; see, in general, Knapp *op. cit.* (n. 36) 148.

89. However it does seem that local coins were elsewhere used to pay Roman troops. Quinarii from Gaul perhaps were paid to Caesar's troops (Allen, *op. cit.* (n. 90) 202, *op. cit.* (n. 50) 2).

90. D.F. Allen, 'Wealth, Money and Coinage in Celtic Society', *Essays Presented to S. Piggot* (London, 1976), 201; *op. cit.* (n. 50), 93; Knapp, *op. cit.* (n. 36), 14-18.

91. Degrassi 561.

92. A. Dominguez Arranz, *Las cecas ibéricas del valle del Ebro* (Zaragoza, 1979), 173.

93. Villaronga, *op. cit.* (n. 1), 87.

94. Chaves, *op. cit.* (n. 11).

95. Full bibliography in Guadan *op. cit.* (n. 35), 105.

96. *IGCH* 2310, 2319, 2323, 2324, 2326, 2327, 2329 - a total of 82+ coins.

97. *Op. cit.* (n. 11), 106 n.3.

98. Villaronga, *op. cit.* (n. 1) 139 (near Cuenca). Beltran Martinez, *op. cit.* (n. 4) (near Almeria); he also reviews earlier opinions for such locations as Acci (Zobel) and Carthago Nova (Gomez Moreno).

99. Located at Los Villares, Caudete de las Fuentes (Valencia) Ripollés, *op. cit.* 404.

100. Dominguez, *op. cit.* 20, 28, 30 p. 330.

101. Dominguez, *op. cit.* 22 p. 330; Chaves, *op. cit.* (n. 11), 118 n. 4.

102. Villaronga, *op. cit.* (n. 1) 119; M. Paz Garcia y Bellido, 'Las series mas antiquas de Castulo', *Numisma* 138-43 (1980), 97-110.

103. Crawford, *CMRR* 341.

104. Chaves, *op. cit.* (n. 11), 100.

105. Chaves, *op. cit.* 117-119.

106. Crawford, *CMRR* 177-181.

107. Chaves, op. cit. is not blind to these socio-economic factors - 110-11; see also Knapp op. cit. (n. 16), 187-89.

108. Garcia y Bellido, in Chaves op. cit. 121.

109. F. Chaves Tristan, Las monedas Hispano-Romanas de Carteia (Barcelona, 1979).

110. Strabo 3.1.7 (C140) (from Timosthenes) for a native port.

111. Crawford, CMRR 71; Burnett, op. cit. (n. 3).

112. Knapp, op. cit. (n. 16), 15-16.

113. Chaves, op. cit. (n. 11), 114.

114. D.E. Woods, Carteia (Madrid, 1967), F.J. Presedo Velo, Carteia I (Madrid, 1982).

115. Beltran Lloris op. cit. (n. 4) for the Castra Caecilia finds. Many questions remain about this find; Hildebrandt has promised a new, thorough study. The latest denarius RRC 335/3c is from about 96 BC.

116. Chaves, op. cit. (n. 11), 107-108.

117. Plutarch Sert. 3; the Sertorian war with its war needs and concomitant increase in local taxes - Metellus raised taxes which Caesar later lowered - Chaves op. cit. 109.

118. Garcia y Bellido, op. cit. (n. 102) for an interesting discussion of the special coinage habits of the mines. The early Castulo coins seem on the same standard as those of Kese (Villaronga op. cit.) while Kese's coins are preternaturally common in the Sierra Morena mines, a puzzling fact as Garcia y Bellido admits.

119. Burnett, op. cit. (n. 3), 128.

120. Crawford, AIIN 1982, 140-41; Villaronga, AIIN 1982, 223.

121. Crawford op. cit. 140.

122. F. Chaves Tristan, Las monedas de Italica (Seville, 1973).

123. E.g. Chaves op. cit. (n. 11), 106; Beltran Lloris, op. cit. (n. 4), 83.

124. Chaves, op. cit. 119. Cf. Burnett, op. cit. (n. 3), 126 (in Italy the mints which continued to produce bronze after the Hannibalic war did so without regard to 'status or significant dates such as 89 BC') and Crawford op. cit. (n. 120), 141.

Additional note: Iberian denarii in action

M.H. Crawford

The purpose of this short note is to draw attention to a striking difference between the circulation pattern of Roman denarii in Spain in the second century BC and that of Iberian denarii.[1] The evidence is as follows:

Hoards including Roman denarii in Spain between 125 and 91

1. Pozoblanco before 1870 - RRCH 174
2. Cordoba after 1945 - Raddatz, 268
3. Segaro 1881 - RRCH 180
4. La Barroca near Gerunda 1953 - RRCH 178
5. El Centenillo 1911 - RRCH 181
6. Montoro = Epora 1936 - RRCH 182
7. Baix Llobregat 1937 - CH 1, 157; L. Villaronga, in XIV Cong. Nac. Arq., 871
8. Sarria near Barcelona 1870 - Gaceta Numismatica 64 (1982), 24
9. Cordoba 1916 - see below
10. Albanchez de Ubeda - Gac. Num. 74-5 (1984), 107
11. Sierra Morena 1920 - RRCH 186
12. Cazlona 1618 - RRCH 188
13. Torre de Juan Abad 1934 - RRCH 189; Acta Num. 1982, 79
14. Penhagarcia about 1920 - RRCH 191
15. Aznalcollar between 1908 and 1919 - M.H. Crawford, A Catalogue of the Roman Republican Coins in the Royal Scottish Museum, Edinburgh (Edinburgh, 1984), xi
16. Cogollos de Guadix 1959 - Numisma 1978, 25
17. Santa Elena 1903 - RRCH 193
18. Rio Tinto between 1903 and 1910 - RRCH 194
19. Sierra Morena 1929 - RRCH 196
20. Oliva 1848-9 and 1961 - RRCH 197
21. Mogon 1914 - RRCH 200

22. Cazlona shortly before 1978 - Numisma 1978, 19

23. Azuara 1890 - see below

24. Salvacanete about 1930 - see below

25. Portugal - Museu Nacional, Lisbon

26. Pozoblanco 1925 - Bol. Real Acad. Bellas Letras y Nobles Artes de Cordoba 1928, 51; CH 3, 119 is perhaps another parcel

27. Crevillente before 1949 - RRCH 206

28. Orcera 1940 - RRCH 211

29. Idanha-a-Velha 1974 - CH 3, 120

30. San Joao dos Caldereiros 1941 - Arquivo de Beja 1955, 65 and 162

I omit the hoard of 1 Roman 2 Iberian denarii of Soto Iruz, RRCH 185.

Hoards of Iberian denarii

	Group A					Group B				
	1	2	3	4	5	6	7	8	9	10
Iltirta(salirban)	173			1				1		
Ikalesken		49		45	55	+140	1	8		
Kese	2	2	1	1				2		
Ausesken			3							
Sesars	60									
Sekaisa								1		
Baskunes				3	1		1			
Konterbia				1	2	1	1			
Bolskan	1	3	100	24	233	+20	16	52	400	700
Areikoratikos				2	2	1	2			
Arsaos				1		1	1			
Turiasu				2		1				
Sekobirikes					2	1				
Belikiom									9	3

1 = Lerida (3 Iltirta, 170 Iltirtasalirban); the corresponding bronze issue of Sesars occurs at Numantia (G.K. Jenkins, ANSMN 1958, 59) = 31 on Map

2 = Arcas = 32 on Map

3 = Fuentes de Ebro = 33 on Map

4 = Cordoba (1 Iltirtasalirban); also 1 drachm of Saguntum; the subsequent bronze issue of Kese occurs at Numantia, denarii of Kese in the Segaro hoard

5 = Granada = 34 on Map

6 = Azuel = 35 on Map; the Roman denarii in the hoard are described by J. Zobel y Zangroniz, MNE 4, 277, as a little later than those in the Cazlona hoard, so are late second century

7 = Mogon = 36 on Map

8 = Salvacenete (1 Iltirta); also 2 drachms of Saguntum

9 = Azuara 2

10 = Calatayud (Aluenda) = 37 on Map

Lerida (sometimes known as Hostalrich or Tarrasa) - P.P. Ripollés Alegre, La circulacion monetaria en la Tarraconense Mediterranea (Valencia, 1982), 36

Arcas - L. Villaronga, Los denarios con leyenda icalgusken (Barcelona, 1962), 21; a further small parcel of 7 pieces of Ikalesken, apparently, is published in Gac. Num. 74-5 (1984), 105; the denarius of C. Annius must be extraneous since denarii of Ikalesken are never present in first century hoards.

Cordoba - G.K. Jenkins, ANSMN 8, 1958, 57; RRCH 184; NC 1969, 79

Granada - G.K. Jenkins, NH 7, 1958, 135, suggesting that 2 denarii of Bolskan, 1 of Areikoratikos and the 2 of Sekobirikes are later than the rest of the hoard

Azuel - Raddatz, 199; the pieces of Ikalseken are from Villa del Rio and from part of the same hoard

Mogon - Raddatz, 227

Salvacanete - RRCH 205; Raddatz, 244; Rev. Arch. Bibl. Mus. 79, 1976, 389

Azuara 2 - RRCH 204

Calatayud - F. Mateu y Llopis, NH 1, 1952, 220ff., no. 503

In the Baetis (Guadalquivir) valley Roman and Iberian denarii are of course both present, both imported from elsewhere. But if we look at Spain north-east of the Sucro (Jucar) river, it is at once apparent that Roman denarii circulated in the coastal strip between Barcino and Emporiae, whereas hoards composed exclusively or almost exclusively of Iberian denarii are found inland, in the middle Ebro valley (23,31,33 and 37) or the headwaters of the Sucro and Turis (Guadalariar) (24 and 32).

Imperfectly known hoards which may belong to the second century do not contradict the pattern: Los Villares (Baetis valley), Burgo, Las Casetas, Huesca (middle Ebro valley), Larrabezua (beyond the upper Ebro valley).[2]

The Sucro and Turis basins and the middle Ebro valley were firmly in Roman hands in the wars of the 150s and 130s BC: plausible areas for the levying of taxation in Iberian denarii by the Romans and their use for the payment of Roman soldiers operating from billets in the area.[3]

NOTES

1. I here slightly correct and supplement CMRR, appendices 29-30. These different patterns are discussed above, by Knapp.

SICILY

M.H. Crawford

One would suppose *a priori* that the coinage of Sicily under Roman rule would be relatively straightforward. The area involved is small, it rapidly became a zone of denarius circulation, like Italy, and production of coinage did not last beyond the reign of Tiberius. Yet in fact the picture is extraordinarily complex and also extremely hard to work out.

Let me begin with the circulation of silver. The large-scale circulation of Roman coinage in Sicily, which was one of the factors which made possible a symbiosis of Roman and native systems of reckoning and coins, was in a certain sense the result of an accident. For Roman coinage continued to flow to Sicily in substantial quantities *after* the end of the Second Punic War, in clear contrast to what happened in Spain. No doubt this was in part the result of the presence of Romans and Italians as men of business from soon after the fall of Syracuse.[1] But the principal cause surely lies in the fact that the Romans not only took over the tithe system from Hieron II, but also by *buying* a second tithe followed his practice of shipping grain out of the island in exchange for silver.[2] The difference is that under Roman rule the silver which arrived was not melted down to make new coinage, but circulated as denarii. Thus Sicily rapidly became a zone of denarius circulation, but a zone where native systems of reckoning survived.

The bronze coinage of Roman Sicily - there is no silver - would require a monograph to do justice to its volume and diversity. Apart from the issues of the cities, there are also the coins known as 'Romano-Sicilian', which were certainly struck by the Roman authorities in western Sicily. Despite the monograph by M. Bahrfeldt,[3] their chronology remains for the most part uncertain. What I should like to do here is to raise a number of general issues and then take one small area of eastern Sicily and show the sort of evidence which is available and the nature of the results which are possible.

If one begins with Syracuse, there is no real doubt which issues follow the fall of Syracuse in 212 BC, since the hoard evidence which identifies the issues struck down to that point is very good. There are four later groups:[4]

1) Random die-axis, legend in line(s), open *omega*

2) Fixed die-axis, legend in open line(s), open *omega*

3) Fixed die-axis, legend around, open *omega*

4) Fixed die-axis, legend around, closed *omega*

There are no particular grounds for supposing that there was a long interval in production after the fall of Syracuse and there are over twenty issues in all. If one wished, one could suppose that coinage at Syracuse was relatively continuous between 212 and Augustus (the latest issues occur in the Megara Hyblaea hoard, on which see below).

If one turns away from Syracuse, the pattern is very different. Down to 212/211, the evidence is not too bad, though not as good as for Syracuse. The hoards do give some indication of the material in circulation when the Romans recovered Sicily (Table 1 with *CMRR*, 110-111). After 212/211 they provide almost no help at all. It is not that hoards, even bronze hoards, are entirely lacking. But what they appear to suggest in the middle of the second century BC is the complete Romanisation of the circulating medium of Sicily - Roman silver and Roman asses and a few large bronzes of the period of the Second Punic War still floating around (Table 2).

TABLE 1: Second Punic War hoards in Sicily

Tripi - RRCH 55 and 66; IGCH 2237-8; I no longer think, with P. Marchetti, 491, that we are dealing with two hoards

Aidone 1908 - RRCH 68; Aidone 1909 IGCH 2239; it seems to me that we are dealing with one hoard; the HISPANORVM piece is clearly on grounds of patination extraneous, *contra* G. Manganaro, *Archivo Storico per la Sicilia Orientale* 1969, 291, n.22; the Tauromenium piece likewise, *contra* P. Marchetti, 489, whose account of the issues of the Mamertini and Rhegium supplements that in RRCH 68; the latest Syracusan issue, however, is of the Syracusan democracy

Mandicini - RRCH 71; AIIN 1962-4, 229, P. Marchetti, 490, whose account corrects that in RRCH 71

Montagna di Marzo - RRCH 99; given the loss of most of the hoard during the war it is probably forlorn to argue as does P. Marchetti, 489, compare RBN 1971, 88, n.20, tht we are dealing with two hoards

San Marco IGCH 2236; earlier pieces include KAINON (1), Abacaenum (1)

Grammichele - list based on my own inspection and that of T.V. Buttrey

I view with grave scepticism the report in the sale catalogue, Bonhams 4/12/1980, p. 19, that an anonymous victoriatus (RRC, no.44/1), an anonymous denarius (RRC, no. 75/1c), a denarius of C. Varro and a denarius of C.A(i)lius were found with a silver issue of Hieron II beneath the destruction level of 211 at Morgantina; no pieces later than the very first moments of the denarius system have turned up in the official excavations of Morgantina.

Yet, as we have seen, there is a lot of bronze coinage of Syracuse between 212/211 and Augustus. And there are a number of issues of other mints which have to be placed somewhere after 212/211. One could easily object to the conclusion which Table 2 appears to suggest, by observing that the hoards simply fail to represent fractional bronze coinage. Pursuing this line of argument, one could suggest that we owe to regular excavation knowledge of the one hoard which reveals at the very end of the Republic some diversity of circulation of small bronze coins. I refer to the Megara Hyblaea hoard (Table 2).

TABLE 2: Second and first century bronze hoards in Sicily

Catania	Morgantina	Avola	Biancavilla
Asses	Asses to 160s BC	Asses to 160s BC	Denarii Victoriatus Asses to 150s BC
	Syracuse to Hieron II Leontini	Hieron II	Hieron II
Mamertini	Mamertini	Mamertini Centuripae	Mamertini Centuripae
Rhegium		Rhegium	Rhegium
	Carthage		

Catania - IGCH 2244
Morgantina - information from R. Ross Holloway (sealed deposit including HISPANORVM issue)
Avola - RRCH 122; also 1 piece of Ptolemy II
Biancavilla - RRCH 127
I have excluded the re-deposited votive offerings from Morgantina, IGCH 2248

Bisacquino	Megara	Campobello	Sicily
Asses Panormus		Asses Panormus	Asses Panormus
	Syracuse Catana Enna as <u>municipium</u>	Syracuse	
		L. Naevius Surdinus	C. Cassius Celer

Biascquino - IGCH 2251; AIIN 23-4, 1976-7, 304; the wear on the asses shows the hoard to be late second or early first century
Megara Hyblaea 1949 - IGCH 2252; G.K. Jenkins, <u>The Coinage of Gela</u> (Berlin, 1970), 117, n. 13
Rhegium: Head of Apollo r./Lyre <u>REG</u> (in monogram) <u>INON</u>
Catana: Gabrici, nos. 9-14
Syracuse: Gabrici, pl. 9, 15 (23); pl. 9, 21 (1); pl. 9, 13 (8); SNG (Cop.) 901-2 (11)
Enna: Gabrici, no. 12
Campobello - IGCH 2253
Sicily - AIIN 3, 1956, 210; also 1 piece of Mamertini, 1 piece of Ebusus

Where does the truth lie? Was there a hiatus in circulation between the Second Punic War and the Late Republic? Or not?

I should like to take one area, not least because it is clear that circulation of bronze coinage in Roman Sicily was fairly localised. The evidence is quite different for different areas and it is likely that the pattern of production was quite different too. The area I should like to consider is eastern Sicily, south of Mount Etna, which is basically a single river system draining east into the sea.

Apart from brief glances at Syracuse, I should like to deal with Aetna, Centuripae, Menae, Catana and Leontini.

The late issues of Aetna, Centuripae and Menae consist of fundamentally similar and internally homogeneous groups, one to each mint:

Aetna 3 unciae + 2 unciae (Gabrici, 2-18)

Centuripae 10 unciae + 6 unciae + 3 unciae
+12 unciae + an uncertain
denomination with XI to which I
shall return (Gabrici, 4-33)[5]

Menae 5 unciae + 4 unciae + 3 unciae
+ 2 unciae (Gabrici, 1-22).

The issues of Menae are remarkable for the diversity of their marks of value. E or for five, four dots, four strokes or for four. But I think that the entire coinage was produced in a relatively restricted period; that the period was the Second Punic War emerges from the presence of specimens of one issue in good condition in the Aidone 1909 and Grammichele hoards (Table 1).

The issues of Centuripae can also be assigned, I think, to the Second Punic War. There are very worn specimens of the largest denomination in the Avola and Biancavilla hoards (Table 2); and some of the obverses of this denomination show a head of Zeus which is very similar to the Head of Saturn on some Roman semisses with corn-ear.[6] I have even wondered whether this issue was produced at Centuripae.

As far as Aetna is concerned, there is no hoard or find evidence known to me, but on the admittedly fallible grounds of style and the rather less fallible grounds of denominational structure, I should assign the issues also to the Second Punic War.

None of these mints ever struck again, apart from a curious group of objects produced at Centuripae. The types are Head of Apollo/Tree, the legend is sometimes in Greek and sometimes in Latin (Gabrici, 34-40). The resemblance most obvious to me is to the late quadrantes of Paestum. I wonder in the case of Centuripae if we are dealing with a real part of the monetary system at all.

Let us turn to Catana and Leontini.

In the case of Catana also much material can be assigned to the Second Punic War.

1) of two associated issues with Busts of Serapis + Isis/Two corn-ears and Head of Silenus/Bunch of grapes (Gabrici, 51-3), the first turns up in a

deposit from Nocera Umbra, which closes during the Second Punic War (see App., no. IX).

2) of those issues with ΙΠ, XII and II (Gabrici, 41-50), the last turns up in the Grammichele hoard already mentioned. In general, the denominational structure recalls the coinage of Centuripae and there is in particular one very close resemblance, between the pieces with XII here and the piece with XI at Centuripae. In think that X = 1/2 and that we have here a piece of 2 1/2 unciae, and at Centuripae a piece of 1 1/2 unciae.

In any case, there is not, within the coinage of Catana, a great quantity to assign to the period 200-50. There are of course two very large groups with different monograms (Gabrici, 4-22); one of these turns up in the Megara Hyblaea hoard, and both belong to the very end of the Republic or the reign of Augustus.

That leaves:

1) Catanaean brother/Catanaean brother (Gabrici, 32-8)

2) Busts of Serapis + Isis/Apollo (Gabrici, 39-40)

3) River god/Caps of Dioscuri (Gabrici, 23-6)

4) Dionysus/Catanaean brothers (Gabrici, 27-31)

Frankly, I have no idea where to date these issues. I would not exclude the possibility that one or more may belong to the first half of the second century BC; but I see no reason for believing this.

At any rate in the case of Leontini, there are clear grounds for believing that the resumption of coinage belongs after the middle of the second century BC.

The late bronze issues of Leontini are, first:

1) Demeter/Sheaf of corn (Gabrici, 9-12)

2) Apollo/Lion walking (Gabrici, 15)

3) Apollo/Two fishes (Gabrici, 17-18).

For this group there is in principle abundant archaeological dating evidence, in the shape of the great cemetery excavated by G. Rizza. The problem is how to interpret the evidence (App., no. VI).

There is no dispute that four specimens of this group turned up in the latest level of the cemetery, either in graves or in the soil surrounding them. Rizza originally dated this level of the cemetery to the second century BC, since he observed in Gabrici that the coins which he found were dated generically to the Roman period. He was briskly picked up by Orlandini who made three points:

1) that the southern end of Leontini was abandoned in the Roman period and that therefore the necropolis was probably also abandoned;

2) that the material is similar to third century BC material from Butera;

3) that the material is unlikely to be separated by over a century from fourth century BC material in the lowest level of the necropolis.

The premise of the first argument is only partly true, since the end of the necropolis was marked (presumably after a gap) by the construction over it of a building of uncertain function in the late second century BC, which clearly indicates some form of occupation in the area. In any case the argument is weak, since habit may well ensure continuing use of a necropolis for a generation even after the habitation has shifted.

The second and third arguments may be considered together. The crucial grave is Grave 45, which contains a pot lid seen by Orlandini as being close to a fourth century pot lid. But it also contains an Ares/Nike bronze of Syracuse (Gabrici, 585-94), which falls about half-way in the sequence of issues which are later than 212 BC. Unless we are to suppose massive issues of Syracuse in the immediate aftermath of the Roman conquest, we are somewhere in the middle of the second century. In my view it is at that point that the Hellenistic coinage of Leontini begins.

There are next two groups of issues, one with LEONT in monogram, another with Warrior reverse and Two corn-ears reverse, the second regularly overstruck on the first (Gabrici, 14, 13, not listed).

Thereafter, the issues which remain belong to the very end of the Republic and I shall return to them in a moment.

At this point, speculation takes over. I have suggested briefly in *CMRR* that the Romans encouraged the revival of local coinage in Sicily after the First Slave War, and this model might accommodate both Catana and Leontini.[7] It might equally be that some of the issues were struck during that war, though if this is so other considerations ensured the continuation of coinage. It might also be that some other reasons applied or that there was no particular pattern at all.

In any case, although there are no marks of value, the issues which I would assign to the late second century are Greek in character.

What is clear is that at a certain point the Romans organised or allowed a monetary system for Sicily which in some ways related locally produced bronze to Roman silver and bronze.

The system was certainly in existence by the time of the Verrines of Cicero, where we read (*II in Verr.* 3, 181) 'For how can there be an agio when everyone uses the same kind of coins?' Since local bronzes were produced in Sicily at least down to the time of Augustus 'the same kind of coins' must refer to the unitary nature of the monetary system and not to the origins of the coins themselves. The Roman character of the monetary system of Sicily emerges from the fact that in the Verrines Cicero always calculated in sestertii (compare Quintilian vi, 3, 80, for the victoriatus = quinarius used as a unit of reckoning under Augustus). But the inscribed accounts from Tauromenium, which are certainly later than the Verrines, reckon in talents, *nomoi*, *heminoma*, *tetralitra* and *litrai*.[8] It is clear that this system must have been compatible with the sestertius as a unit of reckoning, perhaps with a *tetralitron* as the equivalent of a sestertius and a litra as the equivalent of an as.

By the time we get to the end of the Republic, the picture is different. I am fairly sure, though I see no way of proving this, that the bronzes of Catana and Syracuse in the Megara Hyblaea hoard are asses and that the last issues of Leontini, with Demeter and Lion rampant reverses are as and quadrans (Gabrici, 6-8, 16). I have already mentioned the quadrantes or pseudo-quadrantes of Centuripae.

One last word. If the end of the Republic and the reign of Augustus saw the final Romanisation of the monetary system of Sicily, the coinage also provides evidence for the decline of the interior, at any rate in eastern Sicily. It will not have escaped notice that in the area I have been discussing, all the mints with functional coinages in the late Republic, Catana, Leontini, Syracuse, were coastal cities.

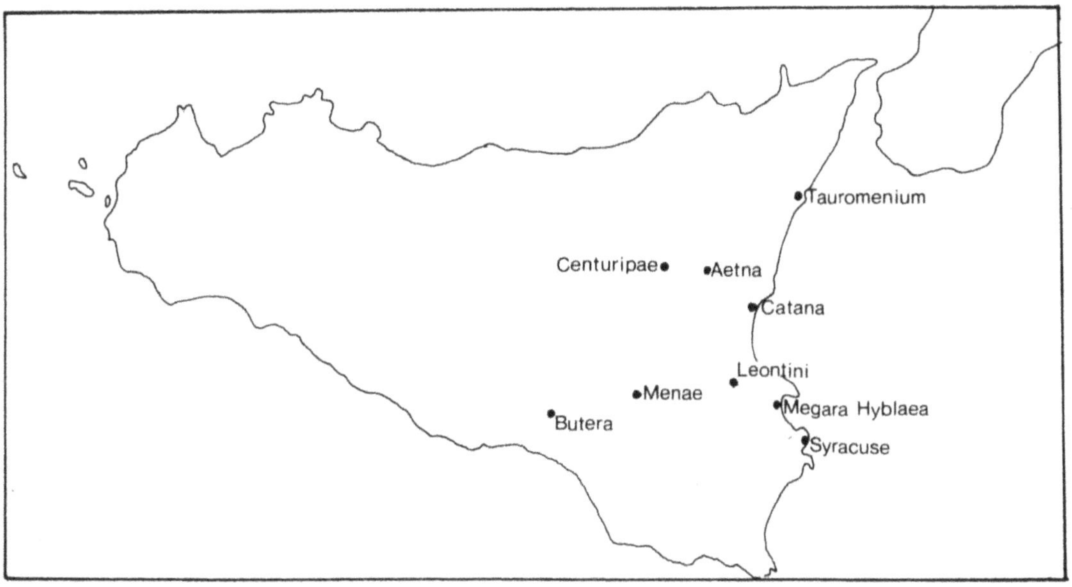

Appendix

This check-list of finds of Sicilian bronze coins in hoards and archaeological contexts of the Hellenistic period is provisional and is intended to serve as a basis for further study. It does not include the hoards which feature in Tables 1-2 or the sealed deposits from Morgantina which are to be published by R. Ross Holloway.

HOARDS

1. Cibali 1894. AIIN 1962-4, 221 = IGCH 2255 (18 bronzes of Syracuse, not 4, as Studi di Num. 1, 64).

2. Cibali 1907. AIIN 1962-4, 223 = IGCH 2254.

3. Megara Hyblaea 1953-7 (?). MEFR 1958, 50-1.

4. Monte Cane 1888. AIIN 1956, 210.

5. Palermo 1980. R. Calciati, Corpus Nummorum Siculorum I (1983), 366-8.

ARCHAEOLOGICAL CONTEXTS

I. Butera. Rass. Med. 7 (1954), 11; Arch. Anz. 1954, 630; Rev. Arch. 1956, 2; Fast. Arch. VI, 630.

II. Erice. NSc 1971, 640.

III. Fontana Calda. AIIN 1955, 213.

IV. Gela. AIIN 1955, 207, with Arch. Class. 1957, pl. 77; ibid. 44, 153, esp. 170-1.

V. Heraclea Minoa. AIIN 1958-9, 296.

VI. Leontini. G. Rizza, NSc 1955, 289; P. Orlandini, Arch. Class. 1956, 210; G. Rizza, Bd'A 42, (1957), 63; Arch. Class. 1959, 78; P. Orlandini, Arch. Class. 1960, 108; F. Coarelli, in Società Romana (1981), I, 6-7.

VII. Lilybaeum. NSc 1971, 662.

VIII. Monte Adranone. Kokalos 1972-3, 241; 1976-7, 451 (note that the excavations provide no evidence for a high date for the Roman denarius).

IX. Nocera Umbra. NSc 1891, 308.

X. Pizzo Cannita. Atti Acc. ... Palermo Ser. 4, 13, 2, 3 (1953), 265-99, at 283-4.

XI. Rhegium. NSc 1957, 394.

XII. Rome. _NSc_ 1953, 148.

XIII. Syracuse. _NSc_ 1938, 296.

XIV. Syracuse. _NSc_ 1954, 363 and 374.

XV. Troina. _NSc_ 1961, 350, 361, 386.

XVI. Tusa. _NSc_ 1959, 293; 1961, 266.

NOTES

1. A. Fraschetti, in _Società Romana_ (1981) I, 51, 'Romani e Italici in Sicilia'.

2. In the period after the Second Punic War covered by Livy, the Romans bought a second tithe in 191, 190 and 189, and again in 171. Denarii perhaps also arrived in Sicily in return for slaves, whose export from Sicily is envisaged in the _lex censoria portus_ and case law arising therefrom, D. 50, 19, 203. Wool was also produced in Sicily, Strabo vi, 2, 7 (273), and perhaps served to clothe Roman armies, _II in Verr._ 2, 5.

3. M. Bahrfeldt, _SNR_ 1904, 331, 'Die römisch-sizilischen Münzen'.

4. I should like to thank Andrew Burnett for sharing his conclusions with me.

5. The series is reduced to disarray by M. Caccamo Caltabiano, 'Sulla cronologia ... delle serie Hispanorum', _QT_ 1985, 159, at 164.

6. Crawford, _CMRR_, Fig. 37.

7. Crawford, _CMRR_, 115.

8. Crawford, _CMRR_, Appendix L.

MACEDONIA

I. Touratsoglou

The defeat of Perseus at Pydna (168 BC) was fatal not only to the Antigonids but also to the Macedonian state itself. Nevertheless, Rome did not immediately proceed to annex conquered Macedonia by transforming it into a regular province, either because she lacked the means to keep so vast a country in subjection, or because she wished to disguise her expansionist aims. The defeated kingdom, stripped of all its foreign possessions, was divided into four departments (merides); land could not be sold across the boundaries and marriages between inhabitants of different districts were not allowed. Every meris was organised as an administrative unit with a capital (Amphipolis, Thessaloniki, Pella and Pelagonia). No attempt was made to exploit the resources of the country; the gold and silver mines were closed, and tribute, now payable to Rome, was halved.

During the following period internal troubles are often mentioned, due either to increasing anti-Roman feelings or to conflicts between privileged classes and the masses.

The attempt of Andriscos in 150-148 BC to restore the monarchy provoked new military intervention by Rome. The suppression of the pretender's revolt brought the decisive end to any dynastic movement; the Senate at last realised that annexation was unavoidable.

The period which extends from 148 BC to the Augustan era is one of the most difficult Macedonia experienced. Although it was up to the Roman governors to defend the province, all the destruction and pillage of barbarian invasions was not without effect on Macedonia itself. And, as well as the barbarians from the north during the second half of the second and the first half of the first centuries, the troops of Mithradates VI also invaded the country in 87 BC, devastating the province. Finally, the two civil wars, first Caesar against Pompey (49-48 BC) and then Brutus and his accomplices against Mark Antony and Octavian (44-42 BC), took place, in their final phases, in northern Greece.[1]

SILVER

Various issues of silver were minted in Macedonia in the late second and early first century BC. The chronology of these is very controversial, the latest scheme, of Crawford,[2] is as follows:

1. After the creation of the four merides:

   a) tetradrachms with Zeus/Artemis Tauropolos (first meris);[3]

   b) tetradrachms with Artemis on shield/club in oak wreath (first and second merides);[4]

   c) tetradrachms with Macedonian shield with whirling star/club in oak wreath (Amphaxitis).[5]

2. From the time of Sulla onwards:

a) tetradrachms with Macedonian shield/club in oak wreath MAKEDONON;[6]

b) tetradrachms with Macedonian shield/club in oak wreath LEG MAKEDONON;[7]

c-d) tetradrachms with Alexander the Great/club, fiscus, and sella in wreath (Aesillas, Suura).[8]

Of these the last (2 c-d) is a very large issue, whose chronology has been much debated in recent years. It should be dated to the years after 94 BC, and circulated until and even later than 65 BC.[9] Its purpose was presumably to cover, during a period of shortages in the Roman treasury,[10] the expenditure required for the expulsion of the Thracian tribes and of the troops of Mithradates VI. They were perhaps issued at mints in Pella, Thessaloniki and Amphipolis.

As well as the issues produced in Macedonia itself, Roman denarii also played an increasingly important part in the silver currency of the area. A study of hoards shows that the "invasion" of Macedonia by the Roman denarius should be dated to the first part of the first century BC, in connection with the movements of the Roman legions to repel the threats from Thrace, and partly from Mithradates's armies. This conclusion is supported by the fact that denarii are often found together with tetradrachms of Aesillas in hoards. The following hoards are relevant:

1. Kerassia, Thessalomiki, 1960, deposited after 76 BC; IGCH 653 = RRCH 283.

2. Thessalomiki area, 1976, perhaps deposited in 75 BC; CH V (1979), 55.

3. Kavala, 1963, deposited 55-50 BC; IGCH 660 = RRCH 336.

4. Macedonia, 1980 (?), deposited c. 54 BC; CH VII (1985), 139.

The three hoards of unmixed Roman coinage from this period are:

1. Hoard from the Ancient Agora of Thessaloniki, deposited around 50 BC; QT 1984, 139-145.

2-3 Hoards from Macedonia, exact find-spot not known, deposited in 55 BC and 35 BC; CH III (1977), 127 and 131.

In contrast, the typical coinage circulating in the second half of the second century BC is mainly Athenian New Style tetradrachms and occasionally Thasian tetradrachms as shown by the hoards: Thessaloniki, 1929 (IGCH 478), Veroia, 1962 (IGCH 479), Macedonia (?), 1958 (IGCH 482) and Serres, 1913 (IGCH 550).[11]

BRONZE

A summary of the coin production in Macedonia during the period from 148/7 or 146 BC (the date of its conversion to a Roman province[12] until 31-27 BC cannot be made without first examining the coinage of the years of the reign of Philip V and of Perseus, as well as of the twenty years or so from 168/7 to 148/7 or 146 BC when the country was, in some respects, a protectorate of Rome. This investigation does not concern so much the coinage of the last two Macedonian kings or of the _merides_[13] as that of the Macedonian cities, since the traditional chronology of their issues within the period 187/6-31 BC (that of H. Gaebler)[14] is, as well known, conventional and, in many cases, erroneous.

The revision of the chronologies which have been proposed in the past, particularly for the issues of the mints of Thessaloniki, Amphipolis and Pella can be made by (a) the examination of all the hoards as a group (table A), (b) study of overstrikes (table B) and monograms (table C) and (c) by comparing and contrasting the types which are often used not only by these mints, but also - and this constitutes the main point of interest for their classification - by the royal issues of the Antigonids and by those issued in the name of the Macedonians and the districts of lower Macedonia.

First results from a preliminary investigation are:

A. The majority of the issues (always bronze) of the three Macedonian cities should be placed in the period 187/6-168/7 BC.[15] First most of the issues from the three mints - that is, those which have iconographic parallels with the coinage of the last Antigonids (both of the royal house itself and of the districts or the issues of the Macedonian nation)[16] - are represented in 90% of the hoards.[17] These hoards are to be dated to the time of Perseus, and probably towards the end of his reign, since issues of the _merides_ (i.e. 168/7-148/7 BC) are usually absent, whereas in some cases issues of early Macedonian kings (e.g. Kassander, Antigonos Gonatas, etc.), Philip V and of Perseus himself are present.

Secondly, these same issues from the same three mints, and only these, have the same style and fabric, and, as is proven by the hoards, were produced in an interrelated sequence.[18] Moreover, the same monograms sometimes occur not only on the various issues of a mint, but also on royal issues as well.[19] Whether this observation also indicates that the same mint was responsible for the city, the royal and the district coinages, would, however require a separate study.

Finally, coins which are not represented in the hoards mentioned above - except for those which, as will be shown, certainly belong to later periods - can be assigned to this early phase on the basis of iconography and fabric.

B. During the following two decades (i.e. 168/7-148/7 or 146 BC) when Macedonia was divided into four _merides_, the coin production of the three mints, which were the capitals of three of the four _merides_, seems to have been reduced considerably and restricted to the beginning of the period.

This conclusion is supported by the consideration that these issues are few in number and follow typologically and stylistically some of the issues of the quaestors C Publilius and L Fulcinius, namely those with the head of the goddess Roma on the obverse, which P. MacKay has correctly dated to 168-166 BC.[20]

This also shows that, in this period too, the three mints and the central government followed a common choice of design.

The assignment to these two decades of certain issues of Thessaloniki and Amphipolis, which recall Roman coinage by using the bifacial bearded head of Janus on the obverse,[21] is, for the moment, problematic. The hoard evidence seems to favour an earlier date, in the final years of Perseus, but the selection of this 'Roman' type makes such a hypothesis most implausible.[22]

Equally problematic is the question of the extent to which during this period, and also in the following period beginning in 148/7 or 146, the Macedonian mints continued to issue coins with some of the same types as in the previous period. This enigmatic category is represented by coins with poorly executed designs, virtually barbaric imitations, which are lighter in weight, smaller in size and crudely struck. They are known from stray finds, museum pieces and from only a single hoard of the middle of the first century BC (the Platania 1969 hoard = *IGCH* 663), which is itself curious in composition.

C. In the period 148/7 or 146 - 32/1 BC, during which the new province was overrun by barbarian hordes and became the theatre of the civil wars, the mints of Thessaloniki, Amphipolis and Pella seem to issue coins only occasionally and for specific events which are related to Roman activities in the east, rather than to those of the cities themselves.[23] Precisely for this reason these issues appear only at isolated points in time and, in contrast to earlier issues which were controlled by state or local authorities, they do not bear monograms, and are not characterised by a common style.

From the later first century, however, events in Macedonia itself directly influenced the coinage. During the stay of Pompey in Thessaloniki in 48 BC, a few months before the battle at Pharsalus, there must have been produced there a relatively small issue which is a copy of a denarius from the mint of Rome of 81 BC.[24] This issue constitutes tangible evidence for a historical event:[25] according to Dio, Pompey was obliged to hold elections for the new magistrates on Roman soil, and therefore decided to solve the dilemma by purchasing a plot of land in the middle of Thessaloniki upon which to perform the customary ceremonies.[26] The reverse of this coin celebrates the new 'Roman soil' by depicting a ploughman tracing the *primigenius sulcus* of Pompey's pseudo-colony.

Until new evidence, especially that of better preserved specimens, appears, the provisional ascription by Grant to the mint of Thessaloniki of the issues which, according to him, were put into circulation by M Acilius for Julius Caesar just after the defeat of Pompey, and by Q Hortensius Hortalus as *praefectus coloniis deducendis* under Brutus,[27] no matter how cleverly presented, still lacks the proof of hoard evidence and of certain Macedonian provenance.

The foundation coinages of Cassandreia, Dium and Philippi are no longer problematic following contributions on the subject by M. Grant, C.H.V. Sutherland, M. Amandry, and P.A. Brunt.[28]

The proclamation of Thessaloniki and Amphipolis as '<u>civitates liberae</u>'[29] by the Triumvirate shortly after the defeat of the Republicans at Philippi saw at Thessaloniki the production of four new issues related to each other by common stylistic characteristics and by the existence of the letter E in the ground of the obverse.[30] In these issues prominence is given to the liberators and to the new relationship between the city and Rome. Using the same example, without enjoying the same status, Pella put into circulation an issue which has the same spirit of celebration.[31] Amphipolis however, even though favoured by the new situation, seems not to have produced any similar new issues.

Another single issue of Thessaloniki, which Gaebler dated to the reign of Augustus,[32] could be assigned to the period 42-32 BC: the Zeus Ammon on the obverse and the eagle on the reverse, following late Ptolemaic prototypes,[33] could reflect the presence of Mark Antony in the East, and be connected with the influence of him and Cleopatra on the city, as known from epigraphic texts and building activities.[34] The extent to which the other cities of Macedonia issued coins during the period of Antony's pre-eminence remains to be investigated.[35] Probably the last chronologically certain Macedonian issue before the proclamation of Octavian as Augustus in 27 BC, but after the victory at Actium, is the Thessalonikan issue of 28/27 BC,[36] on which the new ruler of the world appears as successor to Julius Caesar.[37] This issue inaugurated, in Macedonia, what may be seen as the beginning of the tradition of Roman propaganda on provincial imperial coinage.[38]

TABLE A: HOARDS

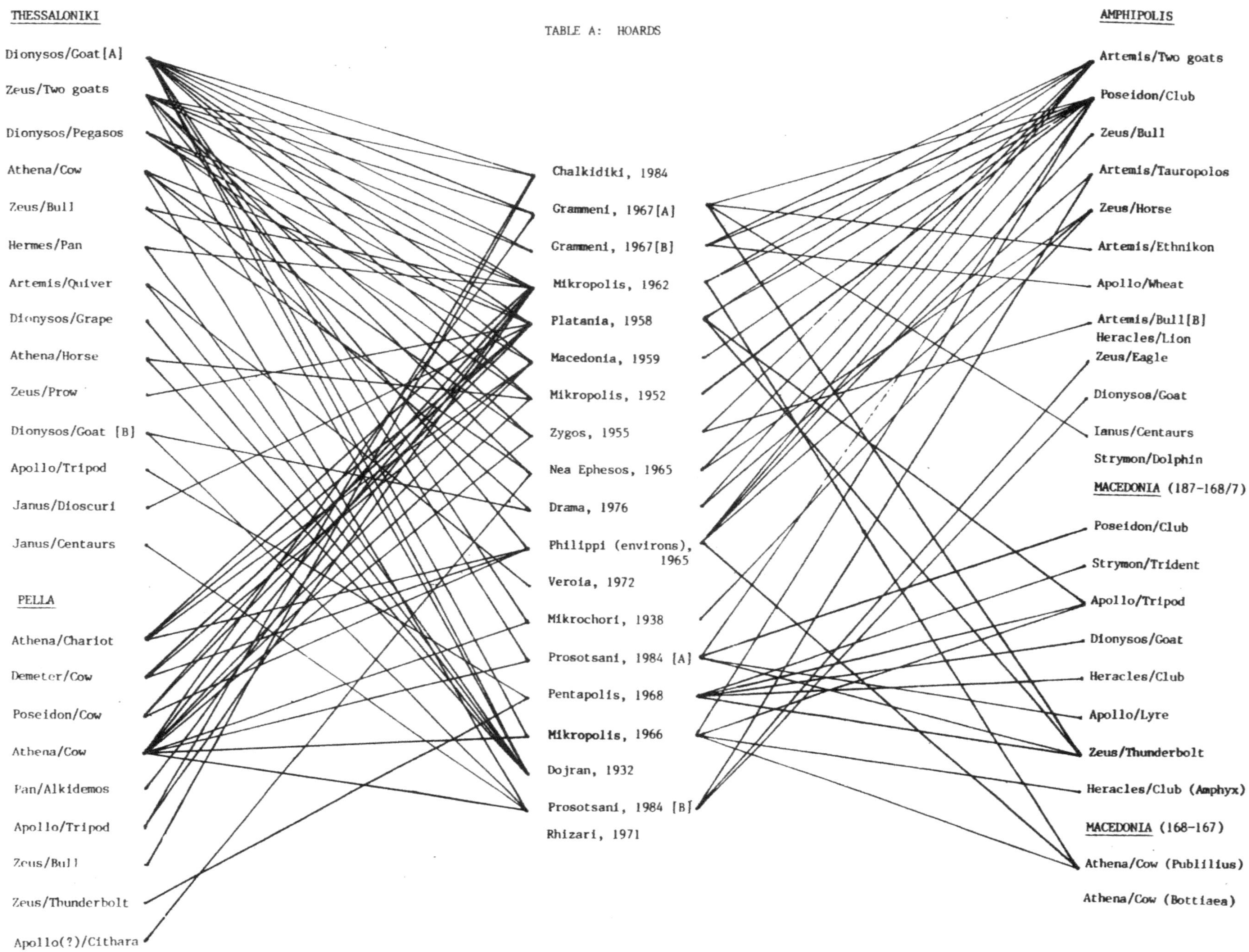

Notes to Table A:

1. The Dojran, 1932 hoard contained also coins of Philip V, Amphipolis, Pella and Macedonia which are not mentioned in IGCH 555. See now I. Mirnik, Numismaticke Vijesti (1986), 44.

2. The Prosotsani, 1984(B) hoard contained also three Amphipolis coins of the early Principate. The fact that the hoard was found in a pot within an unviolated cist grave renders the case peculiar, as the wear of the coins, those of the 2nd century B.C. and those of the time of Augustus, is identical for all specimens. An "enrichment" of the main bulk with three more coins early in the 1st century AD seems nevertheless improbable.

TABLE B: OVERSTRIKES

Thessaloniki	Amphipolis	Pella	Thessaly
Dionysos/Goat[A] (G. XXII, 23)	Zeus(?)/Bull (G. IX. 11)	Athena/Chariot (G. XVIII, 26)	Athena/Horse (SNG Cop. 324-28)
Zeus/Two goats (G. XXII, 25)			
Athena/Cow (G. XXIII, 3)	Hercules/Lion (G. IX, 12)	Athena/Cow (G. XIX, 4)	
Zeus/Bull (G. XXII, 28)	Poseidon/Club (G. IX, 2)		Maroneia
Dionysos/Grape (G. XXII, 21)			Dionysos/Dionysos (SNG Cop. 645-46)
Zeus/Eagle on th. (G. XXIII, 7)	Zeus/Prow (G. IX. 16)		
Zeus/Prow (G. XXIII, 5 and 12)			
Janus/Centaurs (G. XXIII, 9 and 10)			
Macedonia			
Apollo/Tripod (G. II, 28)			

TABLE C : MONOGRAMS

PHILIP V (Mamroth - bronze)

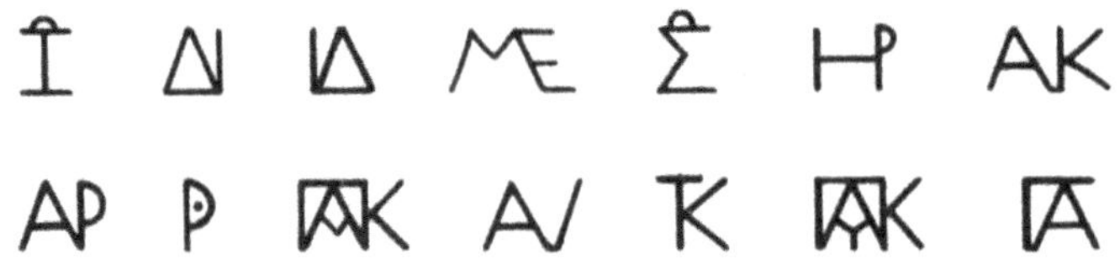

AMPHIPOLIS (*SNG* Cop.)

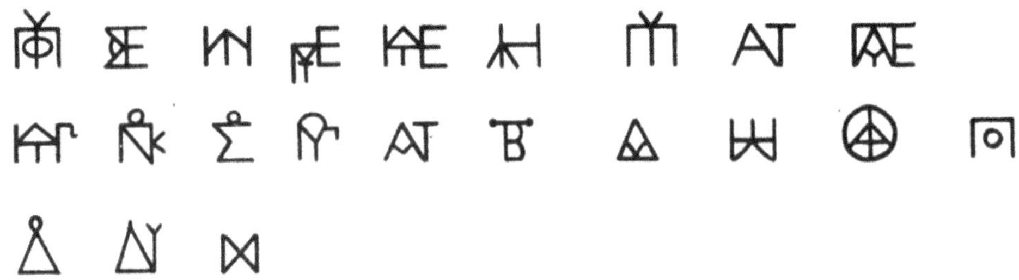

PELLA (*SNG* Cop.)

THESSALONIKI (*SNG* Cop.)

NOTES

1. The above historical sketch is taken directly from the text of F. Papazoglou who has provided an outline of the historical events and the socio-political situation in Macedonia after 168/67 BC, together with the sources and full bibliography: Macedonia 4000 years of Greek History and Civilization (Athens, 1983), "Macedonia under the Romans", 192 ff. The same author had previously presented a critical synthesis of recent research on the political organisation of Macedonia after 148 BC: "Quelques aspects de l'histoire de la province de Macédoine" ANRW II 7.1 (1979) 302 ff. Cf. E.S. Gruen, "Macedonia and the Settlement of 167 BC" in Philip II, Alexander the Great and the Macedonian Heritage, (Washington, 1982), 257-267; F.W. Walbank, 'Via illa nostra militaris: Some Thoughts on the Via Egnatia', Historia 1983, 131 ff. For the second half of the first century BC, see also E.J. Owens, 'Increasing Roman Domination of Greece in the years 48-27 BC', Latomus 35 (1976), 718-729.

2. CMRR 129 and 197, basing his scheme on two hoards (CMRR 197 and 320) published by A. Burnett in CH VII (1985), 54-67. Crawford has revised the positions taken by Gaebler in AMNG, MacKay (note 13) and M. Price, Coinage of the Macedonians (London, 1974), 30 ff.

3. AMNG no. 39. O. Picard raises the question of whether this issue does not, in fact, belong "aux toutes dernières années du Royaume", AIIN (1982), 246.

4. AMNG no. 40.

5. AMNG no. 8. Giovannini believes that "les émissions republicaines de la Macédoine, qui ont une couronne au revers, .. datent de 158 au plus tard, ... ont été mises en circulation dès l'abolition de la monarchie" (Rome, 16).

6. AMNG no. 46.

7. AMNG no. 7. Giovannini does not believe that "les Macédoniens aient pu continuer de frapper monnaie à leur nom après qu'ils eurent été réduits en province romaine", AIIN (1982), 177.

8. AMNG no. 7 and 9; there are also drachms for Aesillas (AMNG no. 8).

9. O. Morkholm, 'The Chronology of the New Style Coinage of Athens' ANSMN 29 (1984), 37-38. In a recent treatment of two new coin hoards from Macedonia, A. Burnett (note 2) casts doubt on the traditional chronology for the magistracy of Aesillas in the 90s proposed by M. Thompson, The New Style Silver Coinage of Athens (1961), 382 and repeated in her article, RN 1973, 54 ff; he rejects two proposals for a lower chronology early in the 60s put forward by D.M. Lewis, NC (1962), 296-299 and H.B. Mattingly, Chiron (1979), 147-169, and does not accept Chr. Boehringer's attempt to reconcile opposing views by assigning Aesillas's coinage a range extending from the years around 90 BC, down to the end of the 60s (SNR 1975, 62). Burnett presents arguments for dating the magistracy of Aesillas to the early years of the 70s, which, as the himself observes, would cause much revision and reassessment of the

prosopography and history of the period. It is, however, questionable whether the degree of wear on the coins in the hoards treated by Burnett may be taken as a decisive criterion which "very clearly puts Aesillas after the 80s and before the 60s". Strangely enough Burnett seems to have overlooked the book by Th. Sarikakis, Romaioi Archontes tes Eparchias Makedonias Part I (1971), 67-69 and especially 174; his article was also written before that of Morkholm had been published. See also now R.S. Fisher, ANSMN 30 (1985), 69-88. See also I. Prokopov, Numismatica 1985(1), 3-11 for a date of 89 BC for the Aesillas coinage and its circulation in Thrace; Prokopov believes that it was intended to pay the Denteletes, allies of Rome by that time.

10. Crawford, RRC p. 637.

11. A. Giovannini states "le monnayage romain ne fait son apparition dans le Nord (de la Grèce) qu'aux environs de 120 et n'y devient fréquent qu'à partir du dernier siècle av. J.-C. (Rome, 20; cf. id. AIIN 1982, 165). M. Crawford more correctly observes: "yet Roman coinage hardly circulated in Greece before Sulla" (CMRR 116). (For further discussion of the denarius in Greece, see the articles by Price and Buttrey, later in this volume).

12. 146 BC is now the preferable date for the conversion of Macedonia into a Roman province after the defeat of Andriskos; see M.G. Morgan, 'Q. Metellus Macedonicus and the province Macedonia', Historia 18 (1969), 422-446 and F. Papazoglou, 'Quelques aspects de l'histoire de la province de Macédoine', ANRW II 7.1. (1979) 307.

13. For the coinage of the last two Antigonids, see the basic studies by A. Mamroth, 'Die Bronzenmünzen des Königs Philippos V von Makedonien', ZfN XLII (1935), 219-251; 'Silbermünzen des Königs Philippos V von Makedonien,' ZfN XL (1930), 277-303; and 'Die Silbermünzen des Königs Perseus', ZfN XXXVIII (1928), 1-28. Cf. also P.R. Franke, 'Zur Finanzpolitik des makedonischen Königs Perseus während des Krieges mit Rom 171-168 v.Chr.', JNG 1957, 31-46. For the period after 168 BC see the decisively important article by P. MacKay, 'Bronze coinage in Macedonia, 168-166 BC', ANSMN 14, 1968, 5-13, especially 12-13. For contrasting views, see Crawford, CMRR 129 and 197.

14. Antike Münzen Nord Griechenlands III. 2 (1935) (cited here as AMNG).

15. After the conclusion of the Roman war against Antiochos (Treaty of Apameia, 188 BC), in which Philip's expectations of Roman concessions had been so decisively disappointed, the latter decided to build up as strong a kingdom as he could, with special care for his northern frontiers, for his relations with the peoples who lived beyond them, and for undertaking new economic measures including the development of the mines. From this period on, thanks to new privileges accorded to the cities and districts of Macedonia, the civic and district mints produced large quantities of coins. For the period and the measures see F.W. Walbank, in Macedonia. 4000 Years of Greek History and Civilisation (Athens, 1983), 165, with bibliography. For the numismatic reform, see especially H. Gaebler, ZfN 36 (1926), 111 ff. and 172; also A. Mamroth, ZfN 40 (1930), 282-283 and 42 (1935), 221.

16. A comparison of the various issues of the Macedonian city mints with those of the royal house and of the districts reveals similarities of

typology and iconography. Many of these types - especially those of the cities - are characteristic for Macedonia. Others, however, are undoubtedly copied or borrowed from the repertories of other Greek cities such as Athens and Thasos. These conclusions lead in turn to the following considerations and proposals:
In working to establish a date of c. 185 BC for the introduction of the New Style Athenian coinage, O. Morkholm was the first to note that the following issues imitated the head of Athena on the obverse of the New Style coinage:

1. The Macedonian bronze issues in the name of the quaestor G. Publilius which P. MacKay had correctly dated to 168/67 BC (see note 13).

2. The Macedonian series in the name of Botteatae from the period of Philip V and Perseus (Gaebler, AMNG 4 nr. 29 pl. XIII, 16).

There is considerable additional evidence to reinforce Morkholm's observations (note 9, 29 ff). The head of Athena on the issues of Pella and Thessaloniki minted within the period 187-167 BC, is also copied from Athenian New Style tetradrachms (Pella issues: Gaebler, op. cit. 93-94 nr. 1-2 pl. XVIII, 26; Thessaloniki issues: Gaebler, op. cit. 119 nr. 12 pl. XXIII, 3). (Editorial note: compare the remarks of M. Price, p. 100 note 3). Imitations of the head of Dionysos on the obverses of the 'New Style' tetradrachms of Thasos and Maroneia provide, on the other hand, the head of the God of wine on the obverse of the Thessalonikan coins of the type Gaebler, op. cit. 118 nr. 4 pl. XXII, 22 and 119 nr. 9 pl. XXII, 21, dated to the period 187-168/7 BC. Thus, the date of the former within the reigns of Philip V and Perseus seems to gain in probability. The earlier dates, previously proposed, thereby lose much of their credibility: G. Le Rider set the beginning of the Thasian coinage at 180 BC (Guide de Thasos (1968), 189-90, "Les monnaies thasiennes"); A. Giovannini dated it after the Third Macedonian War (Rome, 16-17); according to Crawford both the Thasian and Maroneitan tetradrachms probably circulated from 158 BC onwards "in parallel to that of the First and Second (Macedonian) Regions" (CMRR 125 and 131). (Editorial note: compare O. Picard, p. 80).

17. A first attempt to put together the second century BC hoards from Macedonia, mainly of bronze coins, was undertaken by I. Touratsoglou, "The Koufalia, 1966 hoard of 3rd c. Greek Imperials in the Numismatic Collection of the Thessaloniki Museum", in Ancient Macedonian Studies in honour of Charles F. Edson (1981), 317. The number of hoards has been appreciably augmented thanks to the kind assistance of present and past Directors and archaeologists on the staff of the Museums of Thessaloniki, Kavala and Edessa: J. Vokotopoulou, H. Koukouli, M. Siganidou, A. Vavritsas and V. Poulios. I also wish to acknowledge with thanks contributions by M. Oeconomides, Director of the Numismatic Museum in Athens, and I. Mirnik, the Archaeological Museum of Zagreb, and P. Ilisch, the Wesfälisches Landesmuseum für Kunst und Kulturgeschichte.

The majority of the hoards located so far, twenty four in all, come mainly, as was to be expected, from Macedonia itself (23), especially Eastern Macedonia. Most of them come from tombs. In the catalogue, the following abbreviations are used:

NM = Numismatic Museum, Athens.

MK = Archaeological Museum, Kavala.

ME = Archaeological Museum, Edessa.

MV = Archaeological Museum, Veroia.

MACEDONIA

Zygos, Kavala, 1955 (IGCH 552) (NM).

Macedonia, 1959 (IGCH 553) (NM).

Mikrochori, Drama, 1938 (IGCH 551) (NM).

Philippi (environs), c. 1965 (IGCH 483) (Münster).

Chalkidiki, 1984 (NM casts).

Nea Ephesos, Pieria, 1965 (ADelt 21, 1966, 12) (NM).

Grammeni, Drama, 1967(A) (ADelt 23, 1968, 356) (MK).

Granneni, Drama, 1967(B) (ADelt 23, 1968, 356) (MK).

Mikropolis, Drama, 1962 (MK).

Prosotsani, Drama, 1984(A) (MK).

Mikropolis, Drama, 1952 (MK).

Drama, 1976 (ADelt 31, 1976, 303-304) (MK).

Platania, Drama, 1958 (IGCH 554) (NM).

Veroia, 1972 (Makedonika 14, 1974, 172) (MV).

Rizari, Edessa, 1971 (ME).

Platania, Drama, 1959 (IGCH 663) (NM).

Pentapolis, Serres, 1968 (MK).

Mikropolis, Drama, 1966 (NM & MK).

Dojran, 1932 (IGCH 555) (Zagreb).

Grammeni, Drama, 1927 (IGCH 473) (NM).

Prosotsani, Drama, 1984(B) (MK).

Drama, 1929 (NM).

S. Macedonia, 1980 (CH VII, 1985, 102) (dispersed).

OUTSIDE OF MACEDONIA

Galaxeidi, 1967-68 (IGCH 238 = CH II, 1976, 85) (Amphissa).

18. Table A illustrates the distribution of the various issues throughout the hoards and it also provides an approximate chronological sequence of issues within each mint.
Table B collects all the overstrikes known to the author. Overstruck coins (indicating abundant continuous overlapping production) are to be found only within the first two periods proposed in this paper.

19. See Table C, which presents a selection of monograms enabling the reader to make the comparisons for himself. Monograms occur only on coins of this and the following period.

20. ANSMN 14 (1968), 5-11. Although M. Crawford dates the issues with quaestors' names to the period after 168 BC, he believes (evidently in opposition to MacKay's views) that they "cannot at the moment be closely dated" (CMRR, 131).
For the cult of Dea Roma in Macedonia, see C. Fayer, Il culto della Dea Roma. Origine e diffusione nell'Impero (1976) 13 ff, 19, 76-79; R. Mellor, Thea Rome, The worship of the Goddess Roma in the Greek World (Hypomnemata 42, 1975), 107-109. According to C. Edson, the cult of Zeus Eleutherios and Roma was introducted into Macedonia immediately after 148 BC as an expression of gratitude on the part of the inhabitants towards the Romans for liberating them from Andriskos's "tyranny" (HSCP 1940, 133-135). R. Mellor, on the other hand, believes that the cult was introduced directly after the battle of Pydna (op. cit. 163 and ANRW, II. 17. 2, 1981, 962). F. Papazoglou deals with the subject critically (ANRW II 7.1, 1979, 307-308). L. Robert does not take a stand on this point in Rev. Phil. 48 (1974) 211 note 192. For representations of Dea Roma on Roman coins of the Republic, see RRC 721 ff.

21. The vertical line (I) appearing above the head of Janus and the S-shaped line on coins of Thessaloniki and Amphipolis have been interpreted as marks of value, the vertical line standing for an as, the S for a semis (for the vertical line above the Janus head on coins of Thessaloniki, see Gaebler, op. cit. 120-121, nos. 17, 19, 20 with pl. XXIII, 8-10; on coins of Amphipolis ibid., 36 nr. 41 pl. IX, 15. For the S on coins of Thessaloniki, ibid., 120 nr. 18 pl. XXIII, 12; on the coins of Amphipolis, ibid., 36 nr. 42 pl. IX, 16). Two pieces of evidence show that this interpretation is mistaken:

1. The vertical line appears on the abverse of coins of varying sizes and weights: this virtually eliminates the possibility of its being a mark of value (The Janus head is most likely a direct borrowing from Roman coinage).

2. The S, appearing in front of a prow on the reverse of coins from Thessaloniki and behind a male head wreathed with laurel (Zeus?) on the obverse of coins from Amphipolis, does not represent the Latin letter S standing for a semis but depicts a dolphin with its tail pointing upward (ibid., pl. XXII, 12, Thessaloniki, and pl. IX, 16, Amphipolis).

Amphipolis).

B. Mitrea makes no substantial progress in solving the problem of when Roma and particularly Janus first appeared on coins from certain Macedonian cities in the pre-imperial period, nor does he use the more recent literature at least in respect of Macedonia topics: 'Effigies romaines sur les monnaies de la Macédoine et de la Dacie du IIe siècle av. n.è'., QT 1981, 247-259 and especially 247-248. 254. R. Turcan, 'Janus à l'époque impériale', ANRW II 17.1, 397, offers no interpretation of why Janus appears on pre-imperial coins of Thessaloniki and Amphipolis (which he dates, in general, "avant-31") since he evidently takes it for granted that Janus is "un signe de valeur" on Maccedonian coins as on the Roman coins they imitate.

M. Crawford (CMRR 209) gives 70 BC as the probable date of the Janus head issues of Thessaloniki and Amphipolis with no supporting arguments, merely stating that they "reveal the influence of Rome". To these issues he links, for no apparent reason, the Thessalonikan issue of the type: Gaebler, op. cit. 118-119 nr. 6 pl. XXII, 28.

The fact that the Romans thought of Janus as the god with whom everything has its beginning - Statius's "immensi reparator maximus aevi" - could have influenced the Macedonians' choice on Roman coins, see H. Grueber, BMC Republic I, xxii; cf. J. Gagé, 'Sur les origines du culte de Janus', RHR 195 (1979), 3. The asses of 211 BC mark Janus's first appearance as a double-faced and bearded head on Roman coinage (M. Crawford, CMRR 55-56, fig. 17).

22. It is nevertheless obvious that the Macedonian coinage of the period before 168/67 BC had in some cases imitated the technique of a certain issue of Roman denarii, namely the serrati; the bronzes of Philip V of the type Gaebler, op. cit. pl. XXXV, 6 and those of the Macedonians of the type Gaebler, op. cit. pl. II, 19 constitute the proof for this. For the technique and the meaning of the Roman serrati, see M. Crawford RRC II, 581.

23. Cf. A. Giovannini, Rome 34-5.

24. The coin of Thessaloniki: AMNG, 122 no. 26-7 (wrongly dated to the reign of Augustus); for the prototype: RRC 378/1a-c.

25. For the period and the event, see M. Gelzer, Pompeius^{2} (1959), 214-15; J. van Ooteghem, Pompée le Grand (1954), 591-92; E. Meyer Caesars Monarchie und das Principat des Pompejus (1963), 313 ff. Cf. also Th. Mommsen, Römisches Staatsrecht I (1887), 102-103.

26. Dio 41,18,5; 41,43,1-4. Cf. Plut., Pompeius 64,4, Lucan, Pharsalia 5,9,5,11,22, Appian, b.c. II 52,213.

27. FITA 13f., 33f. For Brutus's activity in the East, see E-M. Kniely, Quellenkritische Studien zur Tätigkeit des M. Brutus im Osten (44-42 v. Chr.) (1974), 76ff., with bibliography.

28. Grant, FITA 272-4, Sutherland JRS 1941, 73-81, Amandry RN 1981, 45-67, Brunt, Italian Manpower (Oxford, 1971), 598-9.

29. See Pliny IV. 36 "Thessalonice liberae conditionis"; IV. 38 "Amphipolim liberum (sc. oppidum)". For the status of Macedonian cities before 42/41 BC and after 146 BC, see A.H.M. Jones, 'Civitates liberae et immunes in the East', in Anatolian Studies presented to W.H. Buckler (1939), 109-110. Cf. also R. Bernhardt, 'Die immunitas der Freistädte', Historia, 1980, 190-207 with bibliography.

30. BMC 62, AMNG p. 121, no. 23; p. 113, no. 43; p. 121, no. 22.

31. AMNG pp. 96-97, no. 19, with plate XIX. 9.

32. AMNG p. 128 no. 25, with plate XXIII. 14.

33. Cf. also a coin from Zakynthos dated to 39-32 BC, with the eagle on the reverse and the head of Antony on the obverse (SNG Cop. 489).

34. IG X 2.1, nos. 30, 50, 83, 109 and 124; Chr. Habicht, Gnomon 46 (1974), 489.

35. It would be possible to assign other coins to this period on the basis of iconographic, stylistic and technical similarities with coins in the series, for example, the Pella issue: Gaebler, op. cit. 96, nr. 18 pl. XIX, 8 (the coin from the Münzkabinett in Berlin illustrated by Gaebler was not overstruck, as Gaebler states).

36. According to the reckoning of C. Edson, HSCP 51 (1940), 132.

37. AMC 1110. The theories of R. Martini, 'Monetazione bronzea orientale di Marcus Antonius', RIN 86 (1984), 17 ff., and especially 24-26, 29-31, 41-42 on various aspects of the Thessaloniki mint do not stand up to criticism. Martini's type (f) is simply an issue of the year 28/27 BC and is not dated to 41/40 BC. Type (i), issued in the reign of Vespasian with Titus and Domitian on the obverse, cannot possibly be dated to 40/35 BC, nor can the portraits be identified as Antony and Octavia. Type (t) dates to the last years of Augustus's reign, directly after the adoption of Tiberius and has no connection whatsoever with the year 34/3 BC tentatively suggested.

38. For this 'policy' in issues which Thessaloniki struck in the imperial period, see I. Touratsoglou, Die Münzstätte von Thessaloniki in der römischen Kaiserzeit (Berlin, in press).

PLATE 6

PHILIP V (bronze)

1. Grose II pl. 136, 8.
2. G. III^2 194 nr. 29 pl. XXXV, 9.
3. ZfN XLII pl. VI, 5.
4. G. III^2 nr. 24 pl. XXXV, 1.
5. G. III^2 194 nr. 31 pl. XXXV, 12.
6. ZfN XLII pl. VI, 8.
7. G. III^2 nr. 32 pl. XXXV, 19-20.
8. G. III^2 191 nr. 8-9 pl. XXXIV, 22.
9. G. III^2 191 nr. 11 pl. XXXIV, 24.
10. G. III^2 192 nr. 15 pl. XXXIV, 27.
11. ZfN XLII pl. VII, 10.
12. G. III^2 192 nr. 16 pl. XXXIV, 28.
13. G. III^2 193 nr. 23 pl. XXXV, 21.
14. G. III^2 191 nr. 12 pl. XXXV, 2.
15. G. III^2 193 pl. XXXV, 22 (Philip VI).
16. G. III^2 191 nr. 7 pl. XXXIV, 21.
17. SNG Evelp. 1444.
18. G. III^2 193 nr. 20-21 pl. XXXV, 4.
19. ZfN XLII pl. VII, 7.
20. G. III^2 193 nr. 25 pl. XXXV, 5.
21. G. III^2 194 nr. 30 pl. XXXV, 11.
22. G. III^2 194, nr. 26-27 pl. XXXV, 6-7.
23. G. III^2 192-193 nr. 19 pl. XXXV, 3.
24. G. III^2 192 nr. 17 pl. XXXIV, 29.

PLATE 7

MACEDONIA UNDER PHILIP V and PERSEUS

1. G. III^2 2 nr. 11 pl. II, 22.
2. G. III^2 4 nr. 23, pl. II, 27.
3. G. III^2 4 nr. 22 pl. II, 21.
4. G. III^2 3 nr. 21 pl. II, 26.
5. G. III^2 2 nr. 12 pl. II, 23.
6. G. III^2 3 nr. 16 pl. II, 29.
7. G. III^2 4 nr. 24 pl. II, 28.
8. G. III^2 2 nr. 14 pl. II, 25.
9. G. III^2 2 nr. 13 pl. II, 24.
10. G. III^2 3 nr. 17 pl. II, 30.
11. G. III^2 3 nr. 15 pl. II, 18.
12. G. III^2 2 nr. 10 pl. II, 19.
13. G. III^2 5 nr. 30 pl. XII, 18.
14. G. III^2 5 nr. 31-32 pl. XII, 17.
15. G. III^2 4 nr. 29 pl. XII, 16.
16. G. III^2 5 nr. 33 pl. XII, 15.
17. G. III^2 5 nr. 34 pl. XII, 19.
18. G. III^2 3 nr. 20 pl. VII, 23.
19. G. III^2 3, nr. 19 pl. VII, 22.

MACEDONIA AS ROMAN PROTECTORATE

20. G. I 66-67 nr. 203-206 pl. II, 8.
21. G. III^2 8 nr. 2 pl. III, 10.
22. G. III^2 8 nr. 3 pl. III, 11.
23. G. III^2 8 nr. 4 pl. XII, 21.
24. G. III^2 8 nr. 5 pl. XII, 20.
25. G. III^2 8-9 nr. 6 pl. III, 12.

26. G. III^2 7 nr. 43 pl. III, 8.

27. G. III^2 7 nr. 42 pl. III, 7.

PLATE 8

THESSALONIKI

1. G. III^2 117 nr. 1 pl. XXII, 23.
2. G. III^2 118 nr. 3 pl. XXII, 25.
3. G. III^2 118 nr. 4 pl. XXII, 22.
4. G. III^2 118-119 nr. 6 pl. XXII, 28.
5. G. III^2 119 nr. 12 pl. XXIII, 3.
6. G. III^2 118 nr. 5 pl. XXII, 20.
7. G. III^2 119 nr. 11 pl. XXIII, 2.
8. G. III^2 119 nr. 9 pl. XXXII, 21.
9. G. III^2 118 nr. 2 pl. XXII, 24.
10. G. III^2 119 nr. 10 pl. XXIII, 1.
11. G. III^2 120 nr. 13 pl. XXIII, 4.
12. G. III^2 119 nr. 8 pl. XXII, 26.
13. G. III^2 120 nr. 16 pl. XXIII, 7.
14. G. III^2 120 nr. 15 pl. XXIII, 6.
15. G. III^2 120 nr. 14 pl. XXIII, 5.
16. G. III^2 120 nr. 17 pl. XXIII, 8.
17. G. III^2 120 nr. 19 pl. XXIII, 9.
18. G. III^2 120 nr. 18 pl. XXIII, 12.
19. G. III^2 119 nr. 7 pl. XXII, 27.
20. G. III^2 121 nr. 20 pl. XXIII, 10.
21. G. III^2 121 nr. 21 pl. XXIII, 11.
22. G. III^2 122 nr. 27 pl. XXIII, 16.
23. G. III^2 122 nr. 26 pl. XXIII, 15.

24. SNG Cop. 374.

25. G. III^2 121 nr. 23 pl. XXIV, 3.

26. G. III^2 121 nr. 22 pl. XXIII, 13.

27. G. III^2 121 nr. 24 pl. XXIII, 17.

28. G. III^2 122 nr. 25 pl. XXIII, 14.

29. G. III^2 125 nr. 43 pl. XXIV, 6.

PLATE 9

AMPHIPOLIS

1. G. III^2 33 nr. 23 pl. VIII, 23.

2. G. III^2 35 nr. 35 pl. IX, 10.

3. G. III^2 35 nr. 34 pl. IX, 9.

4. G. III^2 35 nr. 33 pl. IX, 8.

5. G. III^2 35 nr. 36 pl. IX, 11.

6. G. III^2 35 nr. 37 pl. IX, 12.

7. G. III^2 34-35 nr. 32 pl. IX, 7.

8. G. III^2 35-36 nr. 39-40 pl. IX, 3.

9. G. III^2 34 nr. 28 pl. IX, 3.

10. G. III^2 34 nr. 26-27 pl. IX, 1-2.

11. G. III^2 35 nr. 38 pl. IX, 13.

12. G. III^2 36 nr. 43 pl. IX, 17.

13. G. III^2 33-34 nr. 24 pl. VIII, 24.

14. G. III^2 34 nr. 30 pl. IX, 5.

15. G. III^2 34 nr. 31 pl. IX, 6.

16. G. III^2 37 nr. 53 pl. IX, 27.

17. G. III^2 36 nr. 42 pl. IX, 16.

18. G. III^2 36 nr. 41 pl. IX, 15.

19. G. III^2 37 nr. 51 pl. IX, 25.

20. G. III^2 34 nr. 29 pl. IX, 4.

PLATE 10

PELLA

1. G. III^2 93-94 nr. 1-2 pl. XVIII, 26.
2. G. III^2 96 nr. 14-15 pl. XIX, 4.
3. G. III^2 94 nr. 3 pl. XIX, 5.
4. G. III^2 95 nr. 8 pl. XVIII, 30.
5. G. III^2 94 nr. 5 pl. XVIII, 29.
6. G. III^2 94 nr. 4 pl. XVIII, 27.
7. SNG Cop. 265.
8. G. III^2 95 nr. 9 pl. XVIII, 31.
9. G. III^2 96 nr. 17 pl. XIX, 7.
10. G. III^2 96 nr. 16 pl. XIX, 6.
11. G. III^2 95 nr. 10-11 pl. XIX, 1.
12. G. III^2 95 nr. 12 pl. XIX, 3.
13. G. III^2 95 nr. 6-7 pl. XVIII, 28.
14. G. III^2 96-97 nr. 19 pl. XIX, 9.
15. G. III^2 96 nr. 18 pl. XIX, 8.

PHILIP V (Bronze).

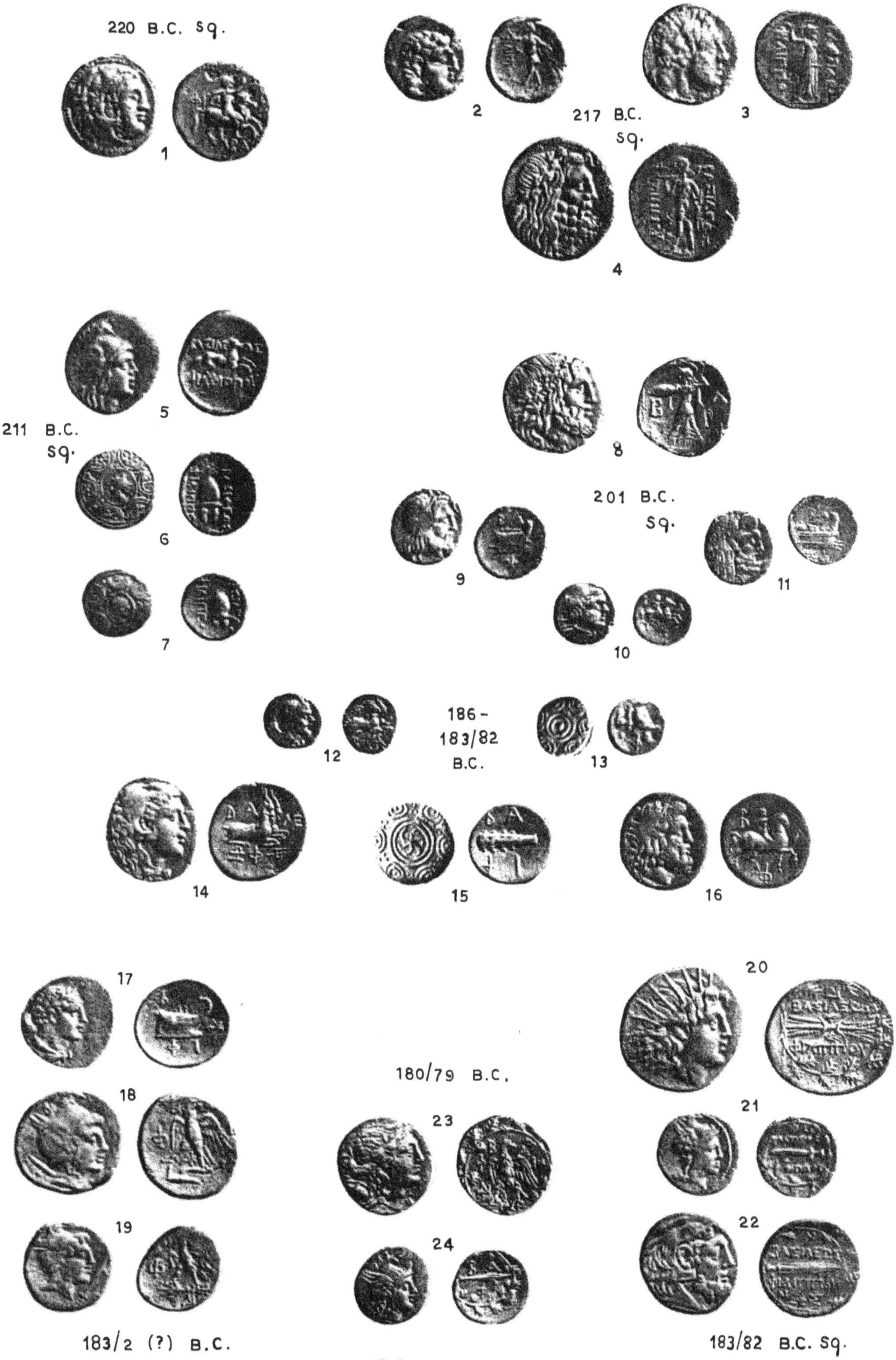

Plate 6.

MACEDONIA UNDER PHILIP V & PERSEUS.

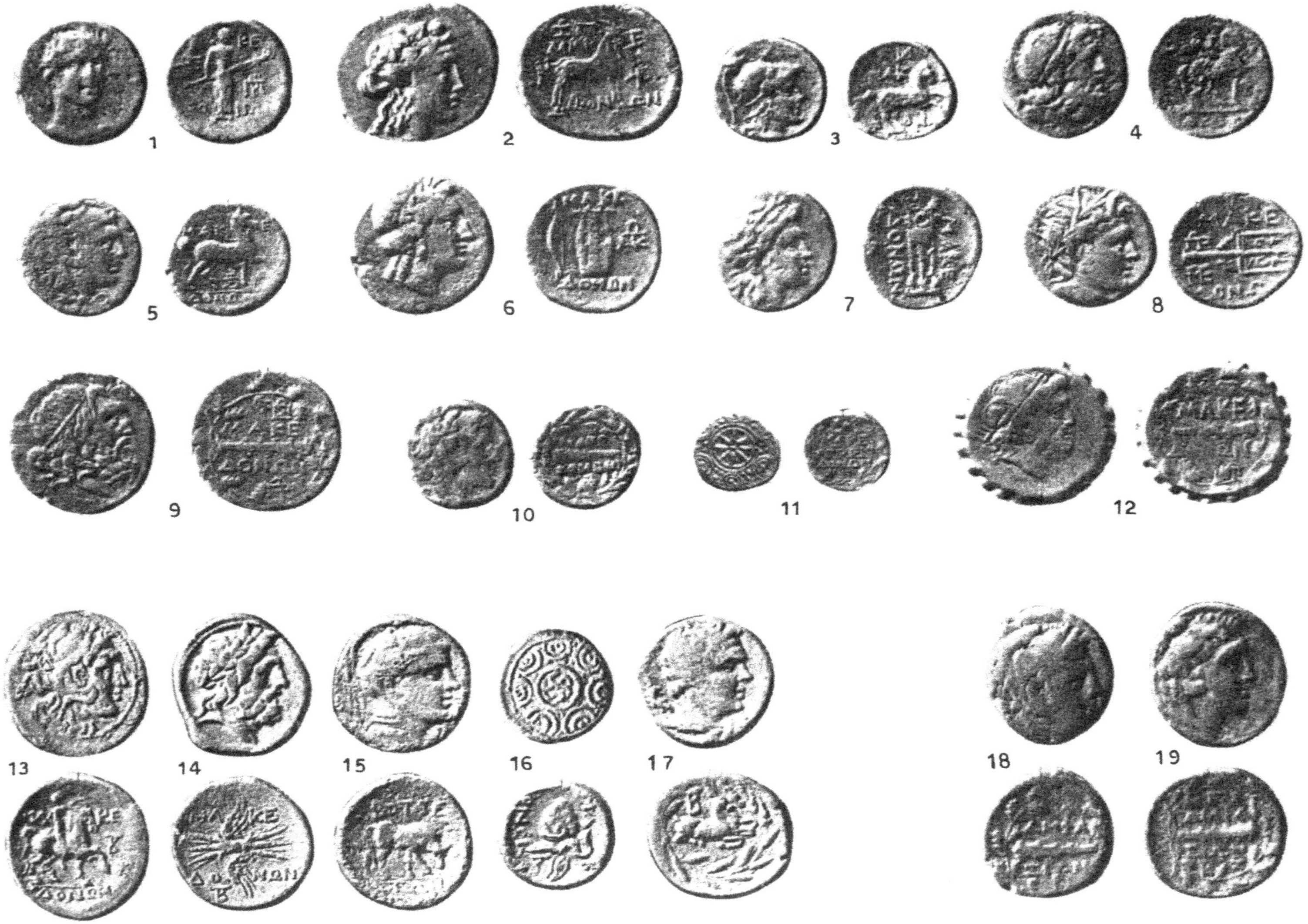

MACEDONIA AS ROMAN PROTECTORATE.

168 - 166 B.C.

20

21

22

23

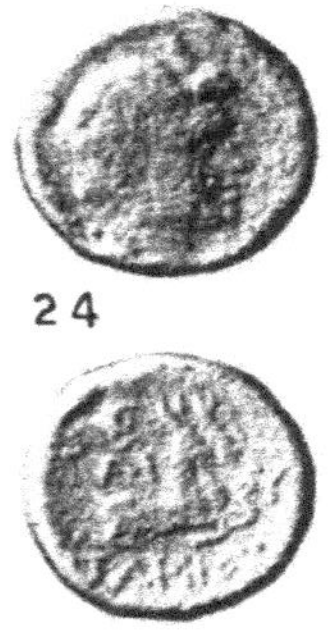
24

166-165 B.C.

25

167-149 B.C.

26

27

Plate 7.

THESSALONIKI 187–168/67 B.C.

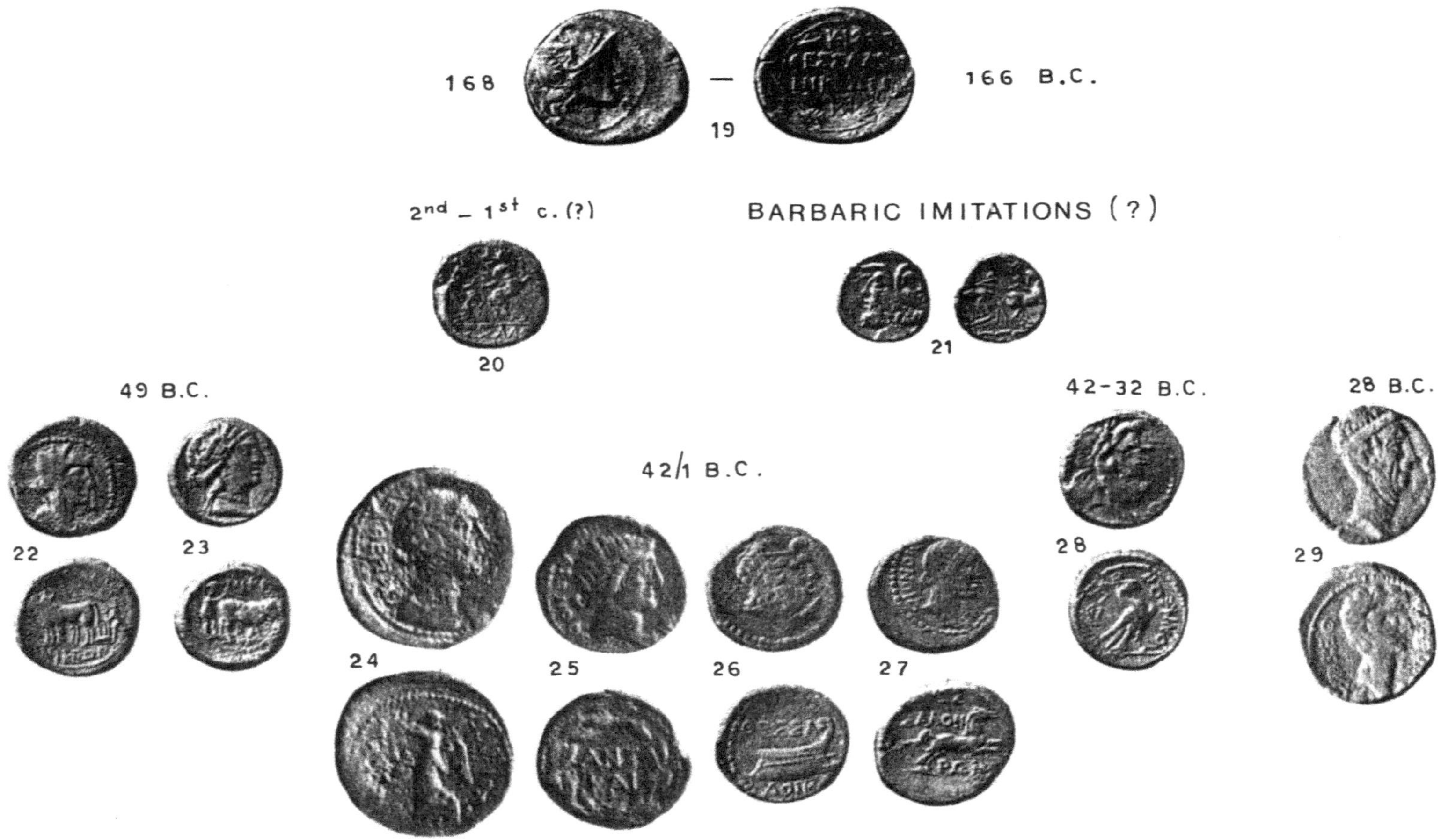
168 — 166 B.C.
19
2nd – 1st c. (?)
20
BARBARIC IMITATIONS (?)
21
49 B.C.
22
23
42/1 B.C.
24
25
26
27
42-32 B.C.
28
28 B.C.
29

Plate 8.

AMPHIPOLIS. 187–168/7 B.C.

1 2 3 4 5 6 7 8 9 10 11 12 13 14 15

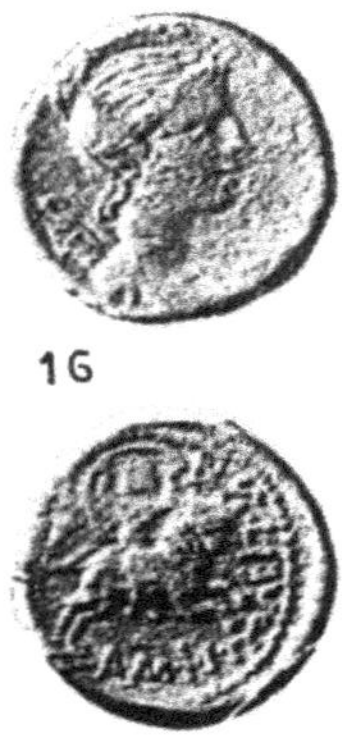

16

17

18

19

168-166 B.C.

20

Plate 9.

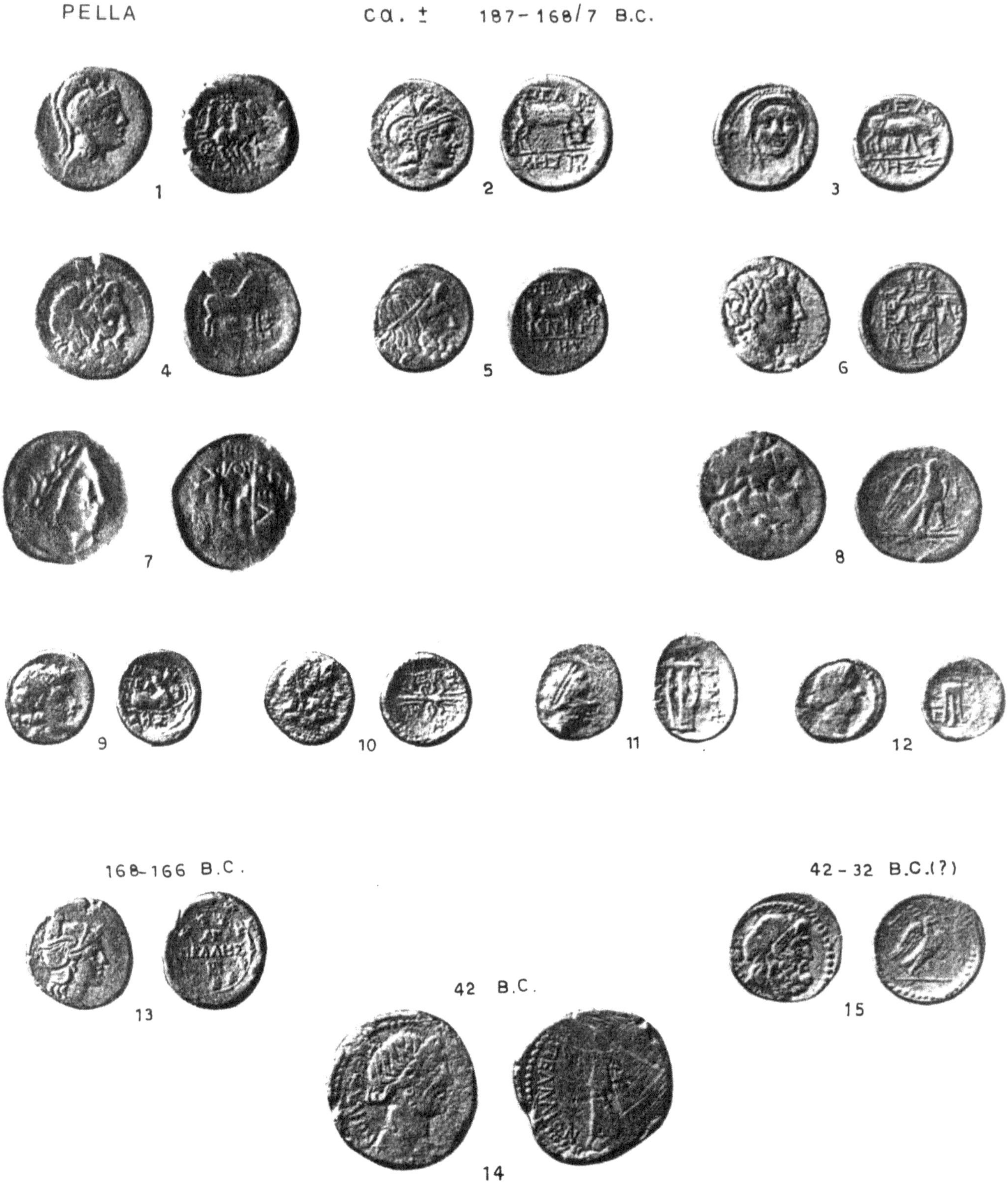
PELLA
ca. ± 187-168/7 B.C.
1
2
3
4
5
6
7
8
9
10
11
12
168-166 B.C.
42-32 B.C.(?)
13
42 B.C.
15
14

Plate 10.

THRACE

O. Picard

Etudier le monnayage en Thrace à la fin de la République romaine, et notamment le contexte juridique, économique et politique de la production et de la circulation de ces monnaies demande d'abord quelques précisions.

Une première remarque sera d'ordre géographique: les monnayages dont nous allons traiter ne sont pas des monnayages thraces, qui sont difficilement datables[1], qui émanent de royaumes ou principautés mal localisés et mal définis, et qui restent rares, sauf peut-être à la fin de la période[2]. Nous allons en fait examiner les émissions des cités grecques de la côte thrace ou des îles voisines. Ce sont toutes des villes indépendantes, alliées de Rome à qui elles doivent d'avoir été délivrées de la domination des rois de Macédoine, ou d'autres souverains comme Antiochos III, ou à tout le moins d'un voisinage pesant[3]: cette liberté retrouvée marque le début de notre période. Si leurs rapports avec les Romains passent régulièrement, après 146, par le gouverneur de Thessalonique, elles n'ont aucune organisation commune, n'appartiennent à aucun organisme régional[4]. D'autre part, cette ceinture côtière occupée par les Grecs ne constitue pas une unité régionale: des cités insulaires comme Thasos ou Samothrace ne sont pas dans la même situation que des cités côtières comme Abdère ou Maronée, exposées aux attaques thraces. L'activité des ports des Détroits comme Sestos ou Byzance dépend au moins autant des échanges maritimes et de la vie de la Propontide, y compris sa côte Sud, que des perturbations du continent thrace. Il faudrait distinguer deux sous-régions: la côte égéenne jusqu'à Ainos, puis les villes de la Propontide et du Pont gauche -- ce qui correspond aux deux grandes catégories de tétradrachmes, les lysimaques posthumes de Byzance et du Pont d'une part, les tétradrachmes au type de Dionysos de Thasos et de Maronée de l'autre.

Le morcellement politique, géographique de la région nous impose de procéder à une brève étude de chaque atelier, avant de dégager les grandes tendances de la période. Pour ce faire, l'examen de l'état actuel de la bibliographie[5] est un peu décevant: alors que les textes épigraphiques, si peu nombreux qu'ils soient, témoignent de la vitalité de ces cités, il n'y aurait, à en juger le BMC et la Syllogé de Copenhague[6], que quatre ateliers à frapper monnaie au deuxième et au premier siècle: Ainos, Maronée, Sestos et Byzance (où les émissions retenues sont en fait, comme l'a montré E. Schönert-Geiss, au plus tôt de l'époque augustéenne). Pour corriger et compléter cette image, nous ne disposons pas, malheureusement, de trésors publiés. Restent les monnaies de fouille, et tout particulièrement les monnaies des fouilles de Thasos, dont je prépare la publication. Les reclassements et redatations que je vais proposer m'ont été suggérés par l'étude de ce matériel considérable, — avec le risque que les conclusions que l'ont peut en tirer ne vaillent surtout que pour les cités de la Thrace occidentale.

I. Thasos: je résumerai, à grands traits, quelques résultats obtenus qu'il ne m'est pas possible d'exposer ni de justifier en détail. Thasos a frappé alors, avec régularité[7], des monnaies d'argent et deux modules de bronze:

1. des tétradrachmes (et quelques rares émissions de drachmes) de poids attique, avec la tête de Dionysos au droit et Héraclès Sôter au revers. Après quelques faibles émissions dont les monogrammes changent régulièrement, la série n'utilise plus que deux ou trois monogrammes pour des dizaines de coins. Une émission porte le nom d'un magistrat romain, Q. Braetius Sura;

2. des grands bronzes aux types d'Artémis et d'Héraclès archer;

3. des moyens bronzes à la tête et aux armes d'Héraclès;

4. une émission de petits bronzes est liée à un épisode particulier du monnayage[8].

Les émissions sont différenciées, pendant la plus grande partie de l'histoire de cette série, par des monogrammes de monétaires et, à la fin, seulement par des caractéristiques stylistiques. Je n'ai pu établir aucun lien entre les bronzes et les tétradrachmes à flan large dont, à vrai dire, je me demande dans quelle mesure, malgré le maintien de l'ethnique THASION, ce sont vraiment des monnaies de la cité. Pour les bronzes, j'ai distingué 22 émissions (17 par les monogrammes, 5 par le style) qui comprennent tantôt les deux modules de bronze, tantôt un seul, auxquelles il faut ajouter l'émission de petits bronzes (no. 4).

La chronologie relative des bronzes est relativement bien assurée, notamment grâce à deux trésors. Elle révèle de nombreuses variations dans le système de contrôle des émissions, ainsi que deux épisodes de contremarquage des monnaies antérieures (c'est lors de l'un d'eux que furent frappés les petits bronzes), et donc une instabilité sensible à la fois dans l'organisation de l'atelier et dans la politique monétaire de la cité. La fin de la série est caractérisée par une dégradation très sensible du style et des poids[9]; la frappe des moyens bronzes est abandonnée dans les six dernières émissions et le poids des grands bronzes des deux dernières tombe au-dessous de celui des bronzes moyens. On observe un même déclin dans le volume des émissions: à une phase d'émissions très abondantes, très proches les unes des autres par le style et, sans doute, par la date, succèdent des émissions à la fois plus maigres et, apparemment, plus espacées dans le temps.

Il est difficile de passer de la chronologie relative à une chronologie absolue. A titre d'hypothèse, je placerais le début de la série vers 180-170[10], et la fin au moment de l'offensive des armées de Mithridate contre Thasos, aux alentours de 91-81[11]. Mais on ne saurait exclure ni que la série ait duré jusqu'à la bataille de Philippes, ni, en sens contraire, qu'elle se soit arrêtée plus tôt, quelque part dans la deuxième moitié du deuxième siècle.

II. Ainos. Certains de ces traits se retrouvent à Ainos dans la série de grands bronzes que Strack[12] place, certainement à juste titre, au deuxième et au premier siècle:

5. Tête de Poséidon à dr. / Hermès nu, debout de face ou de léger 3/4 à g., la tête à g.

La silhouette du revers rappelle très précisément celle d'Héraclès sur les tétradrachmes à flan large de Thasos, ou celle du Dionysos sur les tétradrachmes de Maronée qui sont contemporains. On ne trouve aucun nom ou monogramme de monétaire, mais certaines émissions (ou certains groupes d'émissions) portent un type secondaire: autel allumé, coq, une paire de moutons, un mouton, un demi-bélier ...

La série est abondante et son histoire montre une évolution comparable à celle de la série thasienne, trahissant une détérioration très nette du style et du poids des pièces au fil du temps: le poids s'échelonne entre 13.26g et 4.5g pour les exemplaires catalogués par Strack et il atteint même 3.2g pour une pièce trouvée à Thasos, particulièrement usée, il est vrai. Strack avait déjà bien remarqué que le travail du graveur était de qualité très variable et que la pièce la plus légère avait, associé à un droit de style passable, un revers presque barbare[13]. Ainsi, il est significatif que la perte de poids et la diminution du diamètre, qui lui est concomitante, vont de pair avec la dégradation du style: la dispersion des poids n'est donc pas celle, normale, que présente toute émission de bronzes dont la frappe se faisait <u>al marco</u>; elle est, comme à Thasos, le fruit d'une évolution chronologique, le résultat de la politique monétaire de la cité.

La série est datée par Strack et von Fritze du deuxième et du premier siècle, avec un prolongement possible à l'époque impériale, sur la foi de ce qu'ils considèrent comme des indices d'une influence romaine: forme de la légende, présence d'un grènetis, attribution d'une bourse à Hermès. Si la réalité d'une telle influence me paraît douteuse[14], en revanche la chronologie proposée sort renforcée de ces observations; je ne la modifierais que sur un point: la frappe peut fort bien commencer vers 167[15] mais si nous ne savons pas quand elle s'arrête, je doute qu'elle se soit prolongée très avant dans le premier siècle; en tout cas, la bataille de Philippes marque le <u>terminus ante quem</u> le plus récent.

III. <u>Samothrace</u>. Les fouilles de Thasos permettent de dater du deuxième siècle certains grands bronzes de Samothrace:

6. Tête d'Athéna casquée à dr. / Cybèle à g., ethnique et nom de monétaire.

L'un de ces bronzes a été trouvé sur l'agora de Thasos, associé à un grand bronze thasien no. 2; le nom du monétaire n'est pas lisible.

Cette pièce appartient à une série relativement abondante[16] dont divers exemplaires ont circulé, tout comme les bronzes thasiens, fort longtemps, puisque, selon des informations orales, on en trouve à Samothrace dans des tombes du début de la période impériale. R.S. Poole, dans le <u>BMC</u>, l'avait placée "après Alexandre", et depuis la date de 280 a été reprise partout, pour le début des émissions, sans être justifiée; mais le style n'impose nullement une telle chronologie et les contextes archéologiques mentionnés ci-dessus permettent de conclure que la série samothracienne doit être, en gros, contemporaine des deux précédentes.

Ceci établi, nous pouvons noter que la série présente elle aussi certaines des caractéristiques que nous avons trouvées dans le monnayage contemporain d'Ainos et de Thasos. Si l'identité des modules ne signifie rien, on notera que la mode du deuxième siècle est décidément, dans la région, à la représentation au droit de la monnaie, de la tête d'une des divinités principales de la cité, et au revers, du dieu tutélaire en majesté, debout ou trônant. De nombreux exemplaires (par ex., trois sur les sept trouvés à Thasos) sont contremarqués au droit d'un poinçon en forme de rosace.

IV. Abdère. Les fouilles de Thasos ont également donné dans un contexte contemporain un grand bronze d'Abdère.

9. Tête masculine à dr., imberbe et portant une petite aile sur la tempe et un strophion (plutôt qu'un diadème) / Griffon couché à g., la patte av. dr. levée; devant lui une étoile; ethnique au-dessus et au-dessous.

La pièce appartient à une série où Strack croit pouvoir reconnaître au droit l'effigie d'un souverain lagide (successivement de Ptolémée III à Ptolémée V), et qu'il date en conséquence des années 240 à 202[17]. Mais diverses indications auraient dû prévenir contre une datation aussi haute. La série, fort abondante (Strack en connaît 26 exemplaires, beaucoup plus que pour ses autres numéros; nous en avons trouvé 3 à Thasos), montre elle aussi une détérioration assez sensible du style et du poids, qui, pour les exemplaires réunis par Strack, passe de plus de 6.30g à 3g. D'autre part, les difficultés qu'ont éprouvées les différents commentateurs à choisir entre tel et tel Ptolémée[18] montre bien l'irrégularité du style que souligne Strack. Sur de nombreux exemplaires, une contremarque à la massue (bien visible sur la pièce de la coll. Evelpidis) témoigne d'au moins un épisode[19] de difficultés financières pendant la durée de cette émission. L'ordre des dernières séries hellénistiques d'Abdère est, comme Strack l'avait bien noté, en partie déterminé par la présence de cette étoile à huit branches qui figure régulièrement devant le griffon, alors qu'elle était apparue en contremarque sur les grands bronzes à la tête de Poseidon dont nous allons parler; Strack considérait que la tête de Poseidon était une copie de celle qui figure sur des tétradrachmes royaux macédoniens qu'il attribuait à Antigonos Gonatas et il datait donc ces bronzes des années 250. Or, sans même parler d'une éventuelle influence macédonienne, le style de cette tête me paraît sensiblement plus récent.

L'ordre des dernières émissions hellénestiques d'Abdère pourrait être le suivant:

7. Tête d'Apollon lauré à dr. / Griffon couché à g., deux monétaires (Strack, no. 238-240).

8. Tête de Poseidon à dr. / Griffon couché à g.; une émission anonyme, une datée de Phayl... (Strack, no. 235-236); contremarques à l'étoile ou à la massue.

9. Tête masculine à dr. / Griffon couché à g. étoile.

Il me paraît clair que les no. 8 et 9, et sans doute aussi le no. 7, sont à placer, comme les séries déjà étudiées, au deuxième siècle, avec, pour le no. 9, un prolongement possible au début du premier siècle. La publication des monnaies trouvées dans les fouilles d'Abdère[20] pourrait résoudre la question, mais l'histoire mouvementée de la ville que nous font connaître les rares textes dont nous disposons expliquerait fort bien une succession rapide de séries monétaires dans les années qui suivent la guerre d'Antiochos.

V. Maronée. Le monnayage de bronze de Maronée, pour lequel on attend le corpus annoncé par Schönert-Geiss, pose un problème particulier, ou plus exactement un problème double.

a) Tout le monde s'accorde à placer au deuxième et au premier siècle les tétradrachmes de poids attique avec la tête et l'image en pied de Dionysos Sôter, ainsi que les bronzes aux mêmes types:

10. Tête de Dionysos juvénile à dr. / Dionysos Sôter de 3/4 à g. DIONYSOY SOTEROS à dr. et à g. MARONITON à l'exergue. Monogrammes variés.

11. Mêmes types et même légende. Monogrammes, le plus souvent 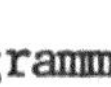 et 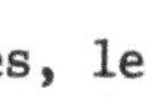. Bronzes de grand module, 27-28 mm. de diamètre, 15 à 16g pour les exemplaires les plus lourds.

12. Mêmes types. MARONITON à dr., eventuellement un monogramme. Petit module, moins de 20mm. de diamètre, 4.5 à 9.75g.

Mais si la date de ces bronzes, qui sont fort nombreux[21], n'est pas douteuse, personne à ma connaissance n'a cherché à analyser les conditions de circulation, d'échange, et en un mot le cours de ces pièces par rapport aux autres émissions de bronze de la cité et aux émissions d'argent. Il est pourtant aisé de constater combien elles sont étranges dans l'ensemble des séries de bronze: le module du no. 11 est inusité, dans ce métal, non seulement à Maronée, mais aussi dans toute la région. Mieux, les types reprennent systématiquement certains traits des monnaies d'argent. Ainsi les modifications de la légende entre la grand module, no. 11, et le petit, no. 12, sont celles-là mêmes que l'on observe entre les tétradrachmes contemporains de Maronée et de Thasos et les drachmes de Thasos[22]. Le diamètre des pièces de grand module est sensiblement le même, ou à peine plus petit que celui des tétradrachmes; le poids des meilleurs exemplaires est exactement celui des tétradrachmes. Le module des no. 10 est le même que celui des drachmes de Thasos. Bref, au métal près, ces pièces s'insèrent mieux dans le monnayage d'argent de la cité que dans celui de bronze.

b) D'autre part Maronée a frappé des bronzes qui paraissent, par leur style et certaines caractéristiques, assez proches des séries que nous venons d'étudier:

13. Tête d'Apollon lauré à dr. / Asclépios debout de 3/4 à dr., la tête à g.; ethnique; divers monogrammes.

14. Tête d'Héraclès à dr. / Cheval galopant à dr.: ethnique. Certaines pièces portent les deux monogrammes 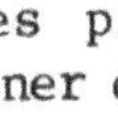 et , d'aucun[23].

On retrouve pour les bronzes no. 13 le même schéma qu'à Ainos, Maronée et Thasos. Le poids de ces pièces, entre 8 et 11g, fait d'eux les bronzes les plus lourds de Maronée, compte non tenu des pièces no. 11, mais il se compare à celui d'autres séries, comme Ainos, Thasos, Samothrace. Il faut surtout noter que les deux monogrammes connus pour le no. 14 sont les mêmes que ceux des pièces no. 11. Ces pièces sont plus légères que les précédentes et semblent bien témoigner de la même dégradation de diamètre et de poids que nous avons déjà observée ailleurs: les exemplaires de Londres et de Copenhague ont 20mm. de diamètre (pour un poids de 7.5g), tandis que la pièce trouvée à Thasos dépasse à peine 15mm. pour un poids de 2.6g!

Ces pièces sont datées, sans plus d'explication, de l'époque impériale[24], mais il est clair qu'elles n'ont rien de commun avec les émissions du premier siècle de l'Empire. Les observations faites, et tout particulièrement l'identité des monogrammes sur les pièces no. 11 et 14, amènent à conclure que l'ensemble des émissions no. 11 à 14 doivent être contemporaines, bien qu'il soit, à première vue, difficile d'expliquer comment elles s'organisent dans un système monétaire cohérent: c'est peut-être cette difficulté qui avait amené à proposer une date manifestement trop basse pour les bronzes no. 13 et 14.

D'autres informations seraient nécessaires pour résoudre cette difficulté, et je ne puis, dans l'état actuel de la documentation, que suggérer une interprétation dont je ne me dissimule pas le caractère hypothétique. Le rapprochement avec les autres cités de la côte thrace semble indiquer que le monnayage de bronze de Maronée à cette époque fut en fait constitué par les deux séries no. 13 et 14, le changement de série étant sans doute à expliquer, comme il est ordinaire[25], par de graves difficultés financières, résultant peut-être elles-mêmes d'une crise plus générale, auxquelles la cité aura cherché un palliatif dans une manipulation monétaire. En revanche les monnaies aux types dionysiaques no. 11 et 12 se rapprochent incontestablement des monnaies d'argent no. 10, non seulement par leurs types, mais par leur répartition en deux modules sur lesquels la légende est disposée de la même manière que sur les pièces d'argent de diamètre (et partiellement de poids) correspondant. J'ai été amené à expliquer par une crise financière l'apparition des bronzes no. 14 qui portent les mêmes monogrammes que les pièces no. 11: je serais tenté de penser, de la même manière, que la frappe de ces pièces en bronze est un exemple supplémentaire d'un phénomène mal connu, mais peut-être plus répandu qu'on ne le croit dans le monde grec, à savoir l'émission de monnaies de métal vil auxquelles la cité impose le même cours qu'à des monnaies d'argent[26].

Quoiqu'il en soit de cette hypothèse, on retiendra que les séries no. 10 à 12 datent du deuxième et du premier siècle, et qu'elles témoignent à la fois de la vigueur du monnayage maronitain et des difficultés que la cité a, par moments, traversées.

VI. A Sestos, un célèbre document épigraphique, le décret pour Ménas, nous atteste de façon certaine la reprise du monnayage de la cité dans les années 160-120, après un temps d'abandon qu'il est impossible d'évaluer[27]. Etudiant ce document, von Fritze a cherché à retrouver les monnaies que Ménas avait fait frapper, en classant l'ensemble du monnayage de la cité. Mais croyant que la lettres A à E qui figurent sur de nombreuses pièces de types différents servaient à dater les cinq premières émissions dues à Ménas, il a été amené à conclure qu'auraient été frappées en même temps et par conséquent auraient circulé parallèlement des pièces qui, tout en ayant le même module et donc la même valeur, auraient eu des types différents. Ceci ne peut se produire que dans des systèmes monétaires comme les Wappenmünzen d'Athènes, les monnaies de Marseille aux types d'Auriol ou les monnaies d'électrum de Cyzique, pour ne citer que quelques exemples, où le type qui occupe la plus grande partie ou la totalité du droit n'est fait qu'un type secondaire, désignant l'émission, et où la valeur de la monnaies était reconnue par l'utilisateur grâce à l'aspect général de la pièce, notamment du revers[28]. Rien n'indique que Sestos ait organisé son monnayage de la sorte et même dans ce cas, il paraît exclu que deux pièces de même module de la même émission aient eu des types différents. L'ensemble du classement et de la chronologie de von Fritze ne peut donc être retenu, il faut chercher une autre explication aux lettres A-E et répartir le monnayage de Sestos sur une beaucoup plus longue période. Ceci noté, il y a incontestablement parmi les séries attribuées par von Fritze à l'activité de Ménas une au moins qu'il faut placer dans la seconde moitié du deuxième siècle, mais je ne suis pas en mesure de reconnaître laquelle: il est en tout cas curieux que, pour une fois qu'un monétaire nous est connu par un document épigraphique, il n'ait pas signé de monnaie à son nom.

VII. Byzance présenterait, si l'on s'en tient à la doctrine admise, un curieux paradoxe. E. Schönert-Geiss a placé les six séries de bronzes hellénistiques au troisième siècle, entre 280-275 et peu après 220[29]: la ville n'aurait donc plus frappé de monnaie de bronze avant la période augustéenne[30], alors même qu'elle frappait une très abondante série de tétradrachmes aux types de Lysimaque[31]. Mais ici encore, ce classement, qui supposerait qu'aient été frappées et qu'aient circulé en même temps des pièces de même module et de types différents, ne peut être retenu. Aux objections antérieures vient s'ajouter le témoignage des contremarques, qui sont différentes selon les différentes séries, ce qui montre bien que les séries se sont succédé dans le temps. En fait, Schönert-Geiss a établi son classement et sa chronologie en s'appuyant presque exclusivement sur les noms des monétaires et sur les homonymies qu'elle constatait d'une série à l'autre. Mais comme ces noms appartiennent, pour la plupart, au fond commun de l'onomastique byzantine et apparaissent assez fréquemment même à travers le petit nombre de documents épigraphiques connus[32], il n'y a pas lieu de conclure, quand cela présente une difficulté, d'une identité de nom à une identité de personne. Il reste donc à reprendre l'examen de ces six séries - dont certaines ont été de durée fort brève -, pour essayer de reconnaître celles qui ont dû appartenir au deuxième et au début du premier siècle: car la richesse de ce monnayage de bronze est telle qu'on peut bien le répartir sur deux siècles et demi.

D'autres villes ont sûrement frappé monnaie pendant cette période, tant sur la côte de la Propontide que sur celle du Pont gauche. Si parmi les premières, Lysimachie[33] ou Périnthe[34] n'ont apparemment pas eu d'autre monnayage que le bronze, les grands ports du Pont-Euxin, comme Callatis, Odessos ou Mesembria[35] présentent le même paradoxe que Byzance: alors qu'on leur connaît des émissions, parfois abondantes, d'or et de tétradrachmes aux types d'Alexandre, on leur refuse tout monnayage de bronze. Mais si les indices sont actuellement trop ténus pour me permettre de proposer de dater du deuxième siècle telle ou telle série, une telle lacune s'explique sans doute davantage par l'état de nos connaissances que par l'histoire monétaire.

Cette série d'analyses locales permet de tirer un certain nombre de conclusions d'ensemble. La première est que le monnayage de l'argent est limité à un petit nombre d'ateliers, une demi-douzaine, qui frappent tous - et le phénomène est nouveau - des tétradrachmes de poids attique, plus exactement de même poids que les tétradrachmes stéphanéphores. Ces émissions peuvent être surabondantes, notamment à Thasos, où il me paraît contestable de vouloir en expliquer le volume par les imitations barbares. Mais deux points sont notables: en dehors des rares drachmes de Thasos, je ne connais pas de monnaie d'argent de petit module. D'autre part je n'ai pu établir aucun lien entre le monnayage d'argent et celui de bronze à Thasos et la situation est la même à Byzance, et dans les villes du Pont qui n'usent mêmes pas de types locaux pour leurs tétradrachmes.

En second lieu, incontestablement, le siècle qui s'étend d'environ 180 à 80 voit un épanouissement du monnayage de bronze des cités grecques de la côte thrace, après les temps de déclin, de repli sur de soi et de très grandes difficultés qu'ont traversés les cités entre 320-300 et 180. Si nous comparons ce siècle avec l'autre grande période de frappe du bronze, le quatrième siècle, deux grandes différences apparaissent. Cet essor du monnayage de bronze n'est pas sans quelques restrictions. Le nombre des ateliers actifs est plus restreint qu'au quatrième siècle: ne semblent pas avoir repris leur production des ateliers comme Orthagoras, Zoné[36], plusieurs cités de Chersonnèse de Thrace, Madytos, Apollonie du Pont, pour ne pas parler de Philippes ou de Néapolis qui sont à la limite de la région. D'autre part, l'étude de détail de ces monnayages nous a montré que des accidents monétaires, des manipulations dont témoignent les changements de types et les contremarques se sont produits dans la plupart des cités. Enfin j'ai cru déceler, sous réserve d'une analyse plus précise, dans diverses cités une détérioration de la monnaie à la fin de la période, comparable à celle qui est manifeste à Thasos.

Mais à ces réserves près, la vigueur du monnayage de bronze, et plus particulièrement des grands bronzes[37] est indéniable. Si nous comparons ce siècle à l'autre grande période de frappe du bronze, la quatrième siècle, une différence majeure apparaît: les petits bronzes qui sont le numéraire le plus important au quatrième siècle (et qui continuent à jouer un rôle très important dans d'autres régions du monde grec), ne constituent plus qu'une fraction tout à fait secondaire du monnayage (comme à Thasos, où ils sont liés à une opération de contremarque), quand ils n'ont pas complètement disparu.

Le rôle monétaire des grands bronzes est d'autant plus important qu'ils constituent le seul instrument disponible pour les petits paiements, alors que les cités avaient émis au cinquième et encore au quatrième siècle un volume très important de petites fractions d'argent. Les tétradrachmes constituent, eux, un monnayage de grande valeur, qui circule très loin, jusqu'au-delà du Danube, manifestement utilisé dans des circuits d'échanges, pour des opérations monétaires qui débordent largement les frontières de la cité et sont entièrement distinctes des paiements auxquels le bronze sert. Aucun des très nombreux trésors de tétradrachmes de Thasos ou de Maronée ne comprenait de pièce de bronze, et inversement les trésors de bronzes thasiens de la période[38] ne comprenait pas de pièce d'argent. Le monnayage de bronze apparaît lui comme le monnayage par excellence de la cité, indispensable tant aux achats de la vie quotidienne qu'aux multiples petits paiements d'une cité démocratique: <u>misthoi</u> des différentes fonctions rémunérées, dépenses régulières de la vie religieuse, dont les comptes de Délos nous montrent tant d'exemples[39].

Toutes les observations confirment le caractère en quelque sorte municipal de ce monnayage. L'étude des divers ateliers a montré que chaque cité avait eu sa politique et son histoire monétaire propres. Les trouvailles des fouilles, dans lesquelles la monnaie locale occupe une place écrasante, attestent que ces bronzes ne circulent guère hors des limites de leur cité et qu'il n'y a pas eu, pour ces espèces, d'entente monétaire comme il y en eut peut-être une pour les tétradrachmes entre Thasos et Maronée.

Cependant ceci n'empêche pas l'existence d'un fait régional: les monnaies de bronze de cités de la côte thrace appartiennent bien à un ensemble, et se distinguent très clairement des bronzes des régions voisines. Certes elles sont très loin de présenter la même homogénéité que les bronzes des cités macédoniennes. Nos cités, je l'ai dit, n'appartiennent à aucun ensemble politique organisé et ne forment même pas une région cohérente. Néanmoins, malgré ces facteurs centrifuges, il n'en demeure pas moins une nette originalité régionale qui peut s'expliquer, en partie, par un effet de mode, les cités adoptant ce qui les a séduit dans le nouveau monnayage de leurs voisins.

Mais le style de l'époque ne suffirait pas à créer un ensemble régional. Celui-ci est plutôt le résultat du milieu géographique et politique auquel ces cités appartiennent: si la circulation du bronze est indépendante des échanges avec le continent thrace, sa production est néanmoins fonction à la fois (dans une mesure qui nous est mal connue) des finances de la cité et de sa bonne marche, disons, pour employer un terme plus vague, de sa prospérité: or celle-ci dépend à son tour des relations commerciales, mais aussi politiques, pacifiques ou conflictuelles, avec le continent thrace. L'arrêt de la frappe du bronze, à la fin de la période, me paraît devoir être mis en relation avec les pressions des Thraces, le pillage de la chôra et l'assaut contre les villes que mentionnent les textes. Cette insécurité culmine avec l'attaque des troupes de Mithridate.

Quel est le rôle de Rome dans cette histoire monétaire? La réponse sera différente pour le monnayage de bronze et pour celui d'argent. Le premier s'inscrit sans aucun doute dans une tradition hellénique d'échanges à l'intérieur de la cité et atteste, quels que soient les changements, encore mal connus, que subit alors la société, la permanence des institutions civiques: le décret de Sestos en l'honneur de Ménas en est un bon témoignage. Je n'ai relevé, malgré ce qu'on a pu dire des monnaies d'Ainos, aucune trace d'intervention romaine dans ce domaine et je note qu'à Thasos les fouilles, qui ne nous renseignent que sur ce type de circulation, n'ont pas donné de monnaie romaine avant les guerres civiles et la bataille de Philippes. L'action de Rome ne se fait sentir, indirectement, qu'à travers sa capacité - ou son incapacité, à la fin de la période - à maintenir la paix et la prospérité nécessaire à l'épanouissement de ces monnayages.

Le cas de l'argent est assurément tout différent, et l'on peut se demander dans quelle mesure il s'agit encore d'un monnayage de cités. Nos tétradrachmes se répartissent en deux catégories. Les lysimaques et les alexandres sont frappés à l'est, dans une région éloignée de la Macédoine, ou les conflits militaires, notamment au temps de Mithridate, maintiennent une situation comparable à celle de la haute période hellénistique. M. Price[40] a montré que certaines émissions reproduisent le portrait de Mithridate Eupator et il est probable que si l'histoire en était mieux connue, elle ferait apparaître les relations de ces monnayages avec les grands événements militaires. Les tétradrachmes à la tête de Dionysos frappés par Maronée et surtout par Thasos ont alimenté d'autres circuits monétaires. Sauf sur une étroite bande côtière le long de la Mer Noire, ils ne circulent pas dans les mêmes régions que les précédents. J'ai noté que ceux de Thasos tout au moins ne portaient plus, très rapidement, les habituelles marques de contrôle et paraissaient donc sortir du cadre institutionnel de la cité. Les lieux de trouvaille des trésors, de part et d'autre de la vallée du Danube, montrent qu'ils sont par excellence l'instrument d'échanges interrégionaux alors que la pénétration du denier romain[41] est encore très lente. L'émission de Sura, dont on ne pourra peut-être proposer d'explication précise qu'une fois le Corpus de la série constitué, confirme qu'un phénomène monétaire d'une telle ampleur n'a pu se réaliser qu'avec l'accord, sinon l'intervention des autorités romaines.

Un autre phénomène est à mettre au compte de l'action de Rome. Les chouettes au quatrième siècle, les émissions royales de poids attique et les alexandres au troisième siècle, constituent une monnaie internationale circulant partout, négociable d'un bout à l'autre du monde grec. Désormais au second siècle, les aires monétaires sont beaucoup plus compartimentées. Dans la zone où circulent les tétradrachmes à la tête de Dionysos, on ne voit guère en dehors d'eux que des tétradrachmes macédoniens et quelques rares tétradrachmes stéphanophores. Les monnaies d'Asie Mineure, de Syrie et de Phénicie ont chacune leur aire de circulation propre. L'unité monétaire du monde hellénistique est brisée.

NOTES

1. Sur ces monnayages des Etats thraces, voir en dernier lieu Y. Youroukova, Coins of the Ancient Thracians (1976): les monnayages qui nous intéressent sont ceux de Mostis, p. 34-39, no. 133-144, de Kotys et de Sadalas, p. 40-41, no. 148-151; voir aussi n. 2. Quant au monnayage de la cité de Kabylé, uniquement de bronze, D. Draganov, - Z. Popov, Kabylé I (1982), p. 18-38 (en bulgare, avec résumé en français), le datent entre la fin du IVe et le début du IIe s.

2. Youroukova, op. cit., p. 46-53, date des années 48-42 le monnayage de Rhaiskouporis (no. 153-157) que l'on date ordinairement des années 12-19 ap. J.-C. Plusieurs de ces pièces ont été retrouvées à Thasos, avec celles de Rhoimetalkés (no. 160-208), qui sont certainement d'époque augustéenne.

3. Cf. les inscriptions et les sources littéraires citées par E. Will, Histoire politique du Monde hellénistique II (1967), 210-211 et 238-239. Pour Maronée, voir D. Triantaphyllou, Thraikè Epitèris 4 (1983), 419-446 et Actes du IXe Congrès Int. d'épigraphie grecque et latine, Athènes 1982 (1984), 278-280.

4. L'expression de B. Holtzmann, BCH 95 (1971), p. 264-265 ("Les cités grecques de la Thrace égéenne, propontique et pontique, entrées peu à peu dans l'orbite de Rome depuis le IIe siècle, dépendirent de la Macédoine aussi longtemps qu'elle demeura la seule province romaine organisée dans la péninsule balkanique") n'est pas heureuse. La seule chose que l'on puisse dire est que les autorités romaines les plus proches pour ces cités sont bien évidemment celles de Thesalonique. Cf. P. Grimal, intr. à l'édition du Contre L. Pison, (1966), p. 54-55.

5. Elle a été commodément rassemblée, en 1965, par E. Schönert-Geiss, JNG 15, 119-193.

6. Ici comme ailleurs, le volume du BMC Thrace (1877), par R. St. Poole, a fixé un cadre chronologique qui a fait très largement autorité. Des volumes de la SNG, nous retiendrons les deux volumes de Copenhague (1942 et 1943), et celui de la SNG Evelpidis I (1970), par R. Evelpidis et T. Hackens.

7. Ce sont les pièces d'argent 51-53 et de bronze 56-59 et 60-66 du 8e groupe distingué par G. Le Rider, in Guide de Thasos (1968), 189-90, qu'il date du deuxième s. et du début du premier av. J.-C.

8. Ce sont les pièces 67-68 du 9e groupe de G. Le Rider, 191. Je ne crois pas qu'il y ait lieu de distinguer un 9e groupe. En revanche les petits modules que Le Rider attribue au 8e groupe (pièces 54-55) me paraissent plus anciens.

9. C'est particulièrement net pour la dernière émission (Guide de Thasos, no. 65-66), dont le poids moyen tombe à environ 2g, alors que les pièces les plus anciennes pèsent entre 9 et 6g, et dont le style est particulièrement barbare. Elle n'a employé qu'un petit nombre de coins.

10. Je reprends la date proposée par G. Le Rider, à la suite de M. Thompson, ANSMN 12 (1966), 61 et n. 4. Le renouvellement des types

thasiens s'inscrit dans la grande mutation monétaire de ces années-là. (Editorial note: compare the remarks of I. Touratsoglou, pp. 62-63, note 6.).

11. Sur l'histoire particulièrement difficile de Thasos dans ces années, voir Chr. Dunant - J. Pouilloux, Recherches sur l'histoire et les cultes de Thasos II (1958), 50-54.

12. M. Strack, Die Antiken Münzen von Thrakien (1912), No. 394-402, pl. V, 23-25: c'est le groupe E de H. von Fritze, 'Die autonomen Münzen von Ainos', Nomisma 4 (1909), 28-32.

13. Voir son commentaire du No. 398, p. 197. Les pièces d'un style très relâché sont particulièrement nombreuses, ainsi le No. 894 de la SNG Evelpidis (daté à tort du Ier-IIe siècle ap. J.-C.) et la plupart des huit exemplaires trouvés à Thasos.

14. Les deux premiers traits n'ont rien de spécifiquement romain. Quant au type d'Hermès à la bourse, il est loin d'être inconnu en Grèce, cf. J. Marcadé, Au Musée de Délos (1969), 341-344.

15. Cette date reste hypothétique, faute de renseignement précis. L'histoire d'Ainos au début du IIe s. est particulièrement mouvementée: cf. Strack, op. cit., 142-143.

16. Un premier aperçu sur les monétaires de cette série est donné par N.B. Phardys, JIAN 1 (1893), 253-262, repris par R. Münsterberg, Die Beamtennamen auf den griechischen Münzen (1913-14), p. 28-29. Sept exemplaires en ont été retrouvés à Thasos, et les deux pièces de Samothrace de la SNG Evelpidis, 1083-1084, appartiennent à cette série.

17. M. Strack, op. cit., Abdère, No. 237, pl. 29-31.

18. M. Strack rappelle que ce roi a été identifié par Imhoof-Blumer d'abord comme Antiochos II, puis comme Ptolémée III, et par Svoronos comme Ptolémée III. Lui-même croit y reconnaître les traits des différents Ptolémée. H. Kyrieleis, Bildnisse der Ptolemäer (1975), 27, déclare ce portrait beaucoup plus grossier que celui qui figure sur d'autres monnaies et ne l'identifie à Ptolémée III que parce qu'il ne peut s'agir ni d'un Séleucide, ni d'un Antigonide, parce qu'il ne ressemble pas à Ptolémée II et parce que c'est sous son règne que les Lagides ont été maîtres d'Abdère. La domination lagide sur Abdère est en fait douteuse et R.S. Bagnall, The Administration of the Ptolemaic Possessions outside Egypt (1976), 158-162, ne la mentionnne pas parmi les possessions lagides en Thrace. J'ai eu tort, Chalcis et la Confédération eubéenne (1979), 163, de suivre l'opinion traditionelle.

19. On trouve sur ces monnaies d'autres contremarques, mais elles n'ont pas la même régularité et ne témoignent sans doute pas d'une mutation monétaire de même ampleur.

20. Les fouilles d'Abdère ont été conduites par D. Lazaridis, pour le compte de la Société archéologique, de 1950 à 1956 (voir les PraktArchEt de 1950, 1952, 1954 à 1956), puis au nom du Service archéologique de 1961 à 1966 (voir ADelt. 17 (1961-62), 245-248; 19 (1964), 376-378 et 20 (1965), 453-61) date à partir de laquelle elles

sont financées par les deux organismes: voir les PrakArchEt de 1966, 1971, 1976, 1978 et 1979. Par la suite elles ont été reprises par Mme Koukouli-Chrysanthaki, voir PraktArchEt (1982), 1-17 et Ergon (1983), 15-18 et (1984), 11-13. Un premier aperçu est donnée par D. Lazaridis Abdère et Dikaia, Cités grecques antiques (1971), en grec.

21. La fouille de Thasos a donné 7 "tétradrachmes" et 10 "drachmes". Mais ce sont les trésors qui montrent l'importance de ces frappes: voir IGCH 663 (Platania, 2 "drachmes"), 934 (Maronée, 31 "tétradrachmes"), 935 (Komotini, 400 "drachmes"), 936 (Podkova, 8+ "tétradrachmes"), 937 (Belinzi, 2 kg. de "tétradrachmes"), 938 (Dzebel, ca. 100 "drachmes"?), 939 (Starveco, ca. 25 "drachmes") et 940 (Ustren, ?).

22. Il faut recourir aux drachmes de Thasos, qui sont d'ailleurs rares dans cette série, Maronée ne semblant pas avoir frappé alors de pièce de ce module.

23. Ce sont les pièces BMC Thrace 83-86 et 87-88, ou SNG Copenhague 635-636 et 634. Les fouilles de Thasos ont donné 6 bronzes à la tête d'Apollon et un à la tête d'Héraclès.

24. La chronologie proposée par le BMC Thrace a été, ici comme ailleurs, fidèlement suivie, ce qui semble d'ailleurs avoir gêné l'auteur de la SNG Copenhague qui a rangé, sur sa planche nos No. 11-12 avant nos No. 9-10, puis noté dans le texte que l'ordre chronologique admis était inverse.

25. Je renvoie à mes remarques 'Numismatique et iconographie: le cavalier macédonien', BCH Suppl XIV (1986).

26. C'est une pratique monétaire bien attestée, depuis les tétradrachmes de bronze saucé frappés par Athènes en 406/5, jusqu'aux drachmes de bronze d'Egypte, en passant par de nombreux autres exemples qui mériteraient une étude systématique.

27. OGIS 339, dont H. von Fritze, 'Die Menas-Inschrift und das Münzwesen der Stadt', Nomisma 1 (1907), 1-13, a étudié les informations numismatiques et L. Robert, RN 1973, 45-53 ainsi que Ph. Gautier, RPhil 56 (1982), 226-231, les informations d'ordre institutionnel. J. Krauss, Die Inschriften von Sestos (1980), No. 1, p. 54, n'apporte rien de neuf.

28. Je prépare à ce sujet une étude à paraître dans les Dialogues d'Histoire Ancienne. Voir en attendant ma note BSFN 36 (1981), 53-55 et la réponse, erronée à mon sens, d'A. Furtwaengler, SNR 61 (1982), 5-25.

29. E. Schönert-Geiss, Die Münzprägung von Byzantion I (1970), 65-72.

30. E. Schönert-Geiss, op. cit. II (1972), a certainement raison de dater de l'époque impériale un certain nombre de fractions de bronze (SNG Copenhague 494-504) que l'on datait auparavant du premier siècle av. J.-C.

31. C'est une des faiblesses du livre d'E. Schönert-Geiss que d'avoir laissé de côté ces lysimaques qui font incontestablement partie du monnayage de la cité. A défaut, on consultera H. Seyrig,

Essays Robinson, 197-199, M.J. Price, NC 1968, 1-12 et M. Thompson, RN 1973, 54-65.

32. L. Robert l'a bien marqué dans l'Index commenté des Stèles funéraires de Byzance (1964), de N. Firatli.

33. La série SNG Copenhague 901-902 et 914-917 pourrait appartenir à notre période.

34. E. Schönert-Geiss, Die Münzprägung von Perinthos (1965), 15, ne place dans la période 280-72 (!) que les deux bronzes de sa 10e série, d'après un vague rapprochement avec des monnaies de Callatis.

35. La seule à avoir frappé monnaie est la Mesembria de la Mer Noire, cf. W. Schwabacher, NC 1942, 94-97. La série Tête féminine / Athéna Promachos (ibid., fig. 4; SNG Copenhague 660-661; SNG Evelpidis 976, datée du "IIIe-IIe s. av. J.-C.") pourrait bien être du IIe s. Pour les alexandres de la région, voir M. Price, NC 1968, 1-12.

36. Les premières monnaies de Zônè ont été publiées par G.F. Hill, NC 1922, 248-249, cf. L. Robert, Hellenica I (1940), p. 80-90 et BullEpigr 1980, 319; 1981, 326, qui montre que la ville fouillée par A. Vavritsas (en dernier lieu Ergon 1984, 16-20) doit être Zônè et non Mesembria.

37. La valeur monétaire de ces grands bronzes est difficile à fixer: à Thasos, je serais tenté de croire qu'ils valent un hémi-obole.

38. A l'exception du trésor de Platania (IGCH 663), qui comprend 4 AR (deux tétradrachmes d'Aesillas et deux deniers) mêlés sà 39 AE, les autres trésors du IIe s. sont composés soit d'argent soit de bronze, alors que les trésors thasiens du IVe comprennent souvent des pièces des deux métaux: voir G. Le Rider, BCH 80 (1956), 1-19 et O. Picard, Actes du IXe Congrès Int. de Numismatique, (Berne, 1979), 123-28.

39. Voir Cl. Vial, Délos indépendante, BCH Suppl X (1984), 18-20, 151-154, 344-346 etc., et mon commentaire CRAI 1985; à Délos, comme dans des villes hellénistiques qui ne frappent plus d'oboles en argent, les mentions de paiements en oboles et fractions d'oboles impliquent en fait des paiements en bronze.

40. Voir no. 35.

41. M. Crawford, CMRR 236-9.

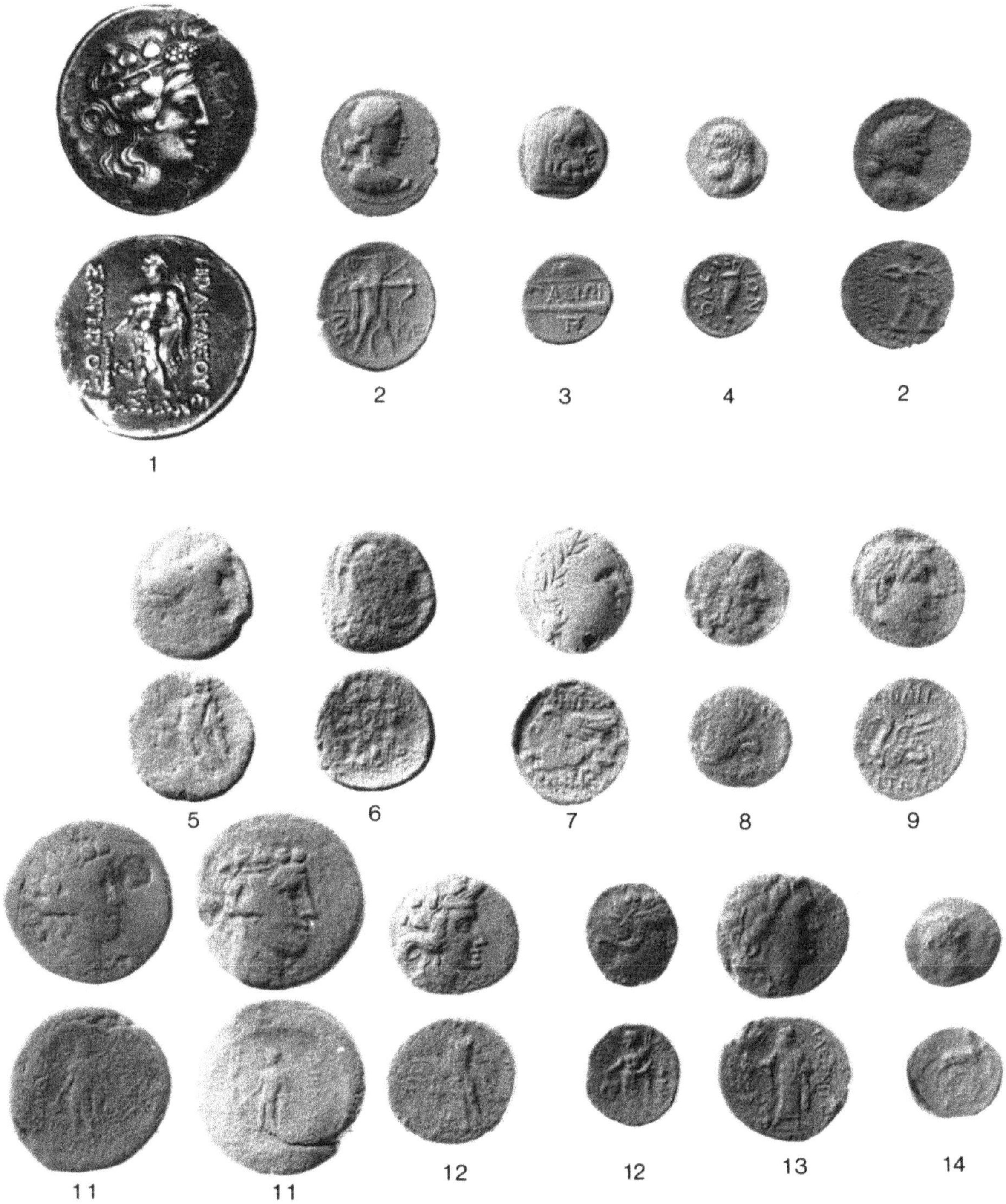

THASOS (1-4), AINOS (5), SAMOTHRACE (6), ABDÈRE (7-9),

MARONÉE (11-14).

Plate 11.

SOUTHERN GREECE

Martin Price

The foundation of the province of Achaea, comprising the whole of central and southern Greece, Thessaly, and most of Epirus, took place only in 27 BC. The details of the political reorganisation in 145 BC have not been preserved. The notion of a Greece freed from the tyranny of Macedonia was clearly attractive, and indirect rule from the province of Macedonia, with most towns declared free, was probably preferred to direct annexation. As far as monetary affairs are concerned, it is not surprising to find that Roman coinage, weights and measures played little part in day to day affairs until the time of the civil wars when Greece was finally absorbed into the political arena of Rome.

The relevant questions here are: what coins were used in the area in the period of the late Republic? what coins were struck in the area during the period? and what function was it intended that such coins should play? If a sufficiently clear pattern should emerge from the answers, then one might conclude that the Romans exercised a particular policy in this regard, even if they baulked at direct annexation.

The main source of information on circulation comes of course from the study of hoards. The Larissa or Sitochoro hoard[1] deposited soon after the foundation of the first Macedonian republic contained large quantities of regal Macedonian coinages and a scattering of regal coinages from further East. It also contained the very last of the tetradrachms of Athens before the New Style coinage began, issues, previously unrecorded, which may be identified with those listed in the Delian inscription as the Attic silver struck before the stephanephori.[2] The presence of this particular group of Athenian coinage and the absence of the New Style issues themselves, combined with the overwhelming evidence from other hoards and the identification of the later issue in the name of King Mithradates as being an issue of Mithradates VI, prove satisfactorily, in my opinion, that this major Attic silver coinage began only after the Roman conquest of Macedonia[3]. Athens as a free city was able to strike an enormous coinage from about 165 to the 40s BC. For more than a century before this her precious metal coinage had been sparse indeed. As, to the north, Thasos and Maronea experienced a resurgence of tetradrachm issues under Roman rule, so Athens was able to create a coinage that was truly international, the coins travelling north into Thessaly, Macedonia, and beyond, south to the Peloponnese and Crete, east to Asia and Syria, and even west to Italy. I do not need to dwell on the chronology or other details of this series, since the arguments have been well debated; but it is worthwhile to point out that in contrast to much of the coinage that was struck in central and southern Greece in the years prior to the mid second century, the New Style coinage is almost entirely of tetradrachms. The sparse issues of drachms and even rarer half drachms were by no means sufficient to provide for the flourishing agora of a major city over a century, and we should reflect on this and on certain other general aspects of this coinage. Thompson lays some stress on the possibility that the control letters found below the amphora on the reverse could be marks identifying the mine[4] from which that particular batch of silver had come. Most commentators, however, state that large scale workings of mines at Laurion during the later Hellenistic period have yet to be found[5] and, although there was a revolt of the mine slaves in the late 130s, there is no trace of the effects of this in the productivity of the New Style coinage which at the beginning of the middle period was rising to particularly high levels. The silver coinage of Athens in the later third and early second century certainly does not reflect major workings of silver mines, and if we cannot show that there were new strikes of silver-bearing ore made to provide for the New Style coinage, we may assume that the newly mined silver continued at about the same rate as before 168, and we must look elsewhere for a further source of silver for the New Style issues.

One obvious source is the vast quantity of silver circulating in Greece prior to the coming of the Romans. This consisted of autonomous and league issues from the fourth century onwards, and in particular the regal Macedonian tetradrachms which in the third century had served beside the fourth century Athenian owls as the main silver currency[6]. These coinages disappear very quickly after the Roman arrival, and a policy of withdrawal and possible recoinage is likely. Another source might be the foreign silver attracted through trade to Delos[7].

At this point should be mentioned two important varieties which have been linked with the activities of Sulla in combatting the menace posed by Mithradates VI of Pontus to Greece[8]. Upon his capture of Athens a small issue of tetradrachms and gold staters was struck at Athens including in the reverse design the name of King Mithradates and the Pontic symbol of the star and crescent combined with the crescent of Athenian owls. Soon after that, in the relative sequence, a major series of imitations of the New Style coinage was struck, apparently not from the main Athenian mint. There are two related series, one with two monograms, the other with a trophy as symbol, and both are thus very different from the contemporary New Style coins which bear the names of three people. Thompson linked the first of these, which unusually contains a number of drachmae, with the Luculleia quoted by Plutarch[9] and in a Delphic inscription,[10] and the second issue with Sulla's activities following the fall of Athens. The identification is likely, and still stands after the revision of her chronology since the idea is easier to accept with the Mithradates issue dated to 86 BC than it would be when that issue was dated c.121 BC.

The idea that the Romans might be using this outwardly city coinage for military purposes strengthens the impression that we must have from any inspection of it, that it was a coinage with a regional significance, a quasi-provincial currency of large denomination, intended to circulate widely in southern Greece and beyond. If any of the cities were paying a form of tribute to Rome as they had previously paid it to the Macedonians,[11] could it be that such payments were even being struck into Athenian coinage?

In this regard I must turn to the inscription at Delphi which specifically insists that the Greeks must accept the Athenian tetradrachms at a value of four drachms of silver[12]. This inscription is certainly of the second century and is usually dated to the 120s. It must therefore refer to the New Style coinage, and Giovannini has suggested[13] that it should be dated before 150 at a time when the New Style coinage might be unfamiliar, when a new coinage might cause uneasiness in the market. However, the inscription is not concerned solely with the general acceptance of Athenian coin. The main concern is that the tetradrachm should be accepted at four silver drachms. This extraordinary phrase has not excited any comment. However, since the silver tetradachm weighed four drachms, the significant word in the inscription would seem to be silver. It is a strange addition, and I can only suppose that it precludes the opposite, that is the passing of the tetradrachm at four bronze drachmae without agio. This would certainly make sense if many people were seeking to exchange the New Style, quasi-provincial coinage for local bronze coins without perhaps paying the normal agio on exchanging bronze for silver. Could they really be arguing that the New Style silver, as a recognised interstate silver currency, should be accepted for four local drachms in bronze? Perhaps they could try, and the Delphic reply took the place of a governor's edict from Macedonia. At any rate the Delphic concern with the Athenian New Style coinage does underline the panhellenic nature of the coinage, and such an explanation would allow the inscription to be dated, as orginally, to the 120s.

This does however raise the question of the value of the bronze coins which were certainly struck in southern Greece by many cities in the period 146-27 BC. In her recent study of Sicyonian bronze coins Warren[14] has listed 18 cities which probably coined during this period in the Peloponnese, and the pattern is not dissimilar in other parts of Greece.

We are all familiar with the 'bronze drachmae' of Ptolemaic papyri[15] in the second and first centuries BC, and if the bronze coins in Greece were valued at more than a small fraction of the obol or a few chalkoi then the above interpretation of the Delphic edict may be considered more credible. A bronze hemiobol at Aegium[16] though of much later date, of the time of Antoninus Pius, does at least allow the possibility of a major fraction of the obol in bronze. There are indications that a bronze drachm was used in Boeotia, although of course one has to be careful that an inscription might use the term bronze to refer to a plated drachm, such as the Delian inscriptions call tin.

In reviewing the Athenian bronze coinage of the period Kroll[18] has become convinced that the major denomination in bronze in the late second and early first century, the so called fulminating Zeus, a series which ends at the time of Mithradates, should be termed a bronze obol. After that the bronze issues at Athens became more substantial in fabric, with fairly continuous issues down to 27 BC or later, after the silver New Style coinage ceased. The new series includes the New Style Parthenos head, and completely replaces the earlier coinage in a very short space of time, suggesting that a reform of the denominations may have taken place[19]. A coinage of bronze drachms is a possibility. The final issue is that with a sphinx that most commentators link with Augustus's signet ring.

It is notable that almost no silver coinage of small denominations was struck in the later Republican times in southern Greece. The Messene property tax inscriptions,[20] possibly as early as the time of Sulla, show the continuing use of <u>chalkoi</u> and accounting with obols and denarii. Although the evidence is not clear cut, one may I think assume a fairly widespread use of bronze coins of denominations higher than in earlier Hellenistic times.

The several hoards of silver from southern and western Greece show clearly the development of the final issues of the Achaean League and Aetolian League. The impression for the Achaean League is very much of hurried emergency issues of half drachms joined at the end by autonomous issues of cities such as those of Argos and Sicyon. The pattern fits with the period of revolt and one may assume that the coinage did not resume after the dissolution of the Achaean League in 146. However, in the Agrinion hoard[21], which does not contain the latest issues of the Achaean League, the accompanying group of Roman denarii clearly continues to 130 BC, and the Diakofto hoard[22] even contained a quinarius of 83 BC. The League half drachms, like the denarius, were suitable for a military currency; and if this coinage had ended by 146 BC, then these hoards show that such coinage remained in people's possession until much later, although how far such coins could have circulated as currency after 146 is uncertain. The latest issues of League coinage in all the hoards are mint fresh, and show no wear from circulation.[23]

Turning to the north however we find that under Roman domination the coinage of Thessalian League flourished. The Aidona hoard[24] containing 4 denarii to 44 BC with 4 Thessalian League staters seems sufficient evidence to show that the League was striking silver in the 40s BC. The staters included the issue in the name of Petraios, who is probably the man named in glowing terms by Caesar and later executed by Brutus in 44 BC. This series bears two names. Helly[25] has been able to show that the name in the genitive can be linked in several instances with the strategos of the League. The other, in the nominative, is perhaps a treasurer or person responsible for the minting. None of this coinage occurred in the Larissa (Sitochoro) hoard from Thessaly itself. The Agrinion hoard, which contained an early half drachm of this series[26] provides a _terminus ante quem_, and a recently published inscription from Thessaly[27] dated 129 mentions a fine of 2 staters 9 obols. A date span of after 168 to 44 BC for the League coinage may now be considered very probable. The coins ciruclated almost entirely within Thessaly, but provided a coinage of relatively small denominations, stater, drachm and half drachm which appear to be lacking further south.

There have been three major studies for cities in this area apart from those of Athens. In Chalkis, Picard[28] recognised a very small issue of tetrobols and a bronze coinage in three denominations during the period under discussion. At Sparta Grunauer[29] could place no silver after 146, but identified a flourishing coinage of bronze in the 40s and 30s including the issue in the name of Atratinus. Franke[30] placed no silver in Epirus after 168, although, again, bronze coinage appears relatively plentiful. The Bakërr hoard (_IGCH_ 559), however, does require that some Epirote silver must date to the time of the Third Macedonian War[31].

In the north-west, however, there are four important silver coinages that deserve mention, although none of them played any significant part in southern Greece. Apollonia and Dyrrachium enjoyed wide circulation in the north, but not at all to the south. The coinage of Corcyra of small denominations in silver and relatively large issues of bronze does not appear to have spread outside the island; and the silver staters of Leucas, if they are to be dated to the period of Roman domination, can likewise only have circulated locally. These would certainly merit further study, even though their influence may be small.

This brief review has been by no means comprehensive, but the pattern that does emerge is that there is one major coinage, the New Style coinage of Athens, and that all other coinages, whether of silver or bronze, were of only local significance.

I would like to turn finally to the question of the introduction of the denarius and of Roman influence on the area. The pattern is again very clear. Occasional examples of the denarius are found in hoards from the second quarter of the second century,[32] and the first appearance in the Delian inscriptions may be dated 153 BC[33]. Significant quantities are not found until the time of Sulla[34], and even then the denarius could hardly have been a major currency in the Achaean world. It is only with M. Antonius that it appears to have enjoyed more widespread use. The quantities of Roman Republican bronze recovered from southern Greece are too insignificant to allow the deduction that the coinage was used at all officially.

The change to the use of Roman denominations is probably to be connected with the physical presence of Romans themselves. At least we know that in Thessaly the reform,[36] the _diorthoma_, that changed the official practice of accounting in League staters to accounting in denarii, only took place after the formation of the province of Achaea in 27 BC - the stater was then reckoned to be 1½ denarii.

The advice that Dio, writing in the third century AD, placed in the mouth of Maecenas recommending Augustus to impose uniform coinage, weights, and measures[37] describes a process that had already begun, but in Greece was not far advanced by 27 BC. At the foundation of the colony at Corinth in 44 BC the bronze coinage followed the Roman denominations, and cities such as Sparta soon followed suit. But the picture is not yet really clear. The cessation of the Thessalian federal coinage and of the New Style coinage at Athens, and the reform of the Athenian bronze coinage, are no doubt related to a growing imposition by Rome of uniformity with the practices of Macedonia. With the institution of the principate the silver coinages Greece had become a phenomenon of the past.

NOTES

1. IGCH 237, to be published in a volume of essays dedicated to C.M.Kraay and O.Morkholm, 1987.

2. H.Nicolet, Studia Paulo Naster Oblata I (Leuven, 1982), 105-114. Cf. ID 1428 II. 77-78 etc.

3. M. Thompson, ANSMN 29 (1984), 29 note accepted the view of O. Markham, ibid., 38-40, that the coinage began in 185-80 BC. Morkholm, however, ignored the evidence of the Sitochoro hoard, and of the several other hoards buried at the time of the Third Macedonian War, as providing merely an argument ex silentio, and he laid stress on the Bakërr hoard (IGCH 559) to argue that the earliest New Style issues must have been struck c.185-180. He omitted to point out that the three Thasian coins in the Bakërr hoard, like those in IGCH 479, 481, 488 etc were more probably struck after 168, and that the first occurrence of New Style coins in the Delian inscriptions was in the 150s. Indeed the New Style issues present in the Urfa, Babylon, Trabzon, and Cilicia 1972 hoards, linked with the deafening silence of many large hoards such as (most recently) Ma'arret en Numan, 1979 (CH VI.37 and VII.98) buried 163/2, document the early period of the New Style from 160-140. Although there is certainly no need to view these as annual issues, a date for the introduction after 168 BC is still preferable from the hoard evidence.

   Morkholm seeks confirmation in the presence of the Athena Parthenos head on the Bottiaean issues in bronze with feeding ox reverse. These varieties, unlike Bottiaean silver, do not provide a straightforward parallel to the coinage of Philip V and Perseus, and most probably belong to the years after the Roman conquest, as do the parallel issues from Pella (BMC 16-28) and Thessalonica (BMC 20-1). The date of the similar head of Athena Parthenos on the bronze coins signed by Poplilius, quoted by Morkholm as being of 168/7, also with feeding ox reverse, is by no means as certain as he maintained. The recent discussion of Burnett (CH VII 54-58) concerning the Makedonon tetradrachms has thrown the chronology of mid second century Macedonian coinages into the melting pot. Unless it can be proved that Poplilius was in office in 168/7, so that it may be assumed, if not proved, that he was copying earlier Macedonian issues of the same types, the very existence of this issue must suggest a post-168 date for all the Macedonian issues of the same types. (Editorial note: compare the remarks of Touratsoglou, p. 63, note 16). The New Style coinage started at about the same time as the wreathed coinages of Chalkis and Eretria, and on the evidence of hoards only shortly before the wreathed coinages of Asia Minor. 185-180 is too early.

4. M. Thompson, ANSMN 1952, 35-48; and New Style, 618-21. Batches of metal delivered to the mint need not have originated at a mine, and so her general theory on the check marks is surely correct.

5. Giovannini, Rome 62 note 128. Cf. Strabo IX.1.23 for the piteous state of Laurion at the time of Augustus.

6. The hoard evidence would suggest that in Greece, unlike Syria, Alexander and other early tetradrachm coinages were replaced from

c.200 BC. Very few survived, e.g., at Sitochoro. For a critique of Giovannini's view, that this change was a political act by Rome, see Kinns, below pp. 105-106.

7. Crawford, CMRR 125, stresses the importance of Delos for the circulation of New Style issues.

8. Thompson, The New Style Silver Coinage of Athens (New York, 1961)

9. Plutarch Lucullus II.2.

10. RN 1935, 1-9

11. O. Picard, Chalcis et la Confédération Eubéene (Athens and Paris, 1979)

12. FD III 2. 139. 1-6

13. Giovaninni, Rome 64-72

14. NC 1984, 21 note 267.

15. E.g. A. Ségré, AJP LXIII.2(1942), 174-192

16. BMC 1-3

17. IG VII.2426. Cf. at Delos ID 1432 Bb.1.12 (tetrobol); 1429 B.11.45 (obol).

18. AJA 1982, 273.

19. Cf. NC 1964, 27-36.

20. E.g. IG V.1.1432-3

21. IGCH 271.

22. IGCH 262.

23. In discussion, C. Boehringer argued for a post-146 date for much of the Achaean League coinage, basing his argument on a study of the Poggio Picenze hoard (IGCH 2056), in which a parcel of Achaean League issues was associated with Sullan denarii and tetradrachms of the time of Mithradates. The make-up of this hoard strongly suggests booty from the Sullan campaigns in Greece, and Thompson The Agrinion Hoard (New York, 1968), 2 has already stressed that its value for chronological purposes is very doubtful. As with the Agrinion and Diakofto hoards one must choose whether the Achaean League issues were circulating at the time of the later Roman issues, or whether a hoard deposited in the 140s was recovered and reburied with additional coinage. I share Thompson's view that the latter is very much more likely.

    There are eight significant groups of Achaean League issues present in the Diakofto, Caserta (IGCH 2053), Western Greece (IGCH 260), and Olympia (IGCH 270) hoards (Argos, Sicyon, Megalopolis, Patrae, Sparta, Dyme, Pallantium, Tegea), not present in Agrinion; and there were two (Elis and Aegium) in Caserta and Western Greece, not present in Diakofto. There is, then, a progression of deposits. The Achaean

League issues in Agrinion were deposited before these in Diakofto, and both before Caserta and Western Greece. All these hoards, though similar, were not deposited at one date. Comparison of wear of parallel issues, and of issues such as those of Corinth which must precede 146 BC, does not permit the obvious deduction made by Boehringer that the deposits were made over the later second and early first century. Rather they give the appearance of a sequence of deposits made over a very short period of time. I would prefer to interpret the evidence to suggest that the silver coinage of the Achaean League ceased in 146, that coins continued to be held as wealth in private possession without being used to any great extent, and that the deposit of the original hoards reflects the troubled times 150-146 BC, with a mass of new issues in the final years of the conflict with Rome. Confirmation is to be found in the comparison of the Aetolian League issues, most of which must have been struck before the dissolution of that League in 168. De Laix (*Californian Studies* 6 (1974), 69) permits a brief flurry of coinage in the 150s. It is the earlier groups which predominate in the hoards quoted above. None were present at Poggio Picenze, but in the other hoards the state of the Aetolian coinage is fully consistent with a deposit in the 140s.

Attractive though Boehringer's suggestion may be, there can be no doubt that some of the Achaean League coinage, such as the Corinthian issues, must have been struck before 146. There is no evidence for any break in the sequence of issues, or other distinction of pre-146 issues, and Boehringer's argument is based on evidence that can hardly be said to be watertight.

24. *IGCH* 351.

25. *RN* 1966, 7-32.

26. Thompson *Agrinion* no. 157.

27. *JRS* 1984, 36-7, 1985, 25.

28. Picard, *Chalcis*, 112-4.

29. It is rather important to emphasise that the half drachms of group VIII belong with the latest issues of the Achaeans in the Caserta and Western Greece hoards, and should be dated 148-6 BC.

30. Cf. P.R. Franke, *Epirus*, 246-7.

31. E.g. the group to be linked with the name of Kephalos, A. Giovannini, *Rome* 105-6.

32. Thebes (IGCH 233) 1; Agrinion (*IGCH* 271) 39.

33. *ID* 1421 Ab 1.3.

34. Peiraeus (*RRCH* 242) 42; Greece (*IGCH* 346) 50.

35. Delos (*RRCH* 465) 649; Euboea (*RRCH* 467) 97; Preveza (*RRCH* 473) 41; (*CH* VII.226) 122.

36. *IG* IX.2.415 b.55-6.

37. Dio LII.30.9. Crawford, CMRR 128 links the late second century reform of commercial weights and measures at Athens with the Roman insistence in 188 BC that Antiochus III pay the indemnity of 12,000 talents with a talent weighing not less than 80 Roman pounds (Polybius XXI.42.19) to suggest Roman influence on a Greek weight system. In the light of the use made of Roman coinage in Greece, this seems a little premature.

ASIA MINOR

Philip Kinns

Roman involvement with the affairs of Asia Minor, previously the meeting place and battleground of the major Hellenistic monarchies, begins in the year 200 BC.[1] For it was Philip V's siege of the city of Abydus on the Hellespont that led to Rome's declaration of the second Macedonian war, and Rome accordingly found herself fighting alongside Rhodes and Pergamum.

Prior to the bequest of Attalus III in 134/3, Roman armies saw active service on Asian soil only in 190 and 189, in the campaign against Antiochus III culminating in his defeat at Magnesia ad Sipylum, and in Vulso's punitive expeditions in Phrygia and the south. The needs of military expenditure are clearly reflected in the large-scale posthumous Alexander issues of such mints as Pergamum, Rhodes and Chios in the first decade of the second century,[2] and the Romans must have made use of such coinages. But apart from those few years before the settlement of Apamea the Romans had no need to concern themselves with the currency of Asia Minor. The assumed role of arbiter of the status quo in the region could be exercised satisfactorily through diplomatic channels - the issue of senatusconsulta and the dispatch and receipt of embassies, and there is no compelling reason to suspect any Roman interference with, or interest in, the coinage circulating there, until the bequest of Attalus forced her hand.

Of course certain Roman political decisions did have profound consequences for the currency of Asia Minor. The expulsion of the Seleucids from cis-Tauric Asia in 188, and the imposition of an indemnity of 10,000 T, the simultaneous awards of territory to Rhodes and Pergamum and the commitment to the freedom of the cities, the subsequent liberation in 166 of parts of Caria and Lycia - such decisions had both an immediate impact on the patterns of coinage in circulation and also engendered further internal changes. The question is, were these effects anything but incidental?

Two recent theories have asserted that there was direct and conscious Roman interference with the coinage before 133, and these need to be considered, if only to be rejected.

Giovannini,[3] seeking an explanation for the disappearance of the posthumous Alexander tetradrachms and the resumed striking of large silver in local types, some time in the second quarter of the second century, has proposed that after their victory at Pydna in 168, and the abolition of the Antigonid monarchy, the Romans ordered the withdrawal of all Macedonian regal coinage, including posthumous tetradrachms in the name of Alexander, and their replacement by new issues. The wreath on the reverse of many second century tetradrachms thus becomes, for Giovannini, a symbol of Rome's victory. This theory will not stand up to detailed examination. On the one hand, the issue and circulation of Alexanders undoubtedly continued well after 168,[4] while the issue of wreathed civic tetradrachms, particularly the new-style coinage of Athens, may have begun well before that date.[5] The existence of contemporary <u>un</u>wreathed issues from a number of mints demonstrates that the wreath motif can have had no such political significance as Giovannini claims, and equally it seems improbable that any Greek or Roman would have seen much connexion between Alexander tetradrachms and the late king Perseus.[6] As for the recently published wreathed Alexanders of Erythrae in Ionia,[7] they would seem to present an insuperable difficulty. Giovannini's theory does not square with the available evidence; his claim that the Romans interfered directly with the currency of Asia Minor in the mid 160s is an unnecessary and misleading hypothesis.

A more recent theory by Szaivert,[8] apparently uninfluenced by Giovannini, is somewhat bizarre. Here the problem is the ending of the Attic weight Philetaerus tetradrachms, and the introduction of the cistophoric coinage. Once again it is suggested that the Romans ordered the change. Szaivert believes that, in anger at Eumenes's activities in the third Macedonian war, the Romans banned him from striking further coinage, and instead encouraged the cities in his kingdom to inaugurate their own federal issues, the cistophori. This is surely pure fiction.

Of course these important changes in the currency of Asia Minor require explanation, but I doubt whether we should look to Rome. It is much more likely that all these developments are indigenous. The first stage seems to have been Eumenes's decision to introduce a closed economy, on the Ptolemaic model, in his kingdom, recently enlarged by the settlement of Apamea. The precise reasons for this move, and in particular, the creation of the new cistophoric coinage (produced under central direction at a number of mints), remain elusive, but a desire to conserve silver must have been a major consideration. Possibly the huge indemnity imposed on Antiochus III by the Romans was causing an unacceptable outflow of the metal from the Pergamene to the Seleucid kingdoms. At any rate there can be little doubt that the cistophori were specifically designed for internal circulation only, for the 33% premium over intrinsic value implied by the 'cistophoric' countermarks on Alexanders and tetradrachms of Side would mean a substantial loss for anyone taking cistophori beyond the borders of Pergamum. The introduction of the cistophori evidently disrupted the free flow of currency in Asia Minor, and I would date this change to the 170s, with Morkholm, rather than the date of 166 proposed by Kleiner.[9]

In the 170s, therefore, the Attic weight Philetaerus tetradrachms will have followed the Seleucid tetradrachms into oblivion as far as the cities of Asia Minor were concerned.[10] In these circumstances the need for a neutral currency such as the posthumous Alexanders had long provided for the cities may well have seemed obsolescent, and the way was open for the resumption of large silver coinage in local types. It rather looks as though the handsome new spread-flan stephanephori or 'wreath-bearers' of Athens started a fashion which soon found favour in western Asia Minor. But this process of replacement was spread over a couple of decades, and must not be over-simplified. The fact is that Alexanders were still being struck in the 160s, at for instance Temnus and Alabanda,[11] while the new local tetradrachms, struck by cities on the borders of the Pergamene kingdom, do not present a unified picture. The tetradrachms of the Ilian confederation commence in the 170s, rare issues of such mints as Samos, Cos, Mytilene and Miletus belong to the 160s,[12] whereas the best known group, the wreathed issues from Aeolis and Ionia, seem to have been struck c.155-145.[13] An interesting aspect of this last group, comprising Aegae, Myrina and Cyme in Aeolis, Colophon, Heraclea, Lebedus, Magnesia and Smyrna in Ionia, is the relative size of the coinages, which seems to bear no relation to the economic importance of the issuing cities. Surprising too is the list of cities which did not participate in this phenomenon. The number of obverse dies used by each city is as follows: Colophon 1, Aegae 4, Lebedus 9, Smyrna 9 (for the monogram reverse issues - those with lion reverse are post-133), Heraclea c. 30, Magnesia, 35, Cyme 78, Myrina 97.[14] That the issues of Lebedus and Smyrna should be similar in scale, and that Heraclea and Magnesia, let alone Cyme and Myrina, whose issues are truly vast, should be so far in advance of them, is surely quite extraordinary, and we are here undoubtedly dealing with something more than straightforward recoinages.

I would suggest that all these issues were produced under Attalid supervision, more often than not with Attalid-supplied silver, and that to a large extent they represent the currency used by the Pergamene kingdom in overseas transactions, from which the cistophori were excluded. The great hoards of these coins discovered in Syria and Cilicia may have got there through trade, particularly the slave trade, but they may also have been sent direct as subsidies to the pretender Alexander Balas, who was very much a creature of Attalus II. Another factor, at least in the issues of Aegae, Cyme and perhaps Heraclea, may be the indemnities secured in 154 from Prusias II, after his war with Attalus.[15]

At any rate, the notion of direct Roman involvement in these important currency developments seems a chimaera, and we can now turn our attention to the period after 133, when Roman intervention can justifiably be expected.

On the eve of the bequest of Attalus, by which the Pergamene kingdom was to become the province of Asia, it is far from easy to form a clear picture of the currency of Asia Minor as a whole. Although the main cistophoric mints, Pergamum, Ephesus, Tralles, Sardes, Apamea, were all in full swing,[16] the number of active mints outside the Pergamene kingdom seems to have been small. The Bithynian and Cappadocian kingdoms both maintained a fairly regular rhythm of coinage production, but Pontus had issued nothing for some decades.[17] There, as in most of the coastal cities, precious metal coinage in circulation must have comprised old issues, often no doubt rather a rag-bag. Small silver was perhaps being struck by the Lycian League, Rhodes, Cos and certain mints in Caria, but except in the north, where the Ilian confederation and Alexandria Troas and perhaps Abydus and Cyzicus remained active, new striking of tetradrachms seems to have ceased some time previously.[18] The precise duration of the bee/stag Attic drachms of Ephesus is unclear. Hoard evidence suggests that they must have commenced before 200, and an issue with EPHESION rather than a magistrate's name perhaps belongs c. 133,[19] so Head's theory that this was latterly an export currency struck alongside the cistophori appears to be correct. There are salutary warnings here against equating coinage with freedom, given the status of Ephesus within the Attalid kingdom.[20]

Although the kingdom as a whole was bequeathed to Rome, Pergamum, Ephesus and apparently some other cities were given their freedom, so that their status was henceforth theoretically identical to that of places like Smyrna. However that may be, the pre-existing cistophoric mints continued striking as before, the only change being that Ephesus now dated her issues by the era of her newly won freedom, year 1 being equivalent to 134/3 BC.[21] Since Rome did not take up her legacy immediately, it seems necessary to conclude that the decision to maintain the cistophoric coinage was taken locally, rather than ordered by Rome.

A curious situation now arises. Whereas the pre-133 cistophori should be regarded as royal issues of the Pergamene kingdom,[22] after 133 they technically become civic issues. Yet at this very moment, with the revolt of Aristonicus, posing as Eumenes III, we are also confronted by cistophori which for the first time are specifically regal, inscribed BA(SILEOS) EY(MENOY), put out by the ephemeral mints of Thyatira, Apollonis and Stratonicea.[23]

By 129/8 Aristonicus had been crushed, and the new province could be organized. By now we must assume that the Roman authorities had also decided to retain the cistophoric coinage system, and much else of the Attalid administrative structure. Simple convenience must have been the main consideration.

De facto the post-133 cistophori serve as the coinage of the new province, but de iure they purport to be civic issues of their respective mints, signed by local magistrates and, in the case of Ephesus, dated by a local era. Perhaps the problem is more apparent than real, for I have already suggested that many of the mid second century civic issues on the Attic standard were actually struck for Pergamum's benefit, and that those coins too were not all that they seem.

The mint of Smyrna appears to introduce a further complication. Before 133 she had struck Homer type Attic drachms and, for a brief period c. 155-145, wreathed tetradrachms with a monogram on the reverse.[24] She had been a free city and was to remain so at least until the Mithradatic revolt, so her political status underwent no change in 133. Yet although a considerable further series of Homer drachms and tetradrachms (now with lion reverse) was to continue until well into the first century, there are also extant rare cistophori from Smyrna, bearing dates 'A', 'B' and 'H'. A hoard provenance (IGCH 1459) shows that they belong in the late second century, but the reason for their issue and the era of their dates are obscure.[25] No doubt the idea of 'minting on commission' can also be invoked here, but when Ephesus and Pergamum were responsible for such an enormous volume of coinage, why should Smyrna be called on to operate as a cistophoric mint?

The only possible explanation for this state of affairs would seem to be that each mint struck bullion for both the Roman government and the local authorities. As a result, although the post-133 cistophori are ostensibly city issues, at any one time the bulk of new coin was probably being put into circulation by the Roman provincial government. By the same token we may presume that the Roman authorities will sometimes have exercised a right of access to non-cistophoric mints, such as Smyrna and Alexandria Troas, when coinage was required for transactions outside the cistophoric zone.

In other words the creation of the province of Asia brought no apparent change to the silver currency of the region. We cannot detect the deliberate suppression of any existing coinage, or point to any obvious innovations. The same applies to the bronze coinage of the cities,[26] and probably also to gold.

At the hands of modern scholars civic gold coinages, whether classical or hellenistic, have tended to suffer from over-interpretation. Of course the various gold issues of Athens, and the late fifth century issues from Sicily, prove that the striking of gold was often the result of dire emergency,[27] but the possibility of regular series struck over long periods, as in fourth century Syracuse or Lampsacus,[28] must never be excluded. Here in Asia almost every issue that is not obviously classical in style has been connected with the Mithradatic revolt, but in fact the third-staters of Erythrae and Teos should be dated c. 300, while the staters of Miletus belong in the second quarter of the second century.[29] As G. K. Jenkins will show in the Akurgal Festschrift, the Hellenistic gold staters of Ephesus, with bust of Artemis on the obverse and statue of Artemis Ephesia on the reverse, form a long series in the late second and early first centuries. Nearly twenty different varieties are now known, and as a result of explicit dates in a few cases and symbols which connect with contemporary cistophori, issues made between 132 and 78 can be identified. Indeed the fact that the two known gold staters of Tralles can now be dated c. 160-150 and c. 140-135, again through connections with cistophori, allows the possibility that the Ephesian gold too may have started in the Attalid period, with staters of fine style and full ethnic <u>EPHESION</u>.[30] Once again, therefore, in the case of gold, as much as with silver and bronze, the new Roman administration apparently did not interfere with the coinage it found in use on its arrival.

The most interesting issues from the early years of the province of Asia are undoubtedly the Ephesian cistophori of year 'IΓ' (13 = 122/1 BC.), and an accompanying unique gold stater in Kayseri, bearing the Latin name 'C.ΑΙΝ.C.F'.[31] These stand out, at least at Ephesus, as the only coins prior to the introduction of the proconsular cistophori in 58 with any specifically Roman content, but there could be no clearer demonstration of the dual nature of the coinage, serving at one time both city and province.

It seems certain that, taking Asia Minor as a whole, the period 133-88 saw a much greater proportion of silver being struck as cistophori than had been the case in the half century after Apamea.[32] Although Bithynia and Cappadocia were coining perhaps more vigorously, and Mithradates VI of Pontus began striking on a large scale after 100, the number of civic silver coinages of any size is now small. For large denominations the Ilian confederation, Alexandria Troas and Smyrna may be mentioned with confidence, along with Alabanda, which apparently made a series of dated reduced weight issues c. 133-100. Drachms and below were being struck by Chios, Cos, Rhodes and the Lycian League. Cibyra provides an exceptional series in the interior, which certainly came to an end at the time of the Mithradatic revolt, but most of the Carian issues (e.g. Halicarnassus, Myndus) seem to be post-Sullan.[33]

The numismatic impact of Mithradates's invasion of Asia and the revolt from Rome merits consideration, particularly since the true picture seems so very different fom what has been suggested in the past.

A major feature was of course the dramatic expansion of Mithradates's own coinage, which will have seen much wider circulation than hitherto, far outside the borders of Pontus. Three mints seem to have been in operation, and for the years 89 to 85 parallel series employ two different eras - the traditional Pontic era beginning in 297 and a new era of Asia beginning at year 1 in 89/8. The latter dates also appear on an exceptional gold series which Mithradates struck at Pergamum.[34]

But the number of special civic issues that can now be associated with the revolt period is relatively small. Gone are the 'Mithradatic' gold issues of Ephesus, Erythrae, Miletus, Teos and Tralles; there is no longer any reason to suppose that the 'liberation' of the cities from Roman rule was marked in this way. Troxell[35] has recently suggested that a revival of striking by the Lycian League and Rhodes can reasonably be connected with this difficult time, but the stimulus in those two cases came rather from resistance to Mithradates, <u>not</u> acceptance of his programme. The Rhodian issues, incidentally, if they do belong to, the mid 80s, include the plinthophoric gold series, dated by Hackens to the late second century.

The most remarkable numismatic testimony to the Mithradatic revolt comes from Smyrna.[36] On the one hand there are the gold staters, of which two survive, signed anonymously by the entire board of PRYTANEIS or councillors, rather than a single magistrate. Contemporary with them is a bronze issue, struck in a new large denomination (probably a diobol), with a portrait of Mithradates on the obverse and a figure of Nike on the reverse, whose commemorative significance is clear enough. It comes as no surprise to find that these bronze coins were hastily overstruck with new types (resembling those of current silver tetradrachms, which may imply an emergency measure) after Sulla's victory, or perhaps even before, when it was evident that the tide had turned against Mithradates.[37]

Smyrna then stands out. Also worthy of mention is the large tetradrachm issue of MENEPHRON MENEPHRONOS at Ilium, on part of which the Pontic drinking pegasus appears as a subsidiary symbol; it was evidently struck shortly before the destruction of the city by Fimbria.[38]

But more important perhaps for our understanding of the currency of Asia is the fact that Ephesus, although one of the first cities of support Mithradates, did not interrupt the striking of cistophori. In the absence of a die-study the size of the issues in the years 89-85 cannot be judged,[39] and maybe that it is irrelevant anyway. It seems necessary to conclude that the cistophori, for all their *use* by the Romans, were apparently still not regarded as a Roman coinage.

Sulla's victory brought retribution on the Greeks of Asia. His imposition of an indemnity of 20,000 T, which by 70 had become a staggering debt of 120,000 T, thanks to the activities of Roman moneylenders, must have devastated the finances of the cities.[40] The clearest evidence of such an effect is seen in some of the bronze coinages of Ionia, where a rash of overstriking, countermarking and successive re-coinages can be observed. The process of demonetisation followed by new issues will have acted as a form of taxation.[41]

At Smyrna it was not only the Mithradates bronzes that were overstruck. Apparently all the Homer and Cybele bronzes, the top two denominations (obol and half-obol) of the current series which had been in regular issue since the early second century, were also called in and overstruck with similar but modified types, distinguished in particular by the absence of a magistrate's name.[42] After this temporary measure, all five bronze denominations were re-issued, in a general re-coinage.[43] Apart from small changes to the types, there was an increase in weight of about 50%, which may suggest a move away from token currency to bronze coins with greater intrinsic value, now that silver issues were smaller and more infrequent. Similarly there are countermarks and overstrikes, and a succession of new types at Teos, and related phenomena at Colophon, Lebedus, Clazomenae and Erythrae.[44]

The impact of the indemnity on the silver coinages of Asia is likely to have been more complex. Analyses of late cistophori undertaken by Walker[45] indicate successive debasements after 85; earlier issues had been c. 98% fine, but a reduction to c.95% is observable in the Ephesian issues of 85-81, while those of 70-68 are only 80% fine. In this way considerable quantities of bullion will have been saved, while the over-valuation of the coinage increased. Post-Sullan hoards contain few pre-85 issues, and it is probable that they had been withdrawn and re-struck. Here it is significant that Apamea and Tralles were re-activated as cistophoric mints in the 80s, perhaps to assist in such a re-coinage, and in order to cope with the inflow of indemnity payments. Apamea had struck no silver between 133 and 88, but now used up 41+ obverses in two decades,[46] while at Tralles the level of production was greatly increased, with a new series dated 1 to 9 on what seems to be a Sullan era.[47]

Outside the cistophoric mints, silver issues are still made after 84, but most come from cities specially favoured by Rome; it is not yet possible to say whether these too are debased to any extent. I refer here to Ilium, Alexandria Troas, Chios,[48] and mints in Caria like Stratonicea and Tabae, whose resistance to Mithradates had been notable.[49] Generally speaking, however, these southern issues belong to the period of the civil wars and later, when all civic tetradrachm coinages had come to an end. Smyrna, for instance, dries up before the middle of the first century,[50] while the last issue from Alexandria Troas is dated 65 BC,[51] and that of Ilium is scarcely later. Bellinger's attribution of a drachm of Ilium to the Augustan period is an aberration, the obverse of the coin in question being by the same hand as another dated by Bellinger himself to the late second century.[52]

Implicit in the observed debasement of the cistophori is greater Roman involvement with the coinage after the Mithradatic revolt, and it now becomes realistic to speak of a province-wide monetary policy. The cost of Lucullus's campaigns against Mithradates in 70-67 seems to be reflected in the increased size and complexity of the Ephesian cistophoric issues of those years, which were only 80% fine. Where before one symbol per year had been the general rule, now there were three or four.[53] But after this burst of coining there was apparently a suspension of new cistophoric issues in 67. At any rate Ephesus suddenly ceased production and all the evidence points to a closure of the other mints as well.[54] Bullion must have been diverted elsewhere, some of it perhaps to the regal mints of Cappadocia, which may have provided coinage for the last campaigns against Tigranes and Mithradates.[55]

A province-wide monetary policy is again seen in operation in the new province of Bithynia and Pontus, formed in 63. No silver was struck, but beginning in 61 and 59 under C. Papirius Carbo, and again under C. Caecilius Cornutus in 56 and C. Vibius Pansa in 47, bronze issues unified as to denominations and types were made at several cities, with the name of the proconsul. The full list seems to be Amisus, Apamea, Bithynium, Nicaea, Nicomedia, Prusa and Tium.[56] Deliberate replacement of the earlier regal issues must have been the motive. This certainly represents a considerable contrast with the non-interventionist policy in the early years of the province of Asia.[57]

A similar picture is presented by the so-called proconsular cistophori, struck under central direction at the mints of Ephesus, Pergamum, Tralles, Laodicea and Apamea between 58 and 49.[58] Yet although the names of the Roman magistrates are prominent, so too on some issues are the local officials who were actually responsible for their production. The process of debasement was now arrested, for the proconsular cistophori are 90% fine.

The re-opening of cistophoric mints in 58, like their closure in 67, argues for a new approach, and it is unlikely to be coincidental that the year 57 saw the institution in Syria, by Gabinius, of the pseudo-Philip provincial tetradrachm coinage.[59]

Before we examine what happened to the currency of Asia in the civil wars, we should consider a significant first century development in the field of base metal coinages. For recent research[60] has shown that the use of orichalcum as a coinage metal began in Asia Minor in the early first century. Hitherto the earliest identifiable usage had been in the issue by C. Clovius in Italy, c. 46 BC,[61] but now we see Mithradates VI using orichalcum, as well as both ordinary leaded bronze and pure copper, in his Pontic civic series, while at Apamea in Phrygia, the site of a cistophoric mint it should be noted, the two highest denominations in a series of four were being struck in orichalcum, the others in bronze, from the early first century onwards. Here then is a clear prototype for the Roman imperial system of base metal issues inaugurated by Augustus.[62]

In this case, therefore, Asiatic practice was to influence Roman coinage. But it must be stressed that prior to the civil wars there is no real evidence that the currency of Asia Minor was in any way affected by the Roman monetary system. Nor is this all that surprising, for the indigenous coinages, precious metal and token, possessed a much greater sophistication and flexibility than anything Rome could offer.

It seems highly probable that Republican denarii played little if any role in Asia Minor before 50 BC. There is still no hoard context of any importance before the 40s, and the evidence from site finds is equally negative.[63] Literary references too, notably in Cicero's letters,[64] suggest that there was no ready convertibility between the cistophorus and the denarius, such as would be expected if the two currencies co-existed to any extent. Given that it remains the case that cistophori travel outside their area of issue only in exceptional circumstances, we seem obliged to conclude that we are still dealing with a closed monetary zone, which will have excluded the denarius. The degree to which the cistophorus was now overvalued is not entirely clear, but the fluctuations in the standard established by Walker, stabilising at c. 90% fine for the proconsular and later issues,[65] tend to corroborate the theory of incompatibility between the two coinages; if the often quoted 'rate' of three denarii to one cistophorus has any validity it can scarcely have applied much before the time of Augustus.

It is not possible to discuss the civil war period in any detail, for in the present state of knowledge there are too many uncertainties. For while Asiatic denarius issues may be quite closely datable, their mints are often unknown; for local Greek issues, by contrast, there are rarely problems of attribution, but chronological indications remain very imprecise.[66] Yet the major developments can be traced.

In 49 the proconsul Lentulus made the first denarius issue on Asiatic soil, probably at Ephesus.[67] Further such Roman issues followed, most notably from the tyrannicides Brutus and Cassius,[68] and from Antony.[69] Much of the metal was undoubtedly supplied by exactions on the local inhabitants, and straightforward plunder, and the coin used to pay troops. So by the time of Augustus's eastern settlements the denarius must have become a component in the currency of Asia Minor,[70] even if the cistophoric system was retained. The massive cistophoric re-coinages by Antony and then Augustus show that it was.[71] The precise role of the denarius (and aureus) in Asia cannot yet be defined, but the results of Sutherland's study of the Pergamene issues of 19-18 are significant.[72] Given that 71+ obverse dies were consumed in the striking of cistophori and only 18+ for the contemporary denarii, it is reasonable to assume that the cistophorus remained the basic unit of currency.

The other half of the picture is provided by the local Greek silver coinages of the time, so far as they can be identified. Although some, such as those of Amyntas of Galatia, both regal[73] and civic[74] conform to traditional Greek models, others, such as the revived silver issues of the Lycian League, which begin in the 40s, and the late first century issues of various Carian cities, show distinct signs of Roman influence. Troxell has demonstrated that the new series of hemidrachms and quarter-drachms from the districts of Cragus and Masicytus are equivalent in weight to contemporary Roman quinarii and sestertii,[75] and their connexion with Roman military activities in Lycia seems beyond doubt.[76] The earliest silver coins of Plarasa-Aphrodisias and Attuda, meanwhile, include issues with the names of <u>three</u> magistrates together, perhaps an echo of the tresviri monetales,[77] and two varieties at Aphrodisias actually bear a denarius value mark.[78]

Under Augustus a few mints still struck silver for local use, such as Chios, Mylasa, Stratonicea and Tabae, and of course the Lycian League,[79] but much of the available precious metal coinage will now have been unequivocally Roman, whether in the form of denarii or cistophori. For the cistophori of Antony and Augustus have completely shed any marks of local responsibility for their production, unlike their proconsular predecessors.

In this survey of the coinages of Asia under the late Republic much has necessarily been passed over. Certain aspects, such as the existence in scores of cities of bronze issues for local use, are of self-evident interest, but in the context of the colloquium can be taken as read.[80] The main theme from our standpoint has been the way in which Rome first made use of the pre-existing cistophoric coinage and eventually, after the Mithradatic revolt, took it over altogether. The denarius enters the scene in the civil wars, and although some local silver was still being struck under Augustus, the complexity and variety of currency in circulation when the Romans arrived had long since disappeared.

NOTES

1. What follows is the paper read at the colloquium, with annotations and a few minor adjustments. It is strictly a general survey, which does not pretend to be comprehensive, the emphasis being on the area of the Roman province of Asia. My aim was to assess the extent of possible Roman influences on the currency struck and circulating in the region between c. 200 and Augustus.
   For the historical background see especially E. Will, Histoire Politique du Monde hellénistique (323-30 av.J.-C.), Vol 2 (2nd edition), (Nancy, 1982), and A.N. Sherwin-White, 'Roman Involvement in Anatolia 167-88 BC,' JRS 67 (1977), 62-75.

2. See Crawford, CMRR 154, with note 3.

3. Giovannini, Rome; idem, 'La circulation monétaire en Grèce sous le protectorat de Rome', AIIN 29 (1982, publ. 1983), 165-81.

4. The late Alexanders of Alabanda and Temnus are crucial. See N.M. Waggoner, 'The Propontis hoard (IGCH 888)', RN^6 21 (1979), 7-29, esp. 21ff.

5. See O. Morkholm, 'Chronology and meaning of the wreath coinages of the early 2nd cent. B.C.', QT 9 (1980), 145-58; idem, 'The chronology of the New Style coinage of Athens', ANSMN 29 (1984), 29-42.

6. So O. Picard, 'Les Romains et les émissions aux types d'Alexander', AIIN 29 (1982, publ. 1983), 245-50.

7. See QT 9 (1980), 154-6.

8. W. Szaivert, 'Stephanephoren und Kistophoren; Die mittelhellenistische Grossilberprägung und die römische Ostpolitik in der Ägäis', Litterae Numismaticae Vindobonenses 2 (1983), 29-55.

9. See O. Morkholm, 'Some reflections on the production and use of coinage in ancient Greece', Historia 31 (1982), 290-305, esp. 300-01, with earlier bibliography. Note the presence of a cistophorus of Apamea, not one of the earliest, in the Sitochoro hoard (NC 142 (1982), Proceedings, p.X.).

10. This may be an over-statement. In discussion both M.J. Price and C. Boehringer stressed the possibility of parallel striking of Philetaerus tetradrachms and cistophori, perhaps at different mints.

11. See above, note 4. But T. Fischer's theory ('Zur Ära der posthumen Alexander-Tetradrachmen pamphylischer Gemeinden', Berichte 125 (Nov. 1981), 1457-8) that the Pamphylian Alexanders are dated by an era beginning in 189/8, taking them down to 157/6, must be rejected.

12. These dates depend on hoard evidence: IGCH 1544 (= H.Seyrig, Trésors du Levant, (Paris, 1974), no.11) for Ilium; CH 4 (1978) no.55, for Samos; the Ma'arret en-Nu'man 1979 hoard (cf. CH 6 (1981). 37, CH 7 (1985).98) is believed to have included tetradrachms of Cos, Mytilene and Miletus. (Information from M.J. Price).

13. So N.F. Jones, 'The autonomous wreathed tetradrachms of Magnesia on-

Maeander', ANSMN 24 (1979), 63-109; K.S. Sacks, 'The wreathed coins of Aeolian Myrina', ANSMN 30 (1985), 1-43. J.H. Oakley, 'The autonomous wreathed tetradrachms of Kyme, Aeolis', ANSMN 27 (1982) 1-37, prefers a slightly earlier date, but the general thrust of the hoard evidence tends to contradict this. All these coinages appear side by side in a series of hoards from the 140s.

14. See Sacks (previous note), 24-6, with note 76.

15. I propose to develop these points in a future article.

16. F.S. Kleiner & S.P. Noe, The Early Cistophoric Coinage, ANSNS 14 (New York, 1977).

17. See W.H. Waddington, E. Babelon, T. Reinach, Recueil général des monnaies grecques d'Asie Mineure, I.1^{2} (Paris, 1925) (Pontus); ibid, I.2, 1908 (Bithynia); O. Morkholm, 'The Cappadocians again', NC^{7} 19 (1979), 242-6.

18. See e.g. Troxell (with a useful summary of the Rhodian issues at p. 80ff, suggesting a gap between c. 150 and c. 100); J.H. Kroll, 'The late hellenistic tetrobols of Kos', ANSMN 11 (1964), 81-117; J. Mavrogordato, 'A chronological arrangement of the coins of Chios', Part III, NC^{4} 16 (1916), 281-355, esp. 307-13 (precise dating impossible); A.R. Bellinger, Troy: The Coins, (Princeton, 1961) (for Ilium and Alexandria Troas, the latter including dated tetradrachms in 135), with essential commentary by L.Robert, 'Monnaies antiques en Troade' (1966). Other silver issues definitely made in the late 140s and early 130s are difficult to identify.

19. Useful hoard evidence includes CH 2.81, CH 5.41, CH 6.37. Two examples of the EPHESION issue are extant, of identical style: Kinns (with 'A' between the stag's legs) and Waddington 1577 (with bee symbol). The controls suggest contemporaneity with the cistophoric tetradrachms of year 1 in 134/3 (Kleiner-Noe (note 16 above) p. 53, series 40). S. Karwiese has confirmed by letter that he had independently come to the same conclusion.

20. So Crawford, CMRR 160. For the status of Ephesus see R.E. Allen, The Attalid Kingdom: A Constitutional History, (Oxford, 1983), 98-121, who does, however, conveniently ignore the Attic weight drachms.

21. See K.J. Rigsby, 'The era of the province of Asia', Phoenix 33 (1979), 39-47.

22. Kleiner-Noe (above, note 16), p. 120ff.

23. Kleiner-Noe, pp. 103-6; for a new issue of year 1 at Thyatira see M. Kampmann, 'Aristonicos à Thyatire', RN 1978, 38-42.

24. See J.G. Milne, 'The autonomous coinage of Smyrna', Part II, NC^{5} 7 (1927), 1-107. Note that his two die-links between the monogram tetradrachms (which can now be dated c. 155-145) and the lion tetradrachms (post c. 133) are imaginary; the obverses and reverses of two coins were mixed up when he was sent casts by the Hague cabinet (loc.cit., p.33 no.157 and p.54 no.200 = J.G. Milne, 'The silver coinage of Smyrna', NC^{4} 14 (1914), P.275 no.4(b) and p.278 no.7(a)).

Whereas his 1914 article (at p. 281) showed the two series linked by obverses 'F' and 'H', in fact 'H' is confined to the first series, 'F' to the second.

25. NC 1927, p. 46 nos. 186-9. Milne's original dating by the 'provincial era' beginning in 134/3 must now be questioned (cf. note 21 above), while his later attempt, in C.J. Cadoux, Ancient Smyrna, (Oxford, 1938), 156 note 4, to associate them with Mithradates was never plausible. For publication of IGCH 1459 (deposited c. 98 BC) see ANSMN 23, (1978), 87-90.

26. Lack of chronological evidence makes late second century issues difficult to pinpoint, but the bronze coinage of Smyrna exhibits a notable continuity.

27. See e.g. C.M. Kraay, Archaic and Classical Greek Coins (London, 1976), 68-9 (Athens), 228 (Sicily).

28. See e.g. C.M. Kraay, op. cit., 231-3 (Syracuse), 250f. (gold in 4th century Asia Minor).

29. I propose to discuss the gold issues from Ionian mints in a paper at the International Numismatic Congress in September 1986. B. Deppert-Lippitz, Die Münzprägung Milets vom vierten bis ersten Jahrhundert v.Chr., Typos 5 (Aarau, Frankfurt am Main, Salzburg, 1984), 121-3, wrongly condemns the Milesian issues as modern forgeries. A reference by Troxell (p. 84) to a gold issue of Priene is mysterious and persumably mistaken.

30. See Jenkins, loc. cit.

31. For the cistophori see F.S. Kleiner, 'The dated cistophori of Ephesus', ANSMN 18 (1972), 17-32 at p. 25 no.19, and now G. Stumpf, 'C.ATINIUS C.F., Praetor in Asia 122-121 v.Chr., auf einem Kistophor', ZPE 61 (1985), 186-90 (a reference I owe to Prof. P.R. Franke). Stumpf identifies this man with Gaius Labeo, mentioned as Strategos (praetor) in Inschriften von Priene 121. The coins therefore apparently bear the name of the governor of Asia. The gold stater is unpublished and was not known to Kleiner or Stumpf.

32. Quantitative justification of this generalisation is scarcely possible in the present state of research. Some of the evidence will be found in notes 16-18 above, to which may be added three studies by Kleiner: 'The dated cistophori of Ephesus' (loc.cit., note 31 above); 'Hoard evidence and the late cistophori of Pergamum', ANSMN 23 (1978), 77-105; 'The Giresun hoard', ANSMN 19 (1974), 3-25. The last is particularly valuable, with a conspectus of the tetradrachms of Mithradates VI (p. 25 = Crawford, CMRR 200) and discussion of many other issues of this period. For a recently discovered tetradrachm of Mithradates V Euergetes, see L. Robert, Journal des Savants 1978, 151-63.

33. See Troxell 80-98, esp. 87 and 95 note 198 (Alabanda).

34. See Kleiner, 'The Giresun hoard' (loc.cit., note 32 above) and M.J. Price, 'Mithradates VI Eupator, Dionysus, and the coinages of the Black Sea', NC[7] 8 (1968), 1-12.

35. Pp.82-4.

36. See Milne, NC 1927, p. 101 no. 340 (AE) and p. 102 no. 344 (AU). A second example of the stater was acquired by the BM in 1936.

37. See J.G. Milne, 'Notes on the Aberdeen University collections', NC^5 14 (1934), 31-2. Milne had previously regarded the Cybele/lion type (= NC 1927, p. 102 no. 345) as earlier than the Mithradates/Nike type.

38. See A.R. Bellinger, *op. cit.* (note 18 above), pp. 33-4 no. T96-9. There are also Mithradatic elements in some of the late silver and bronze of Adramyteum (see H. von Fritze, *Die Antiken Münzen Mysiens I. Adramytion-Kisthene,* (Berlin, 1913), 1-5, 9-25), but more detailed study is required.

39. ANSMN 18 (1972), pp. 26-7, nos. 47-51.

40. Crawford, CMRR 196.

41. For a rationale of countermarks and overstrikes see G. Le Rider, 'Contremarques et surfrappes dans l'antiquité grecque', in *Numismatique Antique: Problèmes et Méthodes* (Nancy-Louvain, 1975), 27-56.

42. See J.G. Milne, 'The autonomous coinage of Smyrna, Part III', NC^5 8 (1928), 131-71, at pp. 132-3, nos. 359-60.

43. *Loc. cit.* (previous note), nos. 361ff.

44. See P. Kinns, *Studies in the Coinage of Ionia: Erythrae, Teos, Lebedus, Colophon, c.400-30 BC,* (unpublished Cambridge Ph.D. diss., 1980), 160-1, 232-8, 269-71, 335-7 etc.

45. D.R. Walker, *Metrology* I, 26-36.

46. See F.S. Kleiner, 'The late cistophori of Apameia', *Essays Thompson,* 119-30.

47. Kleiner, ANSMN 23 (1978), 81 (with note 10).

48. Cf. A.R. Bellinger, *op. cit.* (note 18 above); J. Mavrogordato, 'A chronological arrangement of the coins of Chios', Part IV, NC^4 17 (1917), 207-57.

49. Troxell p.87. For the silver of Tabae see esp. H.A. Troxell and N.M. Waggoner, 'The Robert F. Kelley bequest', ANSMN 23 (1978), 1-41, at 18-23.

50. Milne, *loc.cit.* (note 42 above).

51. Bellinger, *op.cit.,* p. 101 nos. A169-70.

52. Compare Bellinger pl. 6, no. TII9 ('Augustus') with pl. 3, nos. T55 (tetradrachm with same reverse monogram) and T57 (drachm). T55 and T57 are dated by Bellinger late in the period c. 189-133, but L. Robert, *Monnaies antiques en Troade,* p. 72, has shown that they belong at the end of the second century.

53. Kleiner, ANSMN 18 (1972), 27-8, nos.63-74.

54. Crawford, CMRR 200. Cf.Kleiner, ANSMN 23 (1978), 99 etc.

55. Oddly enough the year 68/7 saw an exceptional issue at Alexandria Troas, although this may be pure coincidence. For there exists a unique tetradrachm from that year (233), not known to Bellinger, with a wreath round the reverse (= Glendining sale 21/11/74. 314), possibly in recognition of a Roman victory (?). See now Auctiones S.A. sale 16 (1986), 167, which reveals this issue to be of cistophoric weight (12.11g.). Proof of authenticity would be desirable.

56. See Recueil I.1², p. 73 (Amisus); Recueil I.2, pp. 249-50 (Apamea), 268 (Bithynium); Recueil I.3, pp. 397-8 (Nicaea), 514-5 (Nicomedia); Recueil I.4, pp. 576 (Prusa), 617 (Tium).

57. The 'proconsular' bronze issue from Atarneus in Mysia (H. von Fritze, op.cit. (note 38 above), p. 113 no.350) is of uncertain date, pace Head (HN² p.522, '79-76 BC'). Grant, FITA 394-6, argues for a re-attribution to Adramyteum, c. 35-34 BC.

58. Cf. Crawford, CMRR 206-9, citing J.M. Cody, 'New evidence for the Republican Aedes Vestae', AJA 1973, 43f., for a conspectus of the proconsular cistophori. The unique specimens of Lepidus and Fimbria (the latter with caduceus and Roman standard supplanting the usual reverse type - in Oxford, casts in BM) await convincing explanation; the temptation to connect the latter with Flaccus's legate is obviously strong, but should perhaps be resisted.

59. Cf. Crawford, CMRR 203-9.

60. A.M. Burnett, P.T. Craddock and K. Preston, 'New light on the origins of orichalcum', Actes 1979, 263-8; P.T. Craddock, A.M. Burnett and K. Preston, 'Hellenistic copper-base coinage and the origins of brass', in W.A. Oddy (Ed.), Scientific Studies in Numismatics, BM Occas. Paper no.18 (1980), 53-64.

61. Cf. Crawford, CMRR 196, for the issue of Q. Oppius (= RRC 550), apparently struck at Laodicea ad Lycum in 88; idem p.243 for Clovius.

62. Cf. Crawford, CMRR 258, 260, 266, with earlier bibliography. The 'CA' issues from Asia precede those of Rome itself (C.J. Howgego, 'Coinage and military finance: the imperial bronze coinage of the Augustan east', NC 142 (1982), 1-20).

63. Cf. Crawford, CMRR 252, with note 14. C.Rodewald, Money in the Age of Tiberius, (Manchester 1976), 24-6, collects the almost non-existent evidence for the circulation of the denarius in Asia Minor in the 1st century BC. The hoard from Chios (CH 6 (1981) 46, deposited c. 75 BC) with a denarius of L. Piso Frugi may be the exception that proves the rule.

64. Cicero, Ad Atticum, ii, 6, 2 (59 BC); ii, 16, 4 (59 BC); xi, 1, 2, (48 BC). cf. Crawford, CMRR 160.

65. Loc. cit. (note 45 above).

66. Crawford, CMRR 245 refers to coinages 'which may be regarded as evoked by the preparations of Pompey for resistance against Caesar', naming Teos, Smyrna, Priene and Chios, but no specific issues are cited. The Teos drachms (as SNG Copenhagen 1483) cannot be closely dated, although they are certainly of this general period, while the last Smyrna silver is perhaps rather earlier (Milne, loc. cit., note 42 above). Chios offers several candidates (Mavrogordato, loc. cit., note 48 above), but Priene must now be ruled out. The drachm issue dated by Regling c. 50 BC (K. Regling, Die Münzen von Priene (Berlin, 1927), no. 31) belongs rather to the mid 2nd century.

67. RRC 445/3.

68. RRC 496-508. Troxell, LL 179-81.

69. RRC 516-7ff.

70. Cf. Crawford, CMRR 252, with note 14.

71. See Crawford, CMRR 252, 262; C.H.V. Sutherland et al., The Cistophori of Augustus (London, 1970). Both series are about 90% fine, continuing the standard in use for the proconsular issues of 58-49 (see above, note 45).

72. C.H.V. Sutherland, 'Augustan aurei and denarii attributable to the mint of Pergamum', RN^6 15 (1973), 129-51; RIC I^2, pp. 36-7, 82-3, nos. 505-26.

73. BMC Galatia etc., p.2; S. Atlan, 'Sidede basilan Amyntas sikkeleri' (The coinage of Amyntas at Side), Belleten 39 (1975), 575-611.

74. E.g. the late silver of Sagalassus (HN^2 p.710).

75. Troxell 117-24.

76. Crawford, CMRR 246; Troxell 173-84.

77. E.g. BMC Caria, p. 27 nos. 11-12, p. 271 no. 10A (Plarasa-Aphrodisias); ibid., p. 62 no. 1 (Attuda).

78. Troxell 121; BMC Caria, p.xxxiv.

79. For issues with SEBASTOS or portrait of Augustus, see Mavrogordato, loc. cit. (note 48 above), p. 225 no. 82; A. Akarca, Les monnaies grecques de Mylasa, (Paris, 1959) p. 58; HN^2 p. 625 (Stratonicea); ibid., p. 626 (Tabae); Troxell 148ff, 170ff.

80. Before Augustus civic bronze issues with any specific Roman content or reference are entirely exceptional. Cf. the Ephesian issues with portrait heads of the second triumvirate (BMC Ionia, p. 71).

SYRIA

Hans Roland Baldus

Historischer Abriss

Gn. Pompeius Magnus richtete 64 v.Chr. in dem von König Tigranes d.Gr. übernommenen Rest des Seleukidenreiches die römische Provinz Syrien ein und ordnete im folgenden Jahr die Verhältnisse auch in den südöstlich angrenzenden Nachbarstaaten (s. die Karte S. 122). Provinzhauptstadt wurde die alte Metropole Antiochia am Orontes. Die Grenze der Provinz bildete im Westen natürlich das Mittelmeer, im Norden schied das Amanosgebirge zwischen den Provinzen Cilicia und Syria. Von dort verlief die Grenze westöstlich zum Euphrat bei Zeugma. Der Euphrat bildete auf seinem Lauf in Nord-Süd-Richtung die Machtscheide zur Osrhoëne, dann verlief die Grenze im Bogen entlang der Wüste zum oberen Orontes. Von dort folgte sie dem Tal des oberen Leontes und Jordan, um wenig südlich von Ptolemaïs-Ake, also etwa am Berg Karmel, wieder das Mittelmeer zu erreichen.

Aus oben genannten Daten ergeben sich die Zeitgrenzen der folgenden Betrachtung: Sie reicht von 64 bis 30 v.Chr., wobei allerdings die Entwicklung der Provinzialprägung bis zu einschneidenden Aenderungen unter Augustus - wohl im Jahre 5 v.Chr. - verfolgt wird. Das Augenmerk richtet sich nicht allein auf Prägungen innerhalb der Provinz, in der - wie die Karte zeigt - die Münzstätten übrigens keineswegs gleichmässig verteilt waren, sondern (bis auf zwei am Unterlauf des Orontes) an der Küste konzentriert. Ueber die Provinzgrenzen hinaus sollen auch die Geldausgaben in den angrenzenden Zonen römischer Oberhoheit betrachtet werden, insbesondere in Koilesyrien und den Landstrichen südlich des Sees Genezareth. Denn in dieser Zone lassen sich immer wieder monetäre Einflüsse von Seiten der Provinz nachweisen.

Als Pompeius 64-63 v. im Namen der Republik die Provinz Syrien einrichtete und auch die Verhältnisse im Umland ordnete,[1] fanden die Römer in diesem Raum ein sehr vielgestaltiges Münzwesen vor: Der Münzumlauf, der freilich auch ältere Prägungen umfasste (ein spätes Beispiel ist der Fund von Akbar um 30 v.,[2] mit späten Seleukiden-Tetradrachmen und einem parthischen Exemplar von 33/2 v.), wurde aus zwei aktuellen Quellengruppen gespeist. Zum einen gab es eine ganze Reihe von Städten, die während des Niedergangs des Seleukidenreiches Autonomie und Münzrecht erworben hatten und letzteres durch Emission von Bronzemünzen eher für den lokalen Geldverkehr und (bei einigen von ihnen) auch von Silbergeld für grössere oder über-regionale Transaktionen ausübten; jede Polis hatte ihre eigenen Münzbilder. Selbst bei dem gängigsten Silbernominal, dem Tetradrachmon, gab es keinen einheitlichen Münzfuss,[3] sondern bei den Städteprägungen wenigstens zwei Standards: Arados prägte (bis 44/3 v.) Tetradrachmen von ca. 15,3g, ihm schloss sich Laodicea ad Mare (bis 44/3 v.) mit einem Fuss von ca. 15,1g in etwa an. Demgegenüber hielten sich die weiter südlich gelegenen Städte Sidon und Tyros (auch Askalon, ausserhalb der Provinz) an den ptolemäischen Münzfuss zu ca. 14,3g; ihnen schloss sich Laodikeia später (nämlich nach 44/3 v.) an. Dieser vielgestaltigen Städteprägung standen zum anderen die königlichen, reduziert-attischgewichtigen Tetradrachmen zu etwa 15,4-16,0 g insbesondere aus der Münzstätte der

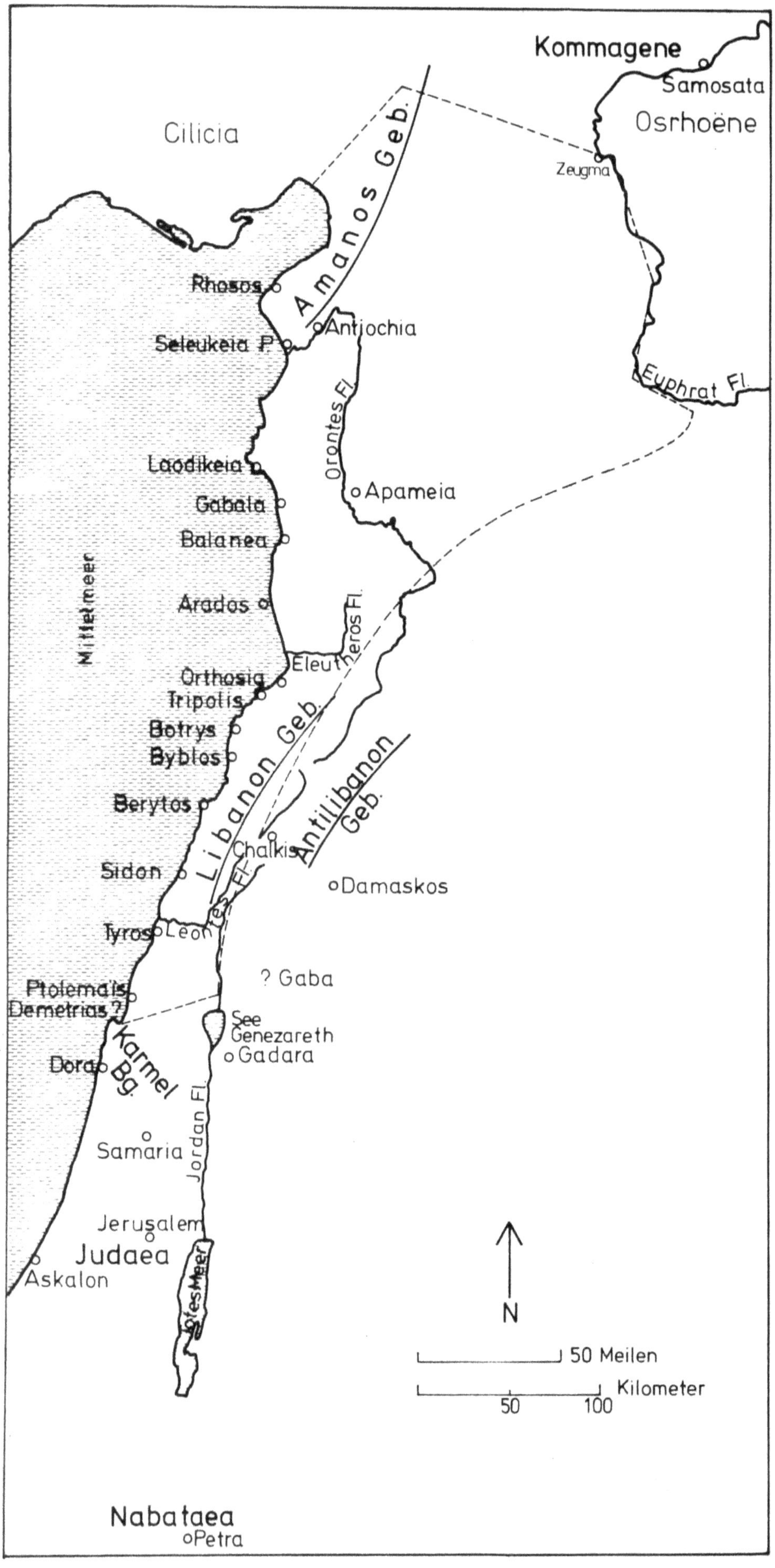
Kommagene
Samosata
Osrhoëne
Cilicia
Amanos Geb.
Zeugma
Rhosos
Antiochia
Seleukeia P.
Euphrat Fl.
Orontes Fl.
Laodikeia
Apameia
Gabala
Balanea
Mittelmeer
Arados
Eleutheros Fl.
Orthosia
Tripolis
Botrys
Libanon Geb.
Byblos
Antilibanon Geb.
Berytos
Chalkis
Sidon
Damaskos
Leontes Fl.
Tyros
? Gaba
Ptolemais
Demetrias ?
See Genezareth
Karmel Bg.
Gadara
Dora
Jordan Fl.
Samaria
Jerusalem
Judaea
Totes Meer
Askalon
N
50 Meilen
50
100
Kilometer
Nabataea
Petra

Residenz Antiochia a.O. gegenüber - letztes übriggebliebenes Nominal der breiteren Palette älterer Seleukidenprägungen, in Mengen etwa von Philippos Philadelphos (Taf.12,A) oder Tigranes d.Gr. emittiert.

Die Römische Republik hat merkwürdigerweise darauf verzichtet, in Syrien ihr eigenes Münzsystem einzuführen:[4] In Crawfords 'Roman Republican Coin Hoards' (1969) ist kein syrischer Schatzfund enthalten, der etwa Denare der Römischen Republik beinhaltet hätte,[5] und in seinem 'Roman Republican Coinage' (1974) ist gerade eine höchst rare Sonderemission von Aurei/Goldstateren enthalten, die aufgrund des Gewichts von ca. 7,84g (das entspricht einem halben reduziert-attischgewichtigen Tetradrachmon) und wegen der typisch Antiochener Randgestaltung (bead and reel-border) mit einiger Wahrscheinlichkeit nach Syrien gelegt wird (Nr. 549): Die Prägung für durchziehende römische Truppen vom Typ 'Jupiterkopf r./Adler auf Blitz l. mit Kopf r., im Abschnitt CN LENTVL' wird dem Statthalter Syriens im Jahr 59/8 v. zugewiesen, Gn. Cornelius Lentulus Marcellinus. Mit dem beschriebenen Befund stimmt überein, dass bei den zeitgenössisch-syrischen Prägungen quasi keine Beeinflussung durch Gewicht oder Darstellungen republikanischer Denare festzustellen ist.

Statt dessen haben die Römer das in Syrien vorgefundene Geldwesen interessanterweise zunächst ohne Aenderungen übernommen: Keine der bis 64 v. prägenden Poleis brach in diesem Jahr ihre Münzproduktion ab,[6] vielmehr wurden die Städteprägungen in Silber und Bronze[7] fortgeführt. Am deutlichsten wird die - die bestehenden Verhältnisse übernehmende - Münzpolitik der Römer bei der Behandlung der königlichen Tetradrachmenprägung in Antiochia a.O.: Sie haben die weit verbreiten Exemplare des Philippos Philadelphos vom Typ 'Diademierter Königskopf r./Thronender Zeus l.' (Taf.12,A) als Provinzialprägung einfach weiter hergestellt; abgesehen von weniger beabsichtigten Aenderungen (z.B. Stil) unterscheiden diese Exemplare nur die Monogramme einiger Gouverneure l. im Feld der Rückseite: Der erste und bezüglich der Prägetätigkeit aktivste von drei bisher identifizierten römischen Offiziellen war A. Gabinius, in Syrien tätig 57 - 55 v. (Taf.12,1). Nach Th. Mommsens Darlegung[8] wurde diesen wie den leichteren städtischen Tetradrachmen von den römischen Eroberern Syriens der gleiche Wert von 4 Denaren zugesprochen.

Das Münzwesen der Provinz Syrien ist im betrachteten Zeitraum bis 30 v. im Prinzip so wie vorgefunden belassen worden, erst unter Augustus wurde stärker in die bestehenden Verhältnisse eingegriffen.[9] Freilich blieb das syrische Münzwesen 64 - 30 v. von den politischen Veränderungen nicht unberührt; diese machten sich zunächst zaghaft, dann deutlicher bemerkbar und wurden in den dreissiger Jahren unübersehbar:

Mit der Einrichtung der Provinz 64 v. oder der Neuordnung der Verhältnisse im Süden 63 v. erhielt eine ganze Reihe von Städten die Freiheit und begann mit der Zählung einer neuen, pompeianischen, Aera. Von den nachstehend behandelten Poleis sind das (jeweils mit Angabe des Epochenjahres): Antiochia a.O. (66 v., nachträglich installiert), Apameia (66 v. wie Antiochia ?), Botrys (64 oder 63 v.), Byblos (64 od. 63 v.), Chalkis a.L. (63 v.), Demetrias a.M. (63 v. ?), Dora (64 od. 63 v.), Gaba (erst 60 v.), Gadara (64 v.), Orthosia (64, od. 63 v.?), Ptolemaïs (64 od. 63 v.) und Tripolis (64 od. 63 v.). Soweit diese Städte in den Jahren kurz vor 64 v. Münzen geprägt hatten - wie das zuletzt genannte Tripolis - wurden die Prägungen einfach mit 'Jahr 1' fortgesetzt. Andere Poleis, deren Münzproduktion vor einigen Jahren abgebrochen war, nahmen sie mit der neuen Datierung (oft aber mit traditionellen Typen) wieder auf: Antiochia a.O.

prägte so nach wenigen Jahren Unterbrechung wieder die gewohnten Bronzen ab Jahr 3= 64/3 v. (bis 17=50/49 v.), Apameia nahm nach einigen Jahren Unterbrechung die Bronzeprägung im Jahr 7=60/59 v. (bis 51/50 v.) wieder auf, Byblos münzte nach 20 Jahren Prägepause Bronzen ab Jahr 3=62/1 v. (bis 26=39/8 v.), Chalkis a.L. gab nach längerer Pause denselben Bronzetyp und anderes Aes ab Jahr 2=62/1 v. heraus. Orthosia emittierte nach einer Unterbrechung (?) wieder Bronzen ab Jahr 1=64/3 v. (bis 24=41/40 v.) und Ptolemaïs gab nach längerer Inaktivität im Jahr 9=56/5 (oder 55/4 v.) Bronzemünzen heraus. Zu den Städten, die vor 64 v. nicht geprägt hatten, jetzt aber mit 'Jahr 1' und späteren Datierungen Bronzen herstellten, gehören Demetrias ad Mare (Jahr 1, 3, 22) und Dora (Jahr 1, erheblich spätere Jahrgänge s. unten). Eine eigene national-nabatäische Münzprägung setzte erst unter römischer Oberhoheit ein; man datierte nach der Regierungszeit des jeweiligen Königs, im Fall Obodas' II. mit 62 v. als Jahr 1. Sidon hielt dagegen an seiner traditionellen Freiheitsära fest, gab aber 64/3 v. nach längerer Unterbrechung die ersten einer Reihe datierter Schekel und Halbstücke heraus. Etwas anders verlief die Entwicklung in Askalon: Die Stadt hielt an Münzprägung und alter Aera fest, verlor oder unterdrückte jedoch den bis 64/3 v. auch getragenen Autonomos-Titel.

Der Bürgerkrieg zwischen Pompeius und C. Julius Caesar hat in der Münzprägung einiger Städte der Region deutliche Spuren hinterlassen: Antiochia a.O. führte eine caesarische Aera ein (49/8 v.=Jahr 1, nachträglich) und trug seit Caesars Besuch 47 v. die zusätzlichen Titel Hiera und Asylos (beides ab 42/1 v. auf den Münzen weggelassen) sowie vor allem Autonomos. Seine Bronzeprägung, in die im Jahr 19 pomp. Aera (=49/8 v.) ein neues Grossnominal (bis 14 g) eingeführt wurde, deren Reversbilder im Anschluss an Caesars Sieg bei Pharsalos 48 v. mit einem Lorbeerkranz umgeben wurden und die in diesen Jahren häufig mit einer Kontermarke versehen wurde, zeigt nach dem Wechsel zu Jahr 2 = 48/7 v. bis 41/40 v. keine wesentlichen Aenderungen. Laodikeia a.M. datierte nach einer caes. Aera mit 48/7 v. als Jahr 1, es liess seit Caesars Visite 47 v. die alten Titel Hiera und Autonomos fort und nahm statt dessen den Namen Julia Laodicea an - ansonsten führte die Stadt ihre Silber- und Bronzeprägung zunächst fort. Ptolemaïs datierte ebenso nach einer caes. Aera mit 48/7 v. als Jahr 1 und nannte sich seit 47 v. statt 'Antiochia in der Ptolemaïs' verkürzt Ptolemaïs; die ersten Prägungen mit der neuen Namensform und neuer Jahreszählung sind Bronzen vom Jahr 5 = 44/3 v. Gabala datierte ab 46 v. gleichfalls nach einer caesarischen Aera, freilich ohne zunächst Münzen zu prägen.

Weitere Modifikationen dieser Jahre sind folgende: Im Jahr 47/6 v. wurde die Prägung der provinzialen Tetradrachmen aus der Münzstätte Antiochia a.O. umgestellt. Statt eines Gouverneur-Monogramms im Feld l. der Rückseite sind die Stücke vom Jahr 3 caes. Aera an im Abschnitt datiert (Taf. 12, 2) und weisen im Feld l. regelmässig das Antiochia-Monogramm auf: Es gibt an, welche der caesarischen Aeren zu gelten hat und wo die Exemplare entstanden sind. Ins Jahr 47/6 v. fallen die ersten Bronzen von Gadara. 44/3 v. wurde der letzte - von Bronze begleitete - Jahrgang aradischer Tetradrachmen ausgegeben. Laodicea a.M., das sich bisher an diesem aradischen Münzfuss orientiert hatte, musste daher fortan nach dem leichteren ptolemäischen Tetradrachmen-Standard prägen, den immerhin auch die Schekel von Sidon, Tyros und Askalon vertraten. In den Jahren 44/3 - 43/2 v. wurde in Apameia nach einiger Abstinenz Bronze vom gewohnten Typ herausgebracht, dann wechselte die Stadt zu neuen Münztypen.

Die Belagerung (und Eroberung) Laodikeias durch den Caesarmörder C.

Cassius hat in der städtischen Münzprägung deutliche Spuren hinterlassen: 44/3 v. bricht die Münzprodukion plötzlich ab. Während der Besetzung werden dann 'Jahr 7' caes. Aera = 42/1 v. datierte Bronzen emittiert, die den Namen Julia unterdrücken und die Stadt altertümlich 'Laodikeia am Meer' ohne Titel nennen; im selben Jahr kehrt man allerdings wieder zur gewohnten caesarischen Umbenennung zurück.

Vergleichbar kurzfristig waren die Aenderungen, die die Partherinvasion von 41 v. in den Bronzeprägungen von Antiochia a.O. und Apameia verursachte: Beide Städte datierten die Münzen der Besatzungszeit nach der auch den Parthern geläufigen seleukidischen Aera (Jahr 272), Antiochia verlor auch seinen Titel Autonomos; allerdings kehrte man im selben Jahr 9 caes. Aera zu gewohnter Jahreszählung und Stadttitulatur zurück. Die Auswirkungen des Einbruchs reichten bis nach Jerusalem, wo die Parther den König Mattathias Antigonos an die Macht brachten. Unter ihm, der sich mehrere Jahre halten konnte, gab es einschneidende Aenderungen im jüdischen Münzwesen. Parallel dazu in Samaria hergestellte Münzen des römischen Favoriten, Herodes d.Gr., nennen erstmals eine Datierung (Jahr 3 = 40 v.).

Die ersten Jahre der Herrschaft des M. Antonius im Osten - bis 38/7 v., dem vorerst letzten Jahrgang der postumen Philippos Philadelphos-Tetradrachmen - brachten nur mässige Neuerungen: Den Titel Autonomos bekamen Rhosos 42 v. und Apameia 41 v. verliehen, beide Städte begannen zum genannten Zeitpunkt auch mit einer neuen Jahreszählung. Rhosos emittierte erste Bronzen im Jahr 6 = 37/6 v., Apameia in den Jahren 2 = 40/39 und 3 = 39/8 v.; ab dem Jahre 38/7 v. kehrte letztere Stadt aus unbekannten Gründen zur Seleukidenära zurück. In besagte Zeit fielen traditionell pompeianisch datierte Bronzeemissionen von Byblos (J. 26 = 39/8 v.) und Demetrias a.M. (J. 22 = 42/1 v.). Letzter Tetradrachmen-Jahrgang von Askalon ist 66 = 39/8 v. (zu Ehren Kleopatras VII.).

Eine neue Erscheinung dieser Jahre ist die Ehrung des Antonius durch Anbringen seines Porträts auf städtischen Münzen: Tripolis emittierte im Jahr 23 = 42/1 v. neben Teilstücken traditionellen Typs Bronzen mit den Bildnissen von M. Anton (Vorderseite) und Fulvia (Rs.). Im Jahr 38/7 v. setzten auch Arados und Ptolemaïs den Kopf des Antonius auf die Averse städtischer Bronzen (bei letztgenannter Stadt: in Lorbeerumrandung).

Im Jahre 37/6 v. erfolgten gewichtige politische Veränderungen, die auch einschneidende Massnahmen beim Münzwesen der Region zur Folge hatten: Antonius schenkte der Kleopatra den zur Provinz Syria gehörenden phönizischen Küstenstreifen vom Eleutheros nördlich Orthosias bis südlich von Berytos, ausserdem überliess er ihr das entsprechende Hinterland, nämlich das Fürstentum Chalkis am Libanon (zu ihm gehörte das Gebiet zwischen Libanon und Antilibanon). Die Königin wurde durch die Uebernahme dieses kompakten Territoriums - durch die 'Rückgabe' vor langem verlorener ptolemäischer Besitzungen - veranlasst, eine zweite Regierungsjahr-Zählung neben derjenigen als Königin von Aegypten einzuführen (Jahr 16 = 1 = 37/6 v.), die doppeldeutige Titulatur Basilissa Kleopatra Thea Neotera zu führen und einen speziellen Ornat (ein Cape, das durch kettenverbundene 'Tasseln' gehalten wurde) zu tragen.

Die Auswirkungen dieser Schenkung im monetären Bereich sind vielgestaltig:[10] In der Antiochener Provinzialprägung wird mit dem Jahr 37/6 v. die Emission der postumen Philippos-Tetradrachmen eingestellt und statt dessen als Gemeinschaftsprägung des Römers und der Königin für die syrisch-phönizischen Gebiete von zweierlei juristischem Status (römische

Provinz, ptolemäisches Königreich) ein Tetradrachmon zu 15g mit den Porträts und Titeln der beiden auf Vorder - und Rückseite herausgebracht (Taf. 12, 3).

Im nördlichen Syrien/Phönizien, das unter direkter Kontrolle des Antonius verblieb, erhielt Balanea die Autonomie, begann eine neue Aera mit 37/6 v. als Jahr 1 und emittierte eine '(Jahr) 1' datierte Bronzeserie, von der das Hauptnominal auf dem Avers den Antoniuskopf zeigt. Einen ähnlichen Antoniusavers weisen aradische Bronzen von 35/4 v. und stadtantiochenische Silberdrachmen der späteren 30er Jahre auf.

In Kleopatras Neuerwerbungen liess die Königin als solche im Jahr 6 = 21 = 32/1 v. in der Münzstätte Chalkis a.L. eine Serie doppeldatierter Bronzenominale mit ihrem Bildnis und Namen als Avers und fehlendem Stadtnamen ausgeben; den Antoniuskopf findet man bezeichnenderweise (ohne Namensnennung) auf der Rückseite von Ganz- und Doppelstück. Einige Poleis des ihr geschenkten Küstenstreifens ehrten die Königin mit städtischen Bronzeprägungen, die ihr Porträt in der 'ägyptischen' Version (!) aufweisen und nach der Schenkungsära von 37 v. datiert sind; bisweilen finden sich noch weitere Aerenangaben: Berytos prägte derartige Bronzen im Jahr 2 = 36/5 v. und im J. 6 = 21 = 50 lokaler Aera = 32/1 v., Orthosia in den Jahren 2 und 3 (36/5 u. 35/4 v.), Tripolis schliesslich im Jahr 2 = 36/5 v. Die kleine Bronzeserie von Botrys aus dem Jahr 28 pomp. Aera = 37/6 v. wird vor dem Herrschaftswechsel emittiert worden sein.

Einigen Nachbarn der mächtigen neuen Herrin im mittleren Syrien schien es ratsam (anders als Gaba in seiner Bronzeprägung des Jahres 25 pomp. Aera = 36/5 v.), die Königin durch Anbringen ihrer Büste in der syrischen (!) Version zu ehren, obgleich die Poleis offenbar nicht zu ihrem eigentlichen Besitz gehörten: Damaskos prägte dergestalt Münzen in den Jahren 37/6 und 33/2 v., die aber gemäss der seleukidischen Aera datiert sind; Ptolemaïs zählte zwar bei seinen Münzen nach Kleopatras Jahr 3 in Syrien/Phönizien = 35/4 v., setzte aber weiterhin den Antonius auf die Münzvorderseite; Dora war es offenbar, das Bronzen mit Antonius und Kleopatra auf dem Avers prägte, die Stücke scheinen jedoch 'Jahr 19' der Königin in Aegypten = 34/3 v. datiert zu sein. Dem Vernehmen nach gibt es Halbe mit dem Porträt des Antonius allein (!). Wenig später wurden eventuell den Normalstücken ähnliche Bronzen mit 'städtischem' Avers (Kopf des Doros) geprägt, die dementsprechend traditionell 'Jahr 32' der pomp. Aera = 33/2 v. datiert sind.

Mit Oktavians Sieg bei Aktium 31 v. und seinem Vormarsch durch Syrien nach Aegypten, wo Antonius und Kleopatra 30 v. den Tod fanden, wurde dieser 'Spuk' schnell beendet: Natürlich wurde die Kleopatraära im mittleren Syrien sofort aufgegeben, man kehrte zu alten städtischen Aeren (Berytos 31/30 v.) oder zur traditionellen Seleukidenära (Chalkis a.L. 31/30 v. unter dem Vertreter des angestammten Tetrarchenhauses, Zenodoros; Tripolis 30/29 v.) zurück. Nicht verwunderlich ist auch, dass Apameia auf Bronzen mit neuen Typen ab 30/29 v. den von Antonius einst verliehenen Titel Autonomos fortlassen musste. Bezeichnend für die restaurativen Tendenzen in der Münzprägung dieser Zeit (31/30 v. Wiederaufnahme aradischer Bronzeprägungen) ist die Provinzialprägung in Antiochia a.O.: Nach Jahren der Ablösung durch die Antonius/Kleopatra-Tetradrachmen (vor 31 v.) wurden mit Jahr 19 caes. Aera = 31/30 v. die postumen Philippos-Tetradrachmen prompt wieder ausgeprägt (Taf. 12, B), allerdings jetzt mit verschlechtertem Silber (bis J. 36 = 14/13 v. sind sie belegt). Die Reformen des Jahres 5/4 v. Chr. leiteten dann zur syrischen Provinzialprägung der Kaiserzeit über: Von da an zeigten die Tetradrachmen stets das Kaiserbild auf dem Avers und wurden sie auch von provinzialen Bronzen (Rv. SC in Kranz) begleitet. Neben diesen Prägungen gab es weiterhin städtische Emissionen, zunehmend traten schliesslich auch Reichsprägungen in Syrien auf.[11]

In den folgenden Abschnitten I Syrische Provinzialprägung in Antiochia a.O., II Städtische Silber- und Bronzeprägungen in der Provinz Syria und III Münzen von Prägeherren ausserhalb der Provinz Syria werden die einschlägigen Münzausgaben der Jahre 64 - 30 v. Chr. auf der Basis jüngerer Literatur und der Handbücher wie BMC (besonders: Galatia... and Syria, W. Wroth, 1899; Phoenicia, G.F. Hill, 1910), B.V. Head, Historia Numorum², 1911, G. Macdonald, Catalogue of the Greek Coins in the Hunterian Collection, University of Glasgow Vol. III, 1905, und IGCH zusammenfassend besprochen.

I SYRISCHE PROVINZIALPRAEGUNG IN ANTIOCHIA A.O.

A. Postume Philippos Philadelphos-Tetradrachmen.

H. Seyrig, Syria, 27 (1950), 6, 8 u. 13-15; Walker, Metrology I, 59 Nr. 2. u 67; Crawford, CMRR 203, 205f., 209; auch 262, 266.

Als Rechtsnachfolger der seleukidischen Könige führten die Römer nach 64 v. Chr. deren Silberprägung als Provinzialprägung (Seyrig 15) fort. Faszinierenderweise verzichteten sie zunächst darauf, eigene Münzbilder und -legenden einzuführen, statt dessen wurden (in Stil und Technik verschlechtert) die in beträchtlichen Mengen geprägten Tetradrachmen des Philippos Philadelphos (92 - 83 v.) (Taf. 12, A) postum weitergeprägt: Av. Diademierter Kopf r., Rv. in Lorbeerkranz: Zeus mit Nike und Zepter l. thronend, Basileos/Philippou - Epiphanous/Philadelphou. Die Nachprägungen (Taf. 12, 1.2.B.) halten bis über das Jahr 30 v. hinaus ihren reduziert-attischen Gewichtsstandard (O. Morkholm, ANSMN 28 (1983), 101 A.27), der Silbergehalt sinkt möglicheweise erst ab 31/30 v. erheblich ab (Walker 67). Wie der Schatzfund IGCH 1578 (= H. Seyrig, Trésors du Levant (1973), Nr. 35) von ca. 55 - 50 v. zeigt, liefen Vorbild (1 Stück) und Nachahmung (21 Exemplare des Gabinius) in der Folgezeit gemeinsam um (ein später Hort: Seyrig, Trésors Nr. 38).

Warum haben die Römer späte Seleukiden-Tetradrachmen weitergeprägt, und weshalb ausgerechnet solche des Philippos und beispielsweise keine des Tigranes? Bei der Londoner Tagung wurde vorgeschlagen (M.J. Price), ersteres damit zu erklären, dass das Vorbild vermutlich eine erhebliche Ueberbewertung erfahren habe, an welche die Bevölkerung gewöhnt gewesen sei. Bei Einführung neuer Typen hätten die Römer vielleicht Schwierigkeiten bekommen können, den künstlich hochgehaltenen Kurswert beizubehalten. Deswegen sei man mit der Kopie des alten Geldes den Weg des geringsten Widerstandes gegangen. Zur zweiten Frage: Genoss Philippos beim Publikum besonderes Ansehen, oder hatten seine Tetradrachmen einen guten Ruf?

Nach Seyrig, der ältere Vorarbeiten Newells und Bellingers zusammenfasste und ergänzte, lässt sich die Produktion in 2 Phasen teilen: In der älteren (Taf. 12, 1) versah man die Stücke rückseitig l. im Feld mit Gouverneurs-Monogrammen, die Verantwortlichkeit und Datierung[12] zugleich angeben. Belegt sind dergestalt Stücke des A. Gabinius 57 - 55 v. (BMC 5; Macdonald III 112 Nr. 4 Taf. LXX, 13; SNG Copenhagen 431), des Crassus von 54/3 v. (Crawford, CMRR 205 Abb. 83) und des C. Cassius von 52/1 v. Wie beim Londoner Kolloquium mit Recht hervorgehoben wurde (A. Burnett), ist die erste Emission (Gabinius) offenbar die bei weitem umfangreichste gewesen. Die Rolle des Gabinius hat auch Crawford vor dem Hintergrund der Annahme stark herausgearbeitet, zwischen Provinzinstallation und Statthalterschaft dieses Mannes seien keine postumen 'Philippi' emittiert worden (ich bin da nicht so sicher): Die monetären Aktivitäten des Gabinius (mit der Konsequenz der Fortführung der Tetradrachmen-Rechnung in Syrien) seien vermutlich im Zusammenhang mit seinen Versuchen einer Steuerreform in Syrien-Palästina zu sehen. Offenbar sei in dem Gouverneur das Mitglied einer Gruppe römischer Politiker dieser Jahre zu sehen, die sich um monetäre und fiskalische Reformen bemüht habe (Crawford, CMRR 203, 205f., 209).

In der jüngeren Phase (SNG Cop. 432f.) kennzeichnete man die Emissionen (Taf. 12, 2) im Feld l. mit dem auch von Augustus-Tetradrachmen bekannten ΑΤ Monogramm (=Antiochia)[13] und mit Datierungen nach der am angegebenen Prägeort (keine städtische Kontrolle!) gebräuchlichen Zeitrechnung im Abschnitt, der caesarischen Aera mit 49/8 v. als Jahr 1 (Seyrig 6 u. 13). Nach Seyrig fallen in die von uns betrachtete Periode 8 Jahrgänge, von 3 = 47/6 v. bis 12 = 38/7 v. (z.B. J. 8 = 42/1 v.: SNG Delepierre 2979). Die Prägung wurde dann, nach einigen Jahren Unterbrechung, im Jahr 19 = 31/30 v. (Taf. 12, B) mit leicht veränderter Reversdarstellung[14] wieder aufgenommen (z.B. SNG Fitzwilliam 5829-5832); derselbe Reverswechsel in der städtischen Bronzeprägung von Antiochia a.O. beweist einmal mehr die Tetradrachmen-Produktion am Dienstsitz der Statthalter.

Die Prägetätigkeit unter Augustus war zunächst relativ gleichmässig und am Anfang offensichtlich auch recht intensiv. Seyrigs Bild der letzten Jahre muss heute etwas modifiziert werden: Letzter Jahrgang der allmählich ausdünnenden Produktion ist nicht J. 30 = 20/19 v., sondern es gibt Stücke vom J. 32 = 18/7, 33 (vgl. Newell, NC 1919, addendum S. 113) und 36 = 14/3 v. (B.M.; so auch die Liste von A. Burnett, die ich einsehen durfte). Mit dem späten Ende verstärken sich die Zweifel an Newells These, dass die ersten Porträt-Tetradrachmen des Augustus mit traditionellem Zeusrevers zum Kaiserbesuch 20/19 v. (Jahr 12 aktischer Aera) geprägt wurden, und man wird lieber Kraays Vorschlag folgen,[15] besser zur alten Lesung ihrer Vorderseiten-Legende (...ΥΠ - IB = COS XII = 5 (bis 3) v.) zurückzukehren:[16] In diesem Fall ist die Reform der Antiochener Tetradrachmen-Prägung nicht in zwei um viele Jahre getrennten Schritten erfolgt, sondern im Zeitraum nur eines Jahres, 5/4 v., unter der Statthalterschaft des Varus. Parallel zum Silber wurden damals auch erstmals provinziale Bronzen ohne Münzstättenangabe (Rv. SC in Kranz) herausgegeben.[17]

Aus Seyrigs Tabelle (13, r. Spalte) ergibt sich der von ihm nicht kommentierte Umstand, dass die Herstellung der postumen Philippos-Tetradrachmen in den Jahren 37/6 bis 32/1 v. ruhte; das Fehlen der Jahrgänge 13-18 bestätigte sich mir sowohl bei der Durchsicht der umfangreichen Burnettschen Materialsammlung als auch der Bestände des British Museum. Ihr besonderes Gewicht erhält diese Beobachtung durch die Tatsache, dass genau in diese Lücke die 37/6 - 32/1 v. aller Wahrscheinlichkeit nach in Antiochia a.O. geprägten Antonius/Kleopatra-Tetradrachmen passen: Offenbar wurde die sozusagen übliche Provinzialprägung durch eine andere Provinzialprägung ersetzt, denn sonst hätte man beide Münzsorten nebeneinander emittieren können (s. auch nachstehendes Kap. B). Die Antiochener Stadtprägung (in Bronze) ist während besagter Jahre 37/6 - 32/1 v. nicht unterbrochen.

B. M. Antonius/Kleopatra-Tetradrachmen.

H. Seyrig, Trésors du Levant (1973), 109f. Nr. 27-32; H.R. Baldus, JNG 23 (1973), 19-43 besonders 26-29 Nr. 1 Taf. 3, 7; ders., SM 33, 1983, 5f. Abb. 3; Walker, Metrology I, 59 Nr. 3 u. 67; Auktion Malter (Encino) 2, 1978, 300; Crawford, CMRR 253.

Die silbernen (Walker: ca. 80%), ca. 15g schweren Tetradrachmen (Walker 59, 3; Morkholm, Studia P. Naster Oblata I, 1982, 146) zeigen (Taf. 12, 3) auf der einen Seite den Kopf M. Antons r., Antonios Autokrator Triton Trion Andron, auf der anderen die Büste Kleopatras VII. r. mit Diadem und einem Schultermantel, der vorn durch perlketten-verbundene Tasseln gehalten wird, Basilissa Kleopatra Thea Neotera, (BMC 53-56, Taf. 19, 3; Macdonald III 147 Nr. 50 Taf. 72, 1; SNG Copenhagen 129). Eine sehr seltene Variante zeigt hinter dem Haupt des Antonius einen Pferdekopf (Svoronos Nr. 1898 Taf. 63, 24).

Der Titel imperator tertium des Triumvirn Antonius steckt die äussersten Zeitgrenzen dieser Prägung ab: Der Wechsel zu ...IMP TER... findet in der Reichsprägung im Jahre 38 v. statt,[18] derjenige zu ...IMP IIII... im Jahre 31 v.,[19] also liegt die mögliche Prägezeit zwischen 38 und 32/1 v. Terminus ante quem für die frühesten Stücke ist das Jahr 276 seleukidischer Aera = 37/6 v.: Damals wurde die besondere Kleopatrabüste der Tetradrachmen zum ersten Mal in Damaskus kopiert (Baldus 32 Nr. 7).

Die ungenannte Münzstätte muss nach dem Auftauchen solcher Stücke im Schatz von Bab/Batna (Seyrig Nr. 39) sowie im levantinischen Antikenhandel und entsprechend der Nachahmung der Kleopatrabüste auch in Dora (?), Ptolemaïs und besonders in Chalkis a.L. im (phönizisch-) syrischen Bereich gelegen haben; von dort gelangten solche Exemplare auch weit nach Norden[20] oder über den Euphrat, z.B. wurde ein Stück 34/3 v. in ein datiertes parthisches Tetradrachmon umgeprägt. Für die Hauptstadt der Provinz, Antiochia a.O. (vgl. BMC 158 Anm.; Head 778f.), spricht über die Wahrscheinlichkeit in se hinaus die Aehnlichkeit des Antoniuskopfes mit demjenigen stadtantiochenischer Drachmen (s.u.); das Gewicht, das T.V. Buttrey einst für eine phönizische Münzstätte plädieren liess, ist mit Seyrig eindeutig nicht ptolemäisch zu nennen. Zu den Gründen der Wahl des verwendeten Standards, der nicht gegen Antiochia als Prägestätte spricht, s. unten.

Die Tatsache, dass keine Stadt als Prägeautorität genannt ist und dass unter anderem an der Umschriftung der Porträts römischer Einfluss deutlich wird, lässt die Tetradrachmen als eine Prägung der römischen Behörden für die Provinz Syria, als eine Provinzialprägung ansehen. Dass die Königin gleichberechtigt neben dem Triumvirn als Prägeherr und Geehrte auftritt (Seyrig 110) - keine Münzseite ist eindeutig als Vorderseite zu erkennen -, versteht man seit der Schenkung des mittelphönizischen Küstenstreifens sowie dessen Hinterlandes (Fürstentum Chalcis sub Libano) 37/6 v. durch M. Antonius an Kleopatra: Beim Umlauf in diesem Gebiet (dokumentiert auch in der dort nachgewiesenen Kopie der Tetradrachmen: Chalkis a.L.) garantierte die Königin für Gewicht und Feingehalt. Als Königin der wiedergewonnenen levantinischen Aussenbesitzungen der Ptolemäer tritt Kleopatra ja wohl auch in ihrem merkwürdigen Prunkgewand und mit dem Namen 'Königin Kleopatra Thea die Jüngere' (Buttrey) auf, wenngleich die Beinamen Thea Neotera gleichzeitig als Anspruch der Reinkarnation von Isis/Astarte/Aphrodite verstanden werden können (s.u. Chalkis a.L.). Der erste grosse 'Schub' solcher Tetradrachmen wird folglich 37/6 v. geprägt worden sein. Ob die

Emission später wieder aufgenommen wurde, lässt sich nicht sicher sagen. Dass die Stücke bis zum Ende der Herrschaft des Paares in dieser Region (und zeitlich darüber hinaus) umliefen, zeigt nicht nur die auffällige Abnutzung vieler auf uns gekommenen Exemplare, sondern auch das Kopieren auf spätdatierten lokalen Bronzen (Chalcis s.L.: 32/1 v.) oder die 'Weiterentwicklung' auf den Antonius/Kleopatra-Denaren von ca. 32 v.;[21] deren mindere Qualität der Gestaltung weicht übrigens genügend von den Antiochener Tetradrachmen ab, um sie nicht derselben Münzstätte zuzuweisen.

Der vorgesehene Umlauf der Tetradrachmen in den Zonen des ptolemäischen und des reduziert-attischen Standards war sicher Ursache der Wahl eines mittleren Gewichts (15g), nicht zufällig ähnlich demjenigen der Tdr. von Arados und Laodikeia vor 44/3 v.

Die Zuweisung dieser Exemplare an die Münzstätte Antiocha a.O. (und ihre Deutung als Provinzialgeld für Syrien/Phönizien) finden ihre Bestärkung durch meine Beobachtung (s.o. Abschnitt A), dass die etwas älteren wie die etwas jüngeren Provinzialmünzen aus Antiochia, die postumen Philippos-Tetradrachmen, genau in den theoretischen Prägejahren 37/6 bis 32/1 v. dieser Antonius/Kleopatra-Stücke aussetzen (Seyrig, <u>Syria</u> 27 (1950), 13 Tabelle): Offenbar weil beide Münzsorten trotz des völlig verschiedenen Aeusseren denselben Charakter hatten und man nicht der einen Provinzialprägung mit der anderen Konkurrenz machen wollte.

II STAEDTISCHE SILBER- UND BRONZEPRAEGUNGEN IN DER PROVINZ SYRIA
alphabetische Anordnung

1 <u>Antiochia a.O., Seleukis und Pieria</u>

H. Seyrig, <u>Syria</u> 27 (1950), 5-15.

Im folgenden werden nur die Münzen behandelt, die die Provinzhauptstadt Syriens in städtischer Regie ausbrachte; zu dem am selben Ort im Auftrag der römischen Machthaber geprägten Geld s.o. Abschnitt I.

Die Stadt führte in der ganzen behandelten Zeit den Ehrentitel <u>Metropolis</u> und datierte zunächst nach einer pompeianischen Aera (66/5 v. = Jahr 1), als deren Epoche rückwirkend Tigranes' Abtretung Syriens an Pompeius 66 v. gewählt wurde. Im Jahr 19(=48/7 v.) dieser Zeitrechnung ging man zu einer ab Pharsalos zählenden caesarischen Aera über (49/8 v. = J. 1), beim Besuch Caesars 47 v. bekam die Polis ausserdem die Titel <u>Hiera</u>, <u>Asylos</u> und besonders <u>Autonomos</u> verliehen. Nur während der parthischen Invasion des Jahres 41/40 v. datierte man - wie Bronzen zeigen (<u>BMC</u> 25; Macdonald III 145 Nr. 31; <u>SNG Copenhagen</u> 81) - nach der Seleukidenära und liess man den Titel <u>Autonomos</u> fort.

In Silber gibt es in den späteren 30er Jahren eine kurzfristige Drachmenemission zu Ehren des Antonius (<u>BMC</u> 52: 3,5g; Crawford, <u>CMRR</u> 255 Abb. 109 l. unten): Antoniuskopf r./Tychekopf r., <u>Antiocheon Metropoleos</u> (aus Platzgründen ohne <u>Autonomos</u> etc.). Diese Stücke helfen bei der Zuweisung der Antonius/Kleopatra-Tetradrachmen an dieselbe Münzstätte (oben I, B), sie sind gewichtsmässig offenbar auf diese ausgerichtet.

Dieser Sonderausgabe steht eine reiche, relativ kontinuierliche Bronzeprägung gegenüber:[22] Vom <u>aes</u> der Jahre 64/3 - 50/49 v. (im Schatz <u>IGCH</u> 1580 von Hama, vergraben gegen 50 v., waren neben 2 unbestimmten AE 49

Antiochener Bronzen bis 53/2 v. vertreten) unterscheiden sich die Stücke von 48/7 v. an durch den seit Pharsalos um die Rückseite gelegten Lorbeerkranz (BMC 26ff.). Die mit neuen Titeln und caes. Aera geprägten Bronzen reichen von 48/7 bis 45/4 v. (SNG Cop. 76f., 79; SNG Fitzwilliam 5927). Nach einigem Hin und Her (Seyrig 13, Tabelle), wozu die erwähnten Modifizierungen des Persereinbruchs im Jahr 41/40 v. gehören, wird 39/8 v. eine regelmässige Produktion aufgenommen (SNG Cop. 82-84), die in den Jahren 37/6-32/1 v. im Gegensatz zur Prägung postumer 'Philippoi' nicht unterbrochen wird und über das Jahr 30 v. hinausreicht.[23] Auf diesen Exemplaren werden Hiera und Asylos weggelassen (BMC 33ff.).

Das Typenspektrum aller dieser Emissionen ist relativ schmal: Am häufigsten trifft man auf die Bronze vom Typ 'Zeuskopf r./Zeus mit Nike und Zepter l. thronend' (BMC 25-35). Andere Bronzen mit derselben Vorderseite haben als Revers 'Tyche mit Ruder und Füllhorn stehend' und 'Dreifuss' (BMC 36; Macdonald III 145 Nr.32f.). Seltener findet man die Kombinationen 'Tychebüste r./Tyche stehend' und 'Tychebüste r./Mohnkapsel zwischen Ähren' (Macdonald III 146 Nr.34f.) sowie 'Artemiskopf/Apollon'. Vielfach hat man zwei, zu Zeiten allerdings auch nur eines oder drei Nominale nebeneinander geprägt, s. die tabellarische Uebersicht bei Seyrig (13, Gewichte: 8f.). Mit der Nominalumstellung des Jahres 19 pomp. Aera = 48/7 v. (Einführung von für Zeit und Region ungewöhnlich schweren Bronzen, maximal 14g) geht für wenige Jahre der Gebrauch des ovalen Gegenstempels 'Apollonkopf mit Bogen r.' einher (BMC 27 u. 35; Macdonald III 145f. Nr.29, 36 u. 38).

2 Apameia, Seleukis und Pieria

H. Seyrig, Syria 27 (1950), 15-20.

Die Stadt setzte in der betrachteten Zeit (und darüber hinaus) eine schon in den Jahren 76/5 - 68/7 v. bestehende Bronzeprägung fort. Ihre Vielgestaltigkeit ist durch die Tatsache bedingt, dass je nach politischen Umständen zu der üblichen Titulatur die Titel Apameon Tes Hieras die Titel Asylos oder Autonomos (mit kai verbunden und im Genetiv) hinzugesetzt wurden und dass man statt der üblichen Seleukidenära gelegentlich andere Zeitrechnungen verwendete. Hinzu kommt ein gewisser Typenreichtum. Es ist am einfachsten, die Komponenten einzeln zu betrachten:

Titel: Bis 41/40 v. führte Apameia den Zweittitel Asylos, von 41/40 bis 30/29 v. dagegen das von Antonius verliehene, daher unter Octavianus wieder verlorene Autonomos.

Aeren: Seit 60/59 v. lässt sich die Verwendung einer pompeianischen Aera nachweisen, deren Epoche im Jahr 66 v. zu liegen scheint (Zweifel an den Benennung 'aktische Aera': BMC LXIV Anm.; 'caesarisch': Macdonald III 191). Während der Besetzung durch die Parther wurde 41/40 v. die Seleukidenära (Jahr 272: BMC 6; Macdonald III 191 Nr. 8) wieder eingeführt. Von 41/40 bis 39/8 v. datierte man nach einer lokalen Freiheitsära des Antonius, ab 38/7 v. wurde diese aber wieder von der Seleukidenära abgelöst.

Prägezeiten und Typen: In den Jahren 60/59 bis 51/50 v. prägte die Stadt in herkömmlicher Weise (vgl. BMC 3-5; Macdonald III 190 Nr. 1-5) verschieden grosse Kleinbronzen der Typen (normal: r.) 'Zeuskopf/Elefant' (SNG Fitzwilliam 5948) - der Revers ist eine Erinnerung an die Garnison der seleukidischen Elefantentruppe -, 'Tychekopf/Nike l.', 'Demeterkopf/Aehre'. Dann scheint die Emissionstätigkeit einige Jahre geruht zu haben. Ab 44/3 v. gab man wieder aes in verschiedenen Formaten und mit neuen Typen heraus:[24] 'Athenabüste/Nike l.' (BMC 6-8), 'Tychekopf/Athena l.' und 'Demeterkopf/Garbe' (SNG Copenhagen 297 von 38/7 v.; 6,29g).

Das Exemplar der Auktion Malter (Encino) 2, 1978, 298 (3,86g/19mm: Kopf des M. Antonius mit ägyptischer Krone r./Dioskurenkappen in Kranz) wurde als fehlbestimmt weggelassen.

3 Arados, Phoenicia

BMC XXXII-XXXV u. 23ff.; Head 790.

Arados datierte seine Münzen nach einer Freiheitsära, deren Jahr 1 dem Jahre 259/8 v. entsprach.

Seine seit 137/6 v. emittierten AR-Tetradrachmen im theoretischen Standard von 15,3g (O. Morkholm, ANSMN 28 (1983), 95ff.) und vom Typ 'Tychebüste r./in Kranz: Nike l. stehend mit aplustre und Palmzweig, Aradion und phönizische sowie griechische Kontrollbuchstaben und das Datum im Feld' wurden nach 64 v. gelegentlich weiterhin emittiert (SNG Copenhagen 55-58: 63/2-56/5 v.; SNG Fitzwilliam 6010-6012: 63/2-62/1 v.; SNG Delepierre 2993: 63/2 v.). Allerdings brach die Prägung nach dem letzten belegten Jahrgang 216 = 44/3 v. (Morkholm a.a.O. 101 Anm. 26) ab.

Diese Tetradrachmen liefen besonders im nördlichen Phönizien um, wie dies drei Horte belegen: IGCH 1581 (mit Korrekturen Morkholms a.a.O. 97f.) wurde um 60 v. vergraben und enthielt 34+ Exemplare der Stadt bis J. 199 = 61/60 v.[25] IGCH 1582 (= H. Seyrig, Trésors du Levant, Nr. 36), in Antarados um 40 v. verborgen, enthielt neben 2 Tetradrachmen Laodikeias a.M. bis Jahr 2 = 47/6 v. auch 16 aradische Exemplare bis J. 216 = 44/3 v. Der Hort IGCH 1618 aus Nahr-Ibrahim (25 km nördlich v. Beirut), vergraben ca. 60 v., enthielt unter 200 AR aradische Stücke bis J. 199 = 61/60 v.

Einzelne Tetradrachmen-Jahrgänge wie 208 = 52/1 v. wurden von Kleinbronzen des Typs 'Köpfe eines Götterpaares (Zeus-?) r./Prora l.' (BMC XXXIV; Head 790) begleitet, vom J. 203 = 57/6 v. stammt wohl das Kleinaes 'Tychekopf r./Schiff l., AP' (BMC XXXV Taf. 38,10; SNG Cop. 73: 1,74 g).

In das Jahr 46/5 v. gehört die Wiederaufnahme der bis 76/5 v. verwendeten Bronze mit den Darstellungen 'Europa-Astarte-Büste r./Stier l. springend', allerdings jetzt durch die hinzugefügten Attribute 'geschultertes Zepter' respektive 'Palmzweig' leicht verändert (BMC 341-344: 6,1-7,1g). Ein weiterer Jahrgang des Typs stammt von 31/30 v. (BMC 345: 8,49g).

In den Jahren zwischen letztgenannten Emissionen ehrte man den Antonius durch Ausgabe von aes mit seinem Porträtkopf auf dem Avers und dem l. springenden Stier der Europa-Astarte auf der Rs.: Bekannt sind derartige Exemplare aus den Jahren 222 = 38/7 v. (BMC 355: 5,94g) und 225 = 35/4 v. (BMC XXXV; Head 790).

4 Balanea (später Claudia Leukas), Seleukis und Pieria

H. Seyrig, Syria 27 (1950), 22-24; besonders ders., RN 1964, 40-42.

Bis 37 v. gehörte die Stadt zur aradischen Peraia und datierte nach der aradischen Aera (259/8 v. = J. 1). Eine Bronze vom Typ 'Tychebüste r./Baal mit Zepter l. in Quadriga, Stadtname' (9,25g/23 mm) ist datiert J. 217 = 43/2 v. Unter M. Antonius gab man dann eine kleine Serie von 3 Bronzenominalen heraus, dessen grösstes (7,25-9,67g/22-24 mm) den Typ 'Antoniuskopf r./Baal ('indischer Dionysos') in Quadriga l.' aufweist (Head 780). Die anderen zeigen 'Tychebüst r./Nike l.' (4,82-7,65 g/18-22 mm) und Hermesbüste mit caduceus r./Aehre' (2,53g/15 mm). Neben dem Stadtnamen und 'Beamten'kürzeln liest man rückseitig '(Jahr) 1'. Die Emission ist ins Jahr 37/6 v. zu datieren: Eine Reihe kaiserzeitlicher Gepräge ist nämlich mit Daten einer Aera von 37 v. versehen. Die Verleihung diverser Privilegien an Balanea durch Antonius war offenbar Ausfluss seines Streites mit Arados im Jahr 38 v.

5 Berytos, Phoenicia

H. Seyrig, Syria 27 (1950), 38 u. 44 Nr. 1-2 m. Abb. 1; zu Kleopatra: H.R. Baldus, JNG 23 (1973), 26,f u. 33; Auktion Malter (Encino) 2, 1978, 291.

Die Polis datierte nach einer Aera, deren Epoche ins Jahr 81 v. fiel und deren Einrichtung offenbar mit guten Beziehungen zu König Tigranes d.Gr. zusammenhängt.

Unter den Bronzen des 1. Jahrhunderts v., deren Reversdarstellungen (Av. Tychebüste r.) sich auf den Kult des dem Poseidon angeglichenen Baal-Berit beziehen (BMC 8-12: Gott im Hippokampenwagen stehend; Delphin mit Dreizack) gibt es gelegentlich datierte Jahrgänge: Belegt ist ein Exemplar mit Meeressymbolen von J. 20 = 62/1 v. (BMC 13: 5,1g/17 mm; Av. Kontermarke 'Stierkopf l., HP'; Rv. im Feld Dioskurenmützen mit Sternen).

Obwohl einige ehedem Berytos zugewiesene Kleopatraprägungen nach Chalkis a.L. gehören (s. unten Kapitel III), verbleiben zwei Bronzeemissionen der Stadt für die Königin, welcher die Polis seit der Schenkung von 37/6 v. untertan war:

Stücke (9,19g/23 mm) mit einer improvisiert wirkenden Kleopatrabüste r. (vgl. das beigegebene, zu  'barbarisierte' La-Phoi-Monogramm)[26] auf dem Av. und Baal in Quadriga mit Triton en face auf der Rs. (Be-Dio) sind auf dem Avers datiert 'Jahr 2' der Königin im neuen Territorium = 36/5 v.

Exemplare (ca. 8-9g/21-23 mm) aus dem Jubiläumsjahr 50 der Stadtära = 32/1 v. tragen neben der Büste der Königin in verbesserter Qualität - gelegentlich - dieses Datum auf der Vs. und die Doppeldatierung nach Regierungsjahren der Monarchin in Aegypten/Phönizien ('Jahr 21', 'Jahr 6') auf dem Rv. Dieser zeigt Baal in Quadriga l. stehend neben den Stadtinitialen BH (BMC XLIX u. LI Taf. 40, 2; Head 790).

Aes ab Jahr 51 = 31/30 v. (SNG Copenhagen 87: 11,70g) dürfte mit den häufigen Poseidon- und Nikedarstellungen (BMC 17ff., auch 16) auf Oktavians Sieg bei Aktium anspielen.

6 Botrys, Phoenicia

H. Seyrig, Syria 31 (1954), 77f. m. Abb.2; A. Kindler, The Coinage of Bostra (1983), 71 Nr. 1 u. 105 Nr. 1 Taf. 1, 1 (falsche alte Zuweisung an Bostra).

Eine kleine Serie autonomer Bronzen mit dem Avers 'Tychebüste r.' ist datiert '(Jahr) 28': Das Ganzstück hat als Rv. das 'redende Stadtwappen', eine Traube (früher: 'Diota': BMC LX), das Teilstück im Durchmesser von 14 mm (oft fälschlich Bostra zugewiesen: BMC Arabia XXVIII Taf. 49, 15) zeigt in Kranz den Baal zwischen geflügelten Löwen r. stehend (ganz ähnlich wie der Baal von Orthosia, s.u.). Das Datum, von dem man früher glaubte, es sei nach der aktischen Aera berechnet (z.B. Head 791), ist wahrscheinlich gemäss der pompeianischen Jahreszählung kalkuliert: Die angeblich augusteische Emission gehört eher ins Jahr 37/6 v., und zwar vor die Uebergabe der Stadt an Kleopatra.

7 Byblos, Phoenicia

H. Seyrig, Syria 31 (1954), 73-76.

Sicher dem 1. Jahrhundert v. zuzuweisende, bilingue Bronzen (phönizischer Stadtname, griechisches Stadtmonogramm B mit Avers Tychekopf r. und Reversen mit Darstellungen einheimischer, ägyptisch beeinflusster Gottheiten (beispielsweise Isis-Astarte l. stehend: BMC LXIX Anm. 1. Taf. 41, 10; SNG Copenhagen 136: 2,61g. Harpokrates mit Füllhorn l. sthd.: BMC 18. Kronos mit mehreren Flügeln l. sthd.: SNG Cop. 137: 6,95g) sind griechisch datiert 'Jahr 3' bis 'Jahr 26'. Gegen die ältere Deutung als nach der aktischen Aera gerechnet (z.B. Head 701) hat Seyrig die Datierung nach einer pomp. Aera von 64 oder 63 v. für wahrscheinlicher erklärt: Die genannten Münzen gehören in diesem Fall in die Jahre 62/1 bis 39/8 v.

8 De(metrias ad Mare), Phoenicia (Küste in der Umgebung des Berges Karmel)

H. Seyrig, Syria 27 (1950), 50-56 Nr. 43 m. Abb.

Autonome Bronzen mit Avers 'Tychebüste r.' sind von einer Stadt De(.....) geprägt, die Seyrig an der südphönizischen Küste lokalisiert hat und die nach Aussage eines Bleigewichtes Demetrias ad Mare hiess. Exemplare mit Rv. 'Zeus mit Adler und Zepter l. stehend' (um 7,4 g/18 mm) sind datiert 'Jahr 1', Stücke von 22-24 mm Durchmesser und mit Revers 'in Kranz: Nike mit Kranz und Palmwedel l.' tragen die Daten 'Jahr 3' respektive 22. Wahrscheinlich sind sie, wie ganz ähnliche Exemplare des nahen Dora, gemäss der pomp. Aera datiert und gehören sie in die Jahre 63/2, 61/60 und 42/1 v.

9 Gabala, Phoenicia

H. Seyrig, RN 1964, 9-28 besonders 16ff. Taf. 1-4 besonders 3.

Die Stadt gehörte bis 47 v. zur Peraia von Arados und datierte nach dessen Freiheitsära (259/8 v. = Jahr 1). Seine bescheidene Aesprägung wurde 86/5 v. wieder aufgenommen, und es existieren datierte Stücke vom Jahr 204 = 56/5, 205 = 55/4 und 207 = 53/2 v. Die Typen sind 'Zeuskopf r./Adler l.' (6,4-9,4g/19-21 mm), 'Tychekopf r./Aehren' (3,62-5,78g/15-18 mm), 'Helioskopf r./Prora l.' (1,93-3,42g/13-16 mm) und 'Medusenkopf von vorn/Biene von oben' (1,65-2,20g/12-13 mm). Seine Münzprägung nahm es nach längerer Pause erst im Jahr 16 einer caesarischen Aera von 46 v., also im Jahre 31/30 v., wieder auf (Seyrig 40).

H. Seyrig, Syria 27 (1950), 26-31; Corpus der Tetradrachmen: O. Morkholm, ANSMN 28 (1983), 89-107 Taf. 13-19.

Die Stadt zählte bei Einrichtung der Provinz nach einer Freiheitsära, deren Jahr 1 wohl dem Jahr 81/80 v. entsprach (=tigranisch), und führte den Doppeltitel Hiera kai Autonomos. Im Jahr 34 = 48/7 v. führte man eine caesarische Aera ein (48/7 v. = J. 1), und bei Caesars Besuch 47 v. bekam die Stadt den Erstnamen Julia verliehen, neben dem Laodikeia aber weiter geführt wurde. Soweit ältere Prägungen über diesen Wechsel hinaus fortgeführt wurden, blieb ihr Erscheinungsbild ansonsten - zunächst - unangetastet.

Die Silber- und Bronzeprägung setzte bald nach der 'Befreiung' 81/80 v. ein (erste Tetradrachmen von Jahr 4 = 78/7 v.). In die betrachtete Periode 64-30 v. fallen die Tdr.-Jahrgänge 17 = 65/4 v., 18, 20, 23-27, 30, 31 sowie 33 = 49/8 v. und spätere; die Bronzen liefern unter anderem den Jahrgang 34 = 48/7 v. (Seyrig 27 mit Anm.). Die Umstellung der Jahre 48-46 v. auf die neue Aera und den neuen Namen erfolgte nach Ausweis der Tdr. über einen Zwischenschritt (Morkholm 93f.): Nach Exemplaren vom Jahr 1 mit alter Legende und vor Stücken vom Jahr 2 mit neuem Namen gab man im Jahr 1 Tdr. mit der 'neutralen' Legende Laodikeon Ton Pros Thalasse heraus. An Tdr.-Jahrgängen der nächsten Jahre sind 3 und 5 = 44/3 v. belegt, Jahr 4 ist offenbar wieder in aes vertreten (Seyrig 27).

Aus Jahr 6 bis Jahr 8 gibt es bislang keine Tetradrachmen, Jahr 7 ist aber durch Bronzen vom Typ 'Tychebüste r./Nike l.' vertreten, die merkwürdigerweise wieder die erwähnte 'neutrale' Legende verwenden (BMC 1f. Taf. 29,1; SNG Copenhagen 323: 4,65g). Nach Seyrig und Morkholm spiegelt sich darin die Besetzung der Polis 43 v. durch den Caesarmörder C. Cassius. Nach Aussage mit dem Datum '7' versehener Bronzen kehrte man im selben Jahr 42/1 v. wieder zum Doppelnamen Julia Laodikeia zurück (Seyrig 30). Derart beschriftete Tdr. gibt es aus den Jahren 9 = 40/39, 18 = 31/30 und 19 = 30/29 v.

In AR wurden in der Berichtszeit allein Tetradrachmen des Typs 'Tychebüste r./in Lorbeerkranz: Zeus mit Nike und Zepter l. thronend' geprägt.[27] Sie sind aus hochwertigem Silber (Seyrig) und wurden nach verschiedenen Standards ausgewogen: Die älteren Exemplare haben ein Gewicht von ca. 15,1g (= leichter aradischer Fuss), die jüngeren (ab Jahr 5 caes. Aera = 44/3 v.) sind nach dem ptolemäischen Fuss von theoretisch (!) 14,3g justiert. Umlaufsgebiet dieser Münzen war nach Aussage dreier Schatzfunde (IGCH 1581 mit Korrekturen Morkholms; IGCH 1582; CH 6, 1981, Nr. 50) insbesondere das nördliche Phönizien und Syrien.

Bei den parallelen Bronzen wurden bis 47 v. die Typen 'Zeuskopf r./Dreifuss' (BMC 11; SNG Cop. 320: 7,87g; beide J. 33 = 49/8 v.) und 'Helioskopf r./Artemis l. stehend' (BMC 12) verwendet. Unter den von 47 v. bis in augusteische Zeit geprägten Bronzen (BMC 13-24 u. 28f.) ist vor 30 v. entstandenes aes schwer zu isolieren: Am ehesten früh sind wohl die Bronzen im traditionellen Typ 'Zeuskopf r./Dreifuss' (BMC 13) und 'Helioskopf r./Artemis l. stehend' (Macdonald III 203 Nr. 8; sicher bei SNG Cop. 324 von 40/39: 8,88g). Ein jüngerer Nachfolger der Sonderemission des Jahres 7 caes. Aera = 42/1 v. stammt vom Jahre 34/3 v. (SNG Cop. 326: 5,29g).

11 Orthosia, Phoenicia

H. Seyrig, Syria 27 (1950), 44 Nr. 3; ders., Syria 31 (1954), 76f.; zu Kleopatra: H.R. Baldus, JNG 23 (1973), 19-43 Taf. 3, besonders Nr. 1-3; Auktion Malter (Encino) 2, 1978, 296f.

Bronzen mit dem Avers 'Tychebüste r.' haben auf dem Revers beim Ganzstück (um 6-7g/22 mm) die Darstellung 'Baal r. stehend zwischen geflügelten Löwen', wie sie schon bei älteren Exemplaren (BMC 1: 7,05g/19 mm, auch LXXVIf. Taf. 41,16: 17 mm, Datierung nach seleukid. Aera; Head 793) vorkam, beim Halbstück das Rv.-bild 'Nike mit Kranz und Palmzweig l.' (BMC 2, auch LXXVI: 3,43g/15 mm). Sie sind rückseitig nach einer Aera datiert, die man früher für aktisch gehalten hat, die aber wohl eher pompeianisch ist. In die Zeit 64-30 v. fallen wahrscheinlich die belegten Jahrgänge 1=64/3 v. (Ganz- und Halbstück), 4, 11, 19 und 24=41/40 v., nach 30 v. sind weitere Emissionen bezeugt (erster Jahrgang 36=29/8 v.).

Die Polis war die nördlichste jenes phönizischen Küstenstreifens südlich des Flusses Eleutheros, den Antonius 37/6 v. der Kleopatra schenkte und in dem sie eine eigene Regierungsjahr-Zählung einführte, 37/6 v. = J. 1. Ihr zu Ehren gab die Stadt 'Jahr 2'=36/5 v. und 'Jahr 3'=35/4 v. (SNG Copenhagen 176) datierte Normalstücke heraus (5,53-8,14g/ca. 20 mm), die statt der Tychebüste älterer Emissionen die diademierte Büste r. der Königin nach alexandrinischem Vorbild zeigen, dahinter einen grob gezeichneten Stern. Die Exemplare von Jahr 2 zeigen ein hervorragendes, vertrauenswürdiges Porträt der alternden Monarchin (Baldus).

12 Ptolemaïs-Ake, Phoenicia

H. Seyrig, RN 1962, 25-50 Taf.1; ders., Syria 39 (1962), bes. 195 Taf.13,2f.; V. Kontorini, RN 1979, 30-41 Taf. 11; zu Kleopatra: H.R. Baldus, JNG 23 (1973), 30 Nr.2 u. 33; Auktion Sternberg (Zürich) 11, 1981, 399.

Namen, Titel, Aeren (RN 1962, 31-34): Ake hiess in der ersten Zeit nach der Provinzgründung offenbar (wieder) 'Antiocheia in der Ptolemaïs', um ab 47 v. nur doch den Namen 'Ptolemaïs' zu führen. Es trug im behandelten Zeitraum die Titel Hiera und Asylos. Man datierte ab 64 oder 63 v. anscheinend nach einer Pompeius-Aera, seit Caesars Visite 47 v. nach einer caes. Aera (48/7 v.=Jahr 1). Auf Prägungen mit Kleopatrabildnis werden deren syrisch-phönizische Herrschaftsjahre (37/6 v. =J. 1) angegeben. Die Daten werden stets vom Jahrzeichen L eingeleitet.

Prägung (RN 1962, 31-35): Ptolemaïs emittierte in der Berichtszeit sporadisch Bronzemünzen:

1. 'Jahr 9' datiert sind zwei Typen mit rückseitig Antiocheon Ton En Ptolemaidi und den Darstellungen 'Tychebüste mit Palmzweig r./Zeus mit Zepter l. stehend' (BMC LXXIX Taf. 42,1-3): Der eine wiegt 6,98-8,56g, zeigt in der Rechten des Gottes eine Aehre (oder Zweig?) und nennt beide Stadttitel, der zweite, einfachere, wiegt 4,88-6,95g (RN 1962, 25ff. Nr.13 u.14). Seyrig (RN 1962, 32) hielt eine Datierung nach einer pomp. Aera für wahrscheinlich. Daraus folgt der Ansatz auf 56/5 oder 55/4 v.

2. 'Jahr 5' caes. Aera= 44/3 v. datiert sind Stücke zu ca. 8-13g/22-25 mm vom Typ 'Zeuskopf mit Palmzweig r./Tyche l. stehend auf Ruderblatt, in

der L. Füllhorn u. Palmzweig, in der R. aplustre u. Ruderpinne' (BMC 11-13; SNG Copenhagen 178f.: 11,6 u. 8,6g). Eine Variante hat einen guten Stil und ist mehrfach mit rechteckiger Kontermarke 'Adler r.' belegt, die andere wirkt gröber und weist keine Stadttitel auf (RN 1962, 25FF. Nr.15f.).

3. 'Jahr 9' caes. Aera=40/39 v. sind zwei Typen datiert: Der erste (RN 1962, 25ff. Nr.17) ähnelt dem besseren des Jahres 5 und wiegt 7,76g, der zweite (Nr.18) kombiniert die gleiche Rückseite mit einem neuen Avers: Büsten r. von Zeus und Tyche (10-13g/23-25 mm).

4. 'Jahr 11' caes. Aera=38/7 v. ist ein Typ zu 10-12g/24-25 mm datiert (RN 1962, 25 ff. Nr. 19), der den Kopf des Antonius r. als imperator (=in Lorbeerumkränzung) auf dem Av. und die gewohnte Tyche auf dem Rv. zeigt; Stadttitel mit kai verbunden (BMC 14 U. LXXXI).

5. 'Jahr 3' Kleopatras in Syrien/Phönizien=35/4 v. sind zumindest einige Stücke des Typs datiert, der denselben Antonius-Avers der unter 4) genannten Exemplare mit der diademierten Büste der Kleopatra r. als Revers kombiniert (RN 1962, 25ff. Nr.20; neben Stadtname und -titulatur im Feld auch IC oder IE; 8,78-9,11g). Bei Vorlage eines 10,36g schweren neuen Exemplares meinte F. Sternberg, im IE Reste eines Zweitdatums gemäss der caesarischen Aera (Jahr 15) erkennen zu dürfen. Baldus äusserte dagegen die Meinung (SM 33, 1983, 8 Anm. 13), wenn schon ein zweites Jahr angegeben sei, wäre Kleopatras 18. Regierungsjahr in Aegypten wahrscheinlicher. Die Bronze variiert die Münzbilder der Antonius/Kleopatra-Tetradrachmen (s. oben I B); dies gilt unter anderem für das geschönte Bildnis der Königin. Dass dieses übrigens auf dem Revers angebracht wurde, hat Seyrig (RN 1962, 35) zu Recht hervorgehoben. An der Zugehörigkeit der Stadt zur phönizischen Schenkung offenbar nicht zweifelnd, hat er daraus ein Sonderverhältnis der Polis zu M. Antonius abgeleitet. Südlich der ausdrücklich Kleopatra nicht übereigneten Territorien von Sidon und Tyros (Fl. Josephus) gelegen, stand Ptolmaïs aber vermutlich nicht unter ihrem Zepter.[28] In diesem Fall erklären sich unsere Münzen zwanglos als 'Verbeugung' vor der Monarchin, vergleichbar Erscheinungen wie in Dora und Damaskos (s. unten Kapitel III).

Nach Aktium wurde die Bronzeprägung vom Typ 'Zeuskopf r. (jetzt in Umkränzung)/Tyche' mit Datierungen nach der caesarischen Aera fortgesetzt.

Die Ptolemaïs zugewiesene Kleopatra-M. Antonius-Prägung mit beider Porträts auf dem Avers und einer stehenden Tyche l. auf dem Rv. gehört wohl in das benachbarte Dora (s. unten Kap. III).

13 Rhosos, Seleukis und Pieria

H. Seyrig, Syria 27 (1950), 32-34.

Um die Mitte des 1. Jahrhunderts v.Chr. ordnete Seyrig undatierte Bronzen ein, auf denen die Stadt die Titel Hiera kai Asylos trägt. Beide Nominale zeigen auf dem Revers einen stehenden Baal von vorn auf Basis, die von Stierprotomen flankiert wird (Attribute: Henkelkreuz zwischen Stierhörnern, Blitz, Schwert, Dioskurenmützen mit Sternen). Das Ganzstück um 8,10g/20 mm hat als Vorderseite: Tychebüste mit Palmzweig r. (Kontermarke: statt aplustre? (Imhoof-B.) vielleicht Tier (Stier?) l.),[29] der Revers ist umkränzt (Imhoof-Blumer, Choix de monn. grecques Taf. 7, 223; ders., Monnaies grecques (1883), 440 Nr. 8; BMC LXX u. LXXXVI; Head 782). Das Halbstück(?) zu ca. 3,18g/17 mm, (teilweise ?) mit denselben

'Beamten'zeichen im Feld l. und im Abschnitt, hat als Av. Stier auf Schild r. stehend, der Rv. zeigt im Feld nur die Sterne der Dioskuren (Macdonald III 210 Nr. 1 Taf. 74, 23).

Auf Nachfolgern der Ganzstücke (jetzt um 7,90g/20 mm) mit ähnlichem Typ (Rv. ohne Kranz und Kontrollzeichen, nur pilei) führt die Stadt den zusätzlichen Titel Autonomos (L. Forrer, Weber Collection (1922-24), Nr. 7991). Nach Seyrig gibt es ein Exemplar (im BM London ?, identisch mit zuvor genanntem Stück?), das 'Jahr 6' der Freiheit von Rhosos datiert sei. S. zeigte an kaiserzeitlichen, nach derselben Aera datierten Münzen, dass die Epoche dieser Zeitrechnung gegen Macdonalds Ansatz wohl auf 42 v. zu datieren ist: Die Autonomie wurde also von Antonius verliehen, die genannte Bronze gehört bei richtiger Lesung in das Jahr 37/6 v.[30]

Auf Stücken des Typs 'Zeuskopf r./Tychebüste r.', die Seyrig nicht erwähnt, die aber im BMC in das 1. Jahrhundert v. datiert werden, nennt die Stadt nur den Titel Hiera (BMC 1: 17 mm; Head 782). Entweder sind sie älter als die zuvor besprochenen oder frühkaiserzeitlich.

14 Seleukeia, Seleukis und Pieria

H. Seyrig, Syria 27 (1950), 28f., besonders 29 Anm. 1.

Seleucia, das die Titel Hiera kai Autonomos trug, prägte nach Abbruch seiner Tetradrachmen-Produktion im Jahr 83 v. nur noch Bronzen, datiert nach der Freiheitsära von 109 oder 108 v. und mit Münzbildern, die sich auf die Stadttyche respektive den Kult des Zeus Kasios/Keraunios beziehen (Head 783): BMC 25ff. Tychebüste r./in Kranz: Blitz und Kissen auf Schemel; BMC 28 Zeuskopf r./Tychebüste r. In die Zeit 64-30 v. fallen die belegten Jahrgänge 65/4, 59/8, 55/4, 37/6 und 30/29(?) v. (Seyrig).

15 Sidon, Phoenicia

BMC CVI-CIX u. 159ff.; Head 797f.

Sidon datierte nach einer Freiheitsära, deren Jahr 1 dem Jahre 111/110 v. entsprach.

Gelegentlich emittierte silberne Schekel (Tetradrachmen ptolemäischen Fusses von 14,3g, de facto eher gut 13g) und Halbschekel (eher knapp 6,5g) zeigten als Avers den Kopf der Tyche r., als Revers in Fortführung ptolemäischer und dann seleukidischer Vorbilder einen Adler mit Palmzweig l. auf prora stehend. Die Beschriftung bestand aus dem Stadtnamen Sidonos oder dann Sidonion mit den Titeln Hiera und Asylos, aus 'Beamten'monogrammen und dem vom Jahrzeichen L eingeleiteten Datum. In die Zeit 64-30 v. fallen die Schekel der Jahrgänge 64/3 v. (erster Jgg. nach längerer Pause) bis 31/30 v. (BMC 105-110; SNG Copenhagen 228f.; Crawford, CMRR, 204 Abb. 82 r. von J. 50 = 58/7 v.) und Halbschekel von 64/3 (SNG Cop. 222: 6,19g), 53/2 und 46/5 v. (BMC 111f.); von letzteren gibt es kaiserzeitliche Nachfolger.

In der begleitenden Bronze für lokalen Umlauf wurde der Stadtname meist zu Sidonion verkürzt und um die Version in phönizischer Schrift und Sprache ergänzt. In den häufigen Schiffsdarstellungen spiegelt sich die alte Bedeutung Sidons als Hafenstadt, in verschiedenen Astarte-Bildern deren besondere kultische Verehrung.

Kleinbronzen vom Typ 'Tychekopf r./Galeere l.' gibt es aus den Jahren 60/59, 58/7 und 56/5 v. (BMC 125-127: 2,51-3,92g; SNG Cop. 224 von 58/7 v.: 2,91g.) sowie zuletzt vom Jahre 44/3 v. BMC Ueberschrift). Der Typus 'Tychekopf r./Astarte l. auf Galeere stehend' kommt im Jahr 53/2 v. vor (BMC 136: 5,33g). Der Typ 'Köpfe von Zeus und Tyche r./Galeere l.' hat in Griechisch die Sonderlegende Sidonos Theas (Thea = Stadttitel) und ist belegt für 47/6 v. (BMC 141: 4,21g; SNG Fitzwilliam 6054: 6,28g).

Den Typ 'Zeuskopf r., Beizeichen/Astarte-Europa auf Stier l.' gibt es in einer älteren Version (62/1 v.: SNG Cop. 225 zu 8,91g; 39/8 v.: BMC 144 zu 6,92g, SNG Cop. 226 zu 7,91g) und in einer jüngeren Variante von 36/5 v., rückseitig ohne phönizische Legende aber umkränzt (BMC 145f.: 5,84-7,65 g; Macdonald III 252 Nr. 23: 7,28g; SNG Cop. 227: 4,61g). Den Typus 'Dionysoskopf r./in Epheukranz: cista und thyrsos mit der Legende Sidonos' kennt man von 59/8 v. (Macdonald 251 Nr. 20f.: ca. 5,1-6,3g), 52/1 v. (Macdonald 252 Nr. 22: 7,28g) und 44/3 v. (BMC 149: 6,69g); es ist fraglich, ob hierbei je der Stadtname auf Phönizisch hinzugesetzt wurde.

16 Tripolis, Phoenicia

H. Seyrig, Syria 27 (1950), 38-43 u. 44 Nr. 4 m. Anm.; zu den Porträtprägungen: H.R. Baldus, JNG 23 (1973) 25f., e und 33f.

Im Jahre 64 v., oder erst 63 v. mit der Beseitigung des Tyrannen Dionysios (mögliche Prägung: BMC CXVIf.) durch Pompeius, begann die Stadt eine neue Jahreszählung. Diese verwendet eine Reihe von Bronzen (mit 'Jahr 1' beginnend: Seyrig, Syria 31 (1954), 80), deren Hauptstücke den Avers Tychebüste mit Stylis und den Rv. Nike auf prora r. stehend, Stern, zeigen (ähnlich, aber später: BMC 24-26).

Ins Jahr 23 = 42/1 v. sind rückseitig zwei Bronzemünzen datiert: Das Hauptstück mit dem Kopf des Antonius r./der Fulvia (früher: Kleopatra, Octavia) r. (BMC 20 u. S.CXVIIf. Taf. 43, 10; Head 799) hat einen Durchmesser von 22 mm (8,92g), das Teilstück mit Av. Weiblicher verschleierter Kopf r.[31] und Rv. Dioskurenmützen (BMC CXVII no. 47,2) hat einen Durchmesser von 16 mm.

Tripolis fiel 37/6 v. wie andere phönizische Poleis als Schenkung des Antonius an Kleopatra und zählte dieses Jahr als Jahr 1 einer neuen Aera. Der Königin zu Ehren wurden in Abwandlung des älteren Hauptnominals Bronzen (8,82-10,1g/22 mm) ausgegeben, die auf dem Avers deren Büste r. zeigen (alexandrinischer Typus, relativ gute Qualität). Die Rückseite zeigt Nike mit Kranz und Palmzweig r. auf prora stehend, gelegentlich einen Stern im Feld, und ist datiert 'Jahr 2' = 36/5 v. (BMC 19 u. S.CXVII; Head 798f.).

Kleinaes vom Typ 'Tychebüste r./Prora r.' (BMC 15-17; SNG Copenhagen 272f.) würde mit dem Jahrgang 29 in dasselbe Jahr 2 Kleopatras (= 36/5 v.) fallen, wäre es nach der Pompeiusära datiert. Daher muss es nach der Freiheitsära zählen, die zwischen 105 und 95 v. beginnt (Seyrig 42); die Stücke gehören also in vorrömische Zeit.

17 Tyros, Phoenicia

Y. Meshorer, Ancient Jewish Coinage 1 (1982), 57-59 u. 2 (1982), 6-9; ders., Festschrift L. Mildenberg (1984), 171-179 Taf. 26; zu Gewicht und

Feingehalt der Schekel: Walker, *Metrology* I 58 u. 67.

Die Stadt, welche die Titulatur *Hiera kai Asylos* führte, datierte nach einer Freiheitsära mit 126/5 v. als Jahr 1. Schon lange vor Einrichtung der Provinz Syria prägte man sehr feine (Walker: ca. 95%) Silberschekel (= ptolemäische Tetradrachmen zu rund 14,3g) und gelegentlich entsprechende Halbstücke mit denselben, letztlich ptolemäische Vorbilder modifizierenden Darstellungen: Av. Belorbeerter Herakles Melkarth-Kopf r., Rv. Adler mit Palmzweig auf *prora* l. stehend, *Tyrou* etc., im Feld Keule, Datum sowie Kontrollzeichen (Head 800). Diese Prägung wurde ab 64 v. ohne Aenderung fortgeführt (*BMC* 146-180; *SNG Copenhagen* 326-328; *SNG Fitwilliam* 6090f.) und lief auch nach 30 v. gut ein Jahrzehnt bis zu einschneidenden Aenderungen weiter. Der Halbschekel ist beispielsweise für J. 87 = 40/39 v. belegt (*BMC* 231: 6,52g).

Die tyrischen Schekel liefen nicht nur im nördlichen Phönizien um, wie der um 60 v. vergrabene Hort *IGCH* 1581 (mit Korrekturen O. Morkholms, *ANSMN* 28 (1983), 97f.) mit 10 Exemplaren bis J. 64 = 63/2 v.[32] und der um 50 v. vergrabene Schatzfund *IGCH* 1621 (= H. Seyrig, *Trésors du Levant* Nr. 47) aus Berytos zeigen, welch letzterer tyrische Stücke bis J. 73 = 54/3 v. enthielt. Ein weiterer Markt für die Schekel tat sich im Lande der Juden auf, das zeigen der Schatzfund *IGCH* 1617 aus Palästina, vergraben nach 61 v., der neben älteren Seleukiden-Tetradrachmen aus Tyros 10 tyrische Schekel der Jahre 45-64 (J. 64 = 63/2 v.) enthielt, und der Fund *IGCH* 1628 aus Jerusalem, vergraben ca. 29 v., mit 9 Schekeln der Zeit 42/1-30/29 v. und 2 älteren tyrischen Tetradrachmen Demetrios' II. Meshorer hat dargelegt, dass die tyrischen Schekel in der frühen Kaiserzeit in Jerusalem nachgeprägt wurden.

Vorrömischen Ursprungs ist der Bronzetyp zu ca. 7g mit Av. Tychebüste mit Palmzweig r., Rv. Galeere l., oben griechisches Stadtmonogramm = TYP, Stadttitel in Monogrammform (*Hier/a, As/y*) und Daten, darunter der Stadtname in phönizischer Schrift und Sprache. In der betrachteten Periode geprägt wurde ein Exemplar (Macdonald III 265 Nr. 16) vom Jahre 35 v. (M.).

Ein neuer Bronzetypus zu rund 8-12g wurde kurz vor Mitte des 1. Jahrhunderts v. eingeführt. Er hat dieselbe Vorderseite wie das Silber, der Rv. zeigt im Eichenkranz die Keule des Stadtgottes, oben in das Stadtmonogramm auslaufend, den phönizischen Stadtnamen sowie das Datum in milesischen Zahlen. Vom selben Jahr wie die zuvor genannte Bronze stammt das Stück *BMC* 268 (dort: 37/6 v.).

III MUENZEN VON PRAEGEHERREN AUSSERHALB DER PROVINZ SYRIA, alphabetische Anordnung.

a *Askalon, Judaea*

A. Spaer, *Festschrift L. Mildenberg* (1984), 229-239 Taf. 35-37.

Die Stadt datierte nach einer Freiheitsära mit 104/3 v. als Jahr 1 und führte in der betrachteten Zeit die Titel *Hiera* und *Asylos*, der Ehrenname *Autonomos* scheint mit Pompeius' Eingreifen unterdrückt oder verloren worden zu sein.

Die Silber-Tetradrachmen der Polis folgen dem ptolemäischen Fuss von ca. 14,3g (O. Morkholm, ANSMN 28 (1983), 95, vgl. 99f.). Ptolemäischen respektive seleukidischen Vorbildern folgend, zeigen sie auf dem Avers diademierte Porträts von Seleukiden oder Ptolemäern, darunter sicher Kleopatras VII. (H.R. Baldus, JNG 23 (1973), 19-43 besond. 25, c Taf.3,6); auf der Rückseite den Adler mit Palmzweig auf Blitz l., den Stadtnamen mit Titeln und im Feld die Taube der Aphrodite-Dekerto (=Stadtwappen) sowie Daten und 'Beamten'zeichen. Das früheste belegte Datum ist 6=99/8 v., in die Zeit 64-30 v. fallen die Jahrgänge ab J.41=64/3 v. (mit Autonomos: SNG ANS 6, 652, dort wie alle Tdr. der Stadt falsch datiert; ohne Autonomos: BMC 18 Taf.12,1): beispielsweise 43=62/1 und 51=54/3 v. (Spaer 238, M-N) oder 50=55/4 v. (BMC 19 Taf.12,2). Die Kleopatrastücke der Jahre 55=50/49 v. (BMC 19 Taf. 12,3; Head 804 Abb. 354), 56(?) und 66=39/8 v. (Baldus op.cit.) beschliessen die Reihe. Umlaufsgebiet der Schekel war nach Ausweis der Schatzfunde nach 64 v. (IGCH 1616, 1622 und 1627) die küstennahe Region südlich des Berges Karmel.

Unter den diversen, meist undatierten Kleinbronzen des späteren 1. Jahrhunderts v. (BMC 21ff.) befinden sich einige vom Typus 'Männlicher belorbeerter Kopf (Askalos?) r. /Prora l., AS' mit Jahresangaben: 56=49/8 und 57=48/7 v. (SNG ANS 6, 661f.: je 3,74g, Av. stempelgleich) sowie 64=41/40 v. (BMC 30 u. LVII Taf.12,8: 4,07g). Eine Bronze vom Jahre 74=31/30 v. weist sehr an die Tetradrachmen erinnernde Darstellungen auf: Bärtiger Kopf (Zeus, Poseidon ?) r./Adler mit Palmzweig l., Taube sowie Datum und AS (BMC 16 u. LVf. Taf. 11, 18: 9,75g).

b Chalcis sub Libano, Coele-Syria

H. Seyrig, Syria 27 (1950) 39 u. 44 Nr.5 bis 49; zu Kleopatra VII.: H.R. Baldus, JNG 23 (1973), 27 u. 30-33 Nr.3, 5 u. 6; Auktion Malter (Encino) 2, 1978, 302f.

Der Herrscher über das Fürstentum in der heutigen Bekaa-Ebene, Ptolemaios Sohn des Mennaios, der im Jahre 73/2 v. eine anonyme, aber J. 240 seleukidischer Aera datierte Bronze vom Typ 'Zeuskopf r./Stehende Dioskuren' herausgebracht hatte (SNG Copenhagen 413: 6,56g), prägte nach der Bestätigung seiner Herrschaft durch Pompeius 63 v. aes desselben Typs (Rv. in Kranz) mit Ptolema Tetrarch und der Datierung 'Jahr 2' (=62/1 v.: SNG Cop. 414, 6,45g); eventuell gibt es Parallelen mit höheren Daten. Undatierte Exemplare desselben Typs geben ihm zusätzlich den Titel Archiereus (BMC 3-5). Doppelstücke ohne Jahr vom Typus 'Zeuskopf r./Adler r. fliegend' (BMC 2; SNG Lewis 1107: 6,13g) weisen nur den Tetrarchentitel auf (Head 783).

Sein Sohn und Nachfolger Lysanias (40-36 v.) prägte Bronzen (BMC 6; SNG Cop. 415f.: 7,39 u. 4,29g), die auf dem Avers ein diademiertes älteres Porträt r. zeigen, dessen Beischrift ΠΤ = Pto an ein postumes Bildnis des Vaters denken lässt. Der Revers 'Athena mit Schild, Speer und Nike l. stehend' nennt Lysanias mit den Titeln Tetrarches kai Archiereus (BMC 6; Head 784).

Von der Beseitigung des Lysanias durch Antonius 36 v. bis zum Regierungsantritt seines Sohnes Zenodoros 31/30 v. (Bronzen dieses Jahres mit Oktaviankopf/Zenodorosporträt und -legende: beispielsweise BMC 7) regierte Kleopatra das ihr von Antonius geschenkte Fürstentum (Head 784). Es ist Seyrigs Verdienst, eine Basilisses Kleopatras (Av.)/ Etous KA tou kai S Theas Neoteras (Rv.) beschriftete, also auf 32/1 v.

doppeldatierte Bronzeserie ohne Münzstätten-Angabe wie bei den Prägungen oben genannter Tetrarchen diesem Fürstentum richtig zugewiesen zu haben; die früher zögernd vorgenommene Zuschreibung an Berytos (BMC LV und 43 Nr.14 Anm.) beruhte auf dem häufigen Auftauchen solcher Exemplare im Beiruter Handel und war angesichts dortiger Münzen zu Ehren der Königin aus demselben Jahr (s. oben II 5), und zwar mit gänzlich anderem Aeusseren, sehr unwahrscheinlich. Angesichts der guten Seyrigschen Argumente für Chalkis sollte sie heutzutage endgültig ad acta gelegt sein.

Alle vier Nominale haben als Avers die diademierte Büste Kleopatras im syrisch-phönizischen Prunkgewand r. sowie die genannte Legende. Das seltene Doppelstück (13,75g/24 mm) und das häufigere Normalstück (BMC Berytus 15; SNG Cop. Phoenicia 383: 5,62g; meist 4,4-8,2g, also gut 6g/ca. 20 mm) zeigen als Reversbild den Kopf des Antonius r., übernehmen also die Münzbilder und die Tatsache der langen Legenden auf beiden Seiten (Rv. s. oben) von den Provinzial-Tetradrachmen M. Antons/Kleopatras der Jahre ab 37/6 v. (s. oben I B). Die seltenen Teilstücke (Halbe ?) zeigen auf dem Rv. entweder 'im Kranz: Nike mit Palmwedel r. eilend' (BMC Berytus 14 Taf. 7,9:17 mm; meist 4,25-5,25g) oder 'Athena l. eilend mit Schild und Speer' (Macdonald III 400 Nr.21 Taf.84,21: 4,18g/16mm).

Während bei den Teilstücken Zweifel an der Reihenfolge der Legendenteile Etous ...S und Theas Neoteras aufkommen mögen, steht bei deren Vorlage, den Doppel- und Ganzstücken, die Doppeldatierung eindeutig am Anfang, dann folgt Theas neoteras. Das lässt erste Zweifel auftauchen, ob T.V. Buttreys (ANSMN 6 (1954) 95ff.) Erklärung der Tetradrachmen-Legende Kleopatras (=Königin Kleopatra Thea die Jüngere, = die Zweite) die allein richtige ist. Dass zumindestens eine Doppeldeutigkeit angelegt und ein anderes Verständnis möglich war, wird bei den anikonen kyrenäischen[33] Antonius/Kleopatra-Bronzen von 31 v. deutlich, bei denen der Name Kleopatras gar nicht mehr begegnet (beispielweise SNG Cop. Ptolem. 692f.: Basil Thea Ne): Thea neotera ist hier eher 'die jugendliche Göttin' (=Aphrodite etc.).

Es ist bezeichend für den Status des Fürstentums Chalkis nach der Schenkung an die Königin, dass Antonius eindeutig auf die Rückseite der Doppel- und Ganzstücke verwiesen wird (Seyrig), im Gegensatz zum Vorgehen bei den Tetradrachmen. Zu letzteren standen die beschriebenen Chalkis-Bronzen als zugehörige Teilstücke aus aes sicherlich in einer klaren Wertrelation.

c Damaskos, Koile-Syria

H. Seyrig, Syria 27 (1950), 34f.; H.R. Baldus, JNG 23 (1973), 32 Nr. 7; Auktion Malter (Encino) 2, 1978, 292-295.

Damascus datierte nach der Seleukidenära und hielt auch daran fest, als es zu Ehren der mächtigen Nachbarin im Fürstentum Chalcis s.L., Kleopatras, zwei Münzemissionen ausgab: Offenbar gehörte die Stadt nicht zu den coelesyrischen Gebieten, die in der Schenkung M. Antons von 37/6 v. enthalten waren.

Die beiden Aesemissionen tragen auf dem Av. die jugendlich-geschönte, diademierte Büste der Königin r. nach dem Vorbild der Antonius/Kleopatra-Tetradrachmen (s. oben I B), auf dem Rv. in Kranz die l. auf Felsen sitzende Stadttyche mit Füllhorn und segnend ausgestreckter Rechten über dem Flussgott Chrysoroas: eine Darstellung in Anlehnung an die Eutychides-Statue von Antiochia a.O., die schon von Damaskener *aes* beispielsweise Tigranes' d.Gr. (*BMC* Seleuc. 9f. Taf. 27,7) bekannt war. Die ersten Kleopatrabronzen sind datiert Jahr 276 seleuk. Aera = 37/6 v. Das *aes* zu 8,2-13,1g/21-26 mm (dazu gehört *SNG Copenhagen* 419: 11,78g) weist im Feld der Rückseite eine Aehre auf und gibt den vollen Stadtnamen an. Ein Teilstück mit demselben Beizeichen 'Aehre' stammt vom Jahr 277 = 36/5 v.: Jugendliche Büste l./Füllhorn zwischen *cista* (?) und Aehre. Die Legende ist hier zu *Damas* verkürzt (*BMC* 1). Die zweite Kleopatraemission von J. 280 = 33/2 v. umfasst Bronzen, die offensichtlich nur die Hälfte der schwereren Vorgänger wiegen (6,23-6,49g/19-21 mm) und durch die Kurzlegende *Damas* und ein *aplustre* im Feld von jenen unterschieden sind.

Die Stadt beeilte sich bald nach der Uebernahme der Region durch Oktavian, den neuen Herrscher des Ostens durch Emission einer Porträtbronze mit traditionellem Revers zu ehren, datiert J. 283 = 30/29 v. (*AMC* 1479; 7,45g).

d *Dora, Phoenicia*

H. Seyrig, *Syria* 27 (1950), 52 m. Abb. 3,e; H.R. Baldus, *SM* 33 (1983), 5-10 m. Abb.

Dora verdankte seine Befreiung von jüdischer Herrschaft dem Pompeius. Dies feierte man 64 (oder 63 v.) mit der Einführung einer neuen Zeitrechnung und einer Münzemission, für längere Zeit die einzige der Stadt: Beide Bronzen zeigen als Avers eine Tychebüste r., auf den Rückseiten die Legende *DO* sowie die Datierung 'Jahr 1'. Das Normalstück zu 8,4-9g/20-24 mm hat als Reversbild die Tyche mit Ruder und Füllhorn l. stehend (*BMC* 1), das Halbstück weist eine Aehre auf (*BMC* 2: 3,77g/15 mm).

Offenbar ohne zur Schenkung des Antonius an Kleopatra zu gehören, gab man eine Prägung auf das Paar heraus: Den von A. Kindler der Stadt Ptolemaïs-Ake und dem Jahr 30/29 v. zugewiesenen Bronzetyp (6,65-8,86g/ca. 23-24 mm) mit Av. Büste Kleopatras mit Diadem und Prunkmantel vor Kopf M. Antons r. und Rv. Tyche mit Palmzweig und *caduceus* l. stehend (jetzt: Crawford, *CMRR* 253 u. 255 Abb. 109 r. unten) hat Baldus dieser Polis zugewiesen: Dieselbe eher ungewöhnliche Reversdarstellung ist für Dora durch eine Bronze mit vollständiger Stadtlegende gesichert (s. unten). Das als 'Jahr 19' gelesene Datum der Kleopatra-Antonius-Münze nach dem Vorbild der Tetradrachmen (s. oben I B) und vielleicht anlässlich der Hochzeit der beiden Dargestellten geprägt, hat B. auf die Regierung der Monarchin in Aegypten bezogen (= 34/3 v.). Der bemerkenswert ähnliche Revers der Bronze mit Av. Belorbeerter Doroskopf r. ist - liest man das Datum der pomp. Aera nicht (2)32, wie im *BMC* (24: 8,27g/22 mm), sondern 32 = 33/2 v. - ein Jahr später verwendet worden. Y. Meshorer berichtete in London von seiner bevorstehenden Publikation weiterer Antonius-Kleopatra-Stücke der Stadt. Wenn ich richtig verstanden habe, ist dieses *aes* ähnlich pompeianisch datiert wie letztgenanntes Exemplar. Ausserdem gibt es, wie es hiess, Halbstücke für M. Anton allein. Das würde - wie die lokale Datierung - das Verbleiben der ausserhalb der Provinz liegenden Polis unter der Oberhoheit des Antonius bestätigen.

e *Gaba, Galilaea oder Trachonitis*

SNG Fitzwilliam VIII 5975.

Eine Kleinbronze vom Typ 'Behelmter Athenakopf r./Zebu l., Stadtname' ist datiert 'Jahr 25' einer Aera mit 60 v. als Epoche, ist also 36/5 v. entstanden.

f *Gadara, Dekapolis*

Head 787.

Die Polis wurde von Pompeius neugegründet, datierte daher nach einer Aera mit 64/3 v. als Jahr 1 und schmückte die Stadttitulatur später mit dem Namen des Gründers (*BMC* LXXXVI). Während die Existenz einer Emission in *aes* (Rv. zwei Füllhörner) vom J. 8 = 57/6 v. im *BMC* (LXXXVII) bezweifelt wurde, sind Bronzen aus den Jahren 18 = 47/6 v., 25 und 26(?) jetzt sicher belegt (*SNGANS* 6, 1287ff.: 2,9-5,3g); Typ 'Tychebüste r./Füllhorn, Stadtname'.

g *Jüdische Hohepriester und Könige*

Y. Meshorer, *Jewish Coins of the Second Temple Period* (1967), 41-68 u. 121ff. Nr. 18-55 Taf. 4-7; ders., *SNGANS* 6 (1981), 53ff., besonders 135-226; ders., *Ancient Jewish Coinage I, Persian Period through Hasmonaeans,* u. II, *Herod the Great through Bar Cochba,* (1982).

Münzstätte war, abgesehen von Herodes' ersten Jahren 40-37 v., 'natürlich' Jerusalem, Münzmetall allein *aes*.

Die Hasmonäer Judas Aristoboulos II. (67-63 v.) und Johannes Hyrkanos II. (63-40 v.) prägten als Hohepriester zusammen mit dem Hohenrat rein paläohebräisch beschriftete Kleinmünzen (*prutah*) zu etwa 2g für den lokalen Umlauf (*IGCH* 1623-1625): Av. Nennung des emittierenden Gremiums in Kranz, Rv. Granatapfel zwischen Doppelfüllhorn (*SNGANS* 135ff., 139-182); bei letztgenanntem seltene Halbe (Palmzweig/Lilie) und Doppel (Helm/Füllhörner), s. *Jewish Coins* Nr. 21f. respektive 25.

Der mit parthischer Hilfe auf den Thron gelangte Mattathias Antigonos (40-37 v.) reformierte die Prägung: Parallel zu Kleinaes des alten Typs (*SNGANS* 191-194), oft allerdings mit Aehre zwischen Füllhörnern, gab er recht grosse Bronzen zu ca. 14g aus (Nr. 183-188) mit Av. Doppelfüllhorn und übliche Legende, Rv. *Basileos Antigonou* um Kranz; daneben Halbe zu gut 7g (Nr. 189f.) mit vereinfachten Darstellungen; jüdische Schrift um *ein* Füllhorn/griechische Legende wie oben (oft verkürzt) *in* Kranz. Ein abweichender Prutahtyp zeigt 'Leuchter, griechische Legende/Tisch, hebräische Legende' (*Jewish Coins* Nr. 36f.). Ein Schatzfund von mehr als 20 Bronzen des Königs ist aus Jericho bezeugt (*CH* 2, 1976, Nr. 128).

Die Münzprägung Herodes' d.Gr. (40-4 v.), traditionell nach Jerusalem gelegt und daher *nach* 37 v. datiert, wird in Meshorers jüngstem Buch (Vol.2, 5ff. u. 235ff. Taf.1-3) radikal anders angeordnet: Die Prägung des Herodes setzte schon 40 v. mit der Verleihung des Königstitels durch die Römer ein. Da Jerusalem bis 37 v. von Mattathias Antigonos gehalten wurde, sei Herodes 40-37 auf Samaria als Münzstätte ausgewichen. Während dieser Jahre seien die Stücke mit der immobilisierten Datierung 'Jahr 3' (=40 v.) ausgegeben worden; da die Zählung von der Einsetzung als Tetrarch im Jahr 42 v. rechne, werde stets ⳨ = T(E)TP = *tetrarches* hinzugesetzt. Wie sein Konkurrent habe Herodes eine ganze Serie von Nominalen ausgegeben, nämlich vier (5-10g; 3,5-6g; 3-4g; 2-2,75g). Auf den Vorderseiten sind sie stets *Herodou*

Basileos (oder abgekürzt) beschriftet. Mit der Eroberung Jerusalems 37 v. habe die traditionelle hauptstädtische Münzstätte die weitere Prägung übernommen. Der Wechsel spiegele sich nicht nur in den lokalen Funden, sondern zeige sich auch auf den Stücken selbst: Fortfall der Datierung und des schweren Nominals, Aenderung von Stil und Münzbildern. Als solche werden diverse Objekte dargestellt, darunter Gegenstände kultischer Bedeutung und monarchischer Repräsentation. Unter den frühen Münzbildern fielen diverse auf, die von römisch-republikanischen Denaren übernommen seien und eine 'Verbeugung' des Herodes vor seinen Protektoren darstellten. Meines Erachtens ist es nicht nötig, ausgerechnet republikanische denarii als Inspirationsquelle anzunehmen, zumal da diese ja in Judaea nicht umliefen (s. oben). Bei den späteren Münzbildern trete Eigenständiges stärker in Erscheinung.

Die von Meshorer entdeckte Nachmünzung tyrischer Silberschekel durch Herodes begann erst nach 19/8 v. und gehört nicht mehr zur republikanischen Münzprägung Syriens.

h Königreich der Nabatäer

Y. Meshorer, Nabataean Coins (1975) 16-28 u. 80f. Nr. 9-19 Taf.1f.

Mit der Unterwerfung des Königreiches unter römische Oberhoheit durch Pompeius setzte eine nabatäisch beschriftete Münzprägung ein. Münzstätte war Petra, das sich seit Malichos I. durch die Zeichen H-O zu erkennen gab.

Obodas II. (62-60 v.), Sohn Aretas' III., liess eine kleine Repräsentationsprägung in Silber emittieren, und zwar höchst feine (ca. 90%) Halbschekel (ca. 6,7g) und gelegentlich Viertelschekel nach tyrischem Vorbild (beispielsweise SNGANS 6, 1425). Sie zeigen auf dem Avers die relativ hellenisiert wirkende, diademierte Königsbüste, auf dem Rv. den Adler l., Königsnamen und -titel sowie Datierungen 'Jahr 1' bis 'Jahr 3'.

Sein Nachfolger Malichos I. (60-30 v.). sah erst während seines Krieges gegen Herodes d.Gr. die Notwendigkeit, Münzen zu prägen. In das 'Jahr 26' (=35 v.) gehört ein höchst seltener Silberschekel nach dem Vorbild des Vaters; allerdings kommt in den langen Locken der jugendlichen Königsbüste viel deutlicher das einheimische Element zum Vorschein. Der Kriegsfinanzierung diente besonders die erste national-nabatäische Bronzeprägung mit den Daten 'Jahr 27' (=34 v.) und 'J.28' (=33 v.). Die drei Nominale (ca. 10, 5 und 2,5g) haben denselben Avers wie das Silber, auf den Rückseiten begegnen neben dem gewohnten Adler die Darstellungen 'Füllhorn' und 'segnend-grüssende Hand'.

i Königreich Kommagene

Head 775; P.Z. Bedoukian, ANSMN 28 (1983), 71-88 Taf. 11f.

Antiochos I. Theos (ca. 69-34 v.) emittierte ca. 6-7g schwere Bronzen vom Typ 'Büste in armenischer, diademierter Tiara r./Löwe r. schreitend, Basileos Antiochou' (BMC If.; zur Tiara und zum Zodiakallöwen S. BMC XLIVf.) sowie Halbstücke desselben Typs (Bedoukian 88 Nr.27). Aes um 6g gibt es auch mit dem abweichenden Reversbild Adler r. (88 Nr.26).

j Samosata, Kommagene

Head 776.

Städtische Bronzen des Typs 'Zeuskopf r./Löwe r., Samo/sato' (BMC 1-3) sind nach Vorbildern Antiochos' I. geprägt, dessen Residenz Samosata war. Während die Stadtprägung im BMC Galatia etc. nach dem Tod des Königs (dort: um 31 v.) datiert wurde, hielt Head einen früheren Prägebeginn - schon unter diesem Monarchen - für môglich.

English Summary

In 64 BC Pompey established the province of Syria (cf.map p. 122) between the Mediterranean Sea and Euphrates, in the north bordering the province of Cilicia and the kingdom of Commagene, in the south covering a rather narrow strip of the coast down to Mt. Carmel. Antioch on the Orontes, the old Seleucid residence, became the capital and governor's seat. It was Pompey again who in 63 BC settled the affairs in the neighbouring cities and smaller kingdoms of the south-east. The coinages of the whole region are dealt with down to about 30 BC.

Arriving in Syria the Romans met a circulation of manifold coinages from two sources: the royal Seleucid coinage in its last phase was limited to silver tetradrachms of reduced Attic weight (nearly 16g), mainly from the mint of Antioch. On the other hand, quite a number of free cities issued their own coinage in bronze for local use, or in bronze and silver. Among civic silver, circulating in a wider area than aes, there was neither uniformity of type nor weight because there were two zones of coin-standards. Some coastal cities of the south followed the Ptolemaic tetradrachm (shekel) of ca. 14.3g, some of northern Phoenicia and Syria used a standard between reduced-Attic and Ptolemaic, around 15.3 - 15.1g for the same denomination.

The Romans did not introduce their denarii to Syria, but took over the traditional coinages. Till imperial times there is no hoard of Roman coins in Syria, no denarius issue is with certainty attributed to this province (an exception is the rare gold issue, RRC 549) and none of its types was copied there. Instead, the provincial authorities continued to strike Seleucid tetradrachms of reduced Attic weight with types taken over from king Philip Philadelphis (pl.12,A). This Roman coinage for provincial use in the 50s was at first signed by monograms in Greek of governors like Gabinius (pl.12,1), Crassus and Cassius; later it was dated by the years of the Caesarian era of Antioch, the latter's monogram replacing the earlier one of Roman officials (pl.12,2). Besides these provincial tetradrachms civic silver (and/or bronze) continued to be struck for a while on the two standards mentioned: Sidon, Tyre and Ascalon issued further shekels (and halves) of Ptolemaic weight, being followed by Laodicea after its former model Aradus with its higher standard ceased to issue in the later 40s, and by the Nabateans who preferred half and quarter-shekels. Down to the reign of Augustus there was a steady reduction in the number of civic silver mints, but no basic change of the traditional Syrian coinage.

Of course, there were many alterations during the time which reflected the historical events of the period.

Pompey's installation of the province and of a zone of Roman supremacy in the south-east initiated the introduction of Pompeian eras in a dozen kingdoms and free cities of the region minting at that time or slightly later; some of them began coining with these events. In the earlier 40s the struggle between Pompey and Caesar caused further changes. For example, the battle of Pharsalus in 48 and Caesar's visit to Syria a year later led Antioch to change its denominations and the reverse design of its bronze, to introduce a Caesarian era and to style itself _Autonomos._ Laodicea changed its dating-system too, and from that time on was called _Julia Laodicea._ In the late 40s the siege and occupation of the city by Caesar's murderer Cassius caused a hiatus in its series of tetradrachms, and a reintroduction of its old name on _aes_ for a short period. The Parthian invasion at the end of the decade entailed among other alterations a temporary introduction of their dating system (the Seleucid era) at Antioch and Apamea, and even indirectly influenced reforms in late Hasmonean-Herodian bronze coinage. Similar changes of civic titles and eras as before can be observed during Antony's first years in the east (Apamea, Rhosus), a new feature of them being the introduction of his portrait on some civic _aes_ (Aradus, Ptolemais, Tripolis).

Mark Antony's donation of a coastal strip of central Phoenicia and its hinterland (the principality of Chalcis) to Cleopatra VII of Egypt in 37/6 BC caused many alterations of Syrian coinages. In her new territory the queen introduced a second sequence of regnal years, a specially ornate bust and a new titulature (bronzes of Chalcis). While some of the Phoenician cities 'given back' to her began to date civic _aes_ by her Syrian regnal years (or by both regnal dating-systems) and to use her Alexandrian portrait (Berytus, Orthosia, Tripolis), some neighbours outside her territory in- and outside the former province put her Syrian bust on their bronze, but by using different dating-systems or by assigning her the coin's reverse they made it clear that they did not belong to her kingdom proper (Damascus, Dora, Ptolemais). As a counter-part to these coinages some northern cities, which stayed under direct Roman control, put Mark Antony's head on civic bronze (Balanea) or even silver (Antioch).

The principal alteration may be observed in the Syrian provincial coinage of Antiochene mintage: pseudo-Seleucid silver tetradrachms show a marked and previously insufficiently considered hiatus between the last dated emission in 38/7 BC (after a rather well documented sequence of annual issues from 47/6 on) and the reintroduction of a somewhat different variant (pl.12,B) by Octavian in 31/30 BC (down to 14/3). Just this gap of 37/6 to 32/1 is filled by the new tetradrachms (pl.12,3) of Antonius and Cleopatra (ca. 15g in weight). This confirms their often supposed Antiochene origin, and their predecessor's character as provincial currency. The same status of the new tetradrachm is made clear by the absence of any mention of a civic minting authority. With their portraits surrounded by (Greek) legends, these coins issued by the Roman government for use in Syria show a marked and premature similarity to contemporary Roman _denarii._ It was the division of Syria into the Roman province with reduced territory and with a zone of Roman overlordship mainly in the south-east, on the one hand, and into a nominal part of the Ptolemaic kingdom from 37/6 to 32/1 BC, on the other, that led to a circulation of these coins in territories _de iure_ under two different governments. This is why Cleopatra (with her full new 'Syrian' titulature and costume) and Antony are dealt as joint guaranteeing authorities, thus making it impossible truly to call one side of a coin the 'obverse' and the other the 'reverse'. The intended areas of circulation were the reason for choosing a standard between reduced Attic and Ptolemaic, quite similar to the former Aradian one.

After the battle of Actium in 31 BC the victor Octavian marched to Egypt via the Levant. His arrival in Syria is echoed in contemporary coinage by a marked restoration of earlier conditions. The most obvious was the renewed minting of the posthumous Philip tetradrachms at Antioch from 31/30 on (pl.12,B), while a similar change was the return to traditional eras on some civic aes around 30 BC (Berytus, Chalcis, Tripolis). It was only far later in Augustus's reign, in 5/4 BC, that he added provincial bronze and reformed the Antiochene tetradrachm coinage (from then on showing the emperor's portrait on obverse), thereby marking the final beginning of the imperial coinage of Syria.

ABBILDUNGSVERZEICHNIS TAF.12

Abgebildet sind aus Beständen der Staatlichen Münzsammlung München Beispiele solcher Prägungen, die die Römische Republik selbst durch ihre Repräsentanten in Syrien und für den dortigen Umlauf hat prägen lassen (Nr.1-3); ausserdem Vorbild und Nachfolger dieser Münzen (A, B). Die Photos verdanke ich den Herren Dietrich O.A. Klose und H. Hotter, München.

A Philippos Philadelphos (König von Syrien 92-83 v.)
Tetradrachmon; Antiochia a.O.; 14,39g
Av. Diademiertes Porträt r. Rv. in Lorberkranz: Zeus mit Nike und Zepter l. thronend, Basileos/Philippou-Epiphanous/Philadelphou; im Feld l., unter dem Thron (und im Abschnitt) 'Beamten'kürzel. E.T. Newell, The Seleucid Mint of Antioch (1918) Nr.457.

1 A. Gabinius (Gouverneur Syriens 57-55 v.)
Tetradrachmon nach dem Vorbild von A; Antiochia; 14,64g gelocht. Beschreibung im Prinzip wie A, jedoch l. im Feld XB = A GABIN.

2 Römische Republik unter Caesar im Jahre 46/5 v.
Tetradrachmon nach dem Vorbild von 1; Antiochia; 15,53g. Beschreibung im Prinzip wie 1, jedoch l. im Feld XT = Antioch, im Abschnitt delta = Jahr 4 caes. Aera.

3 M. Antonius (und Kleopatra VII. als Mitbeherrscher Syriens 37/6 - 32/1 v.)
Tetradrachmon; Antiochia; 14,40g.
Av.(?) Kopf M. Antons r., Reste von Antonios Autokrator triton Trion andron Rv. (?) Diademierte Büste Kleopatras im Prunkmantel r., Reste von Basilissa Kleopatra Thea neotera.

B Römische Republik unter Oktavian im Jahre 31/30 v.
Tetradrachmon nach dem Vorbild von 2; Antiochia; 14,45g. Beschreibung wie 2, jedoch im Abschnitt theta iota = Jahr 19 caes. Aera.

ANMERKUNGEN

1 Ueber das vorgefunde syrische Münzwesen und die Prägungen der ersten Jahre als römische Provinz vgl. A.R. Bellinger, Festschrift A.Ch. Johnson (1951), 58-67, und zuletzt - sehr knapp - Crawford, CMRR 201-206 u. 209.

2 IGCH 1583 = H. Seyrig, Trésors du Levant anciens et nouveaux (1973), Nr.37.

3 Zu den verschiedenen Standards zuletzt: O. Morkholm, Studia P. Naster Oblata, ed. S. Scheers (1982), 139-149, besonders 143ff.; ders., ANSMN 28 (1983), 94-96 u. 98-102.

A

1

2

3

B

Plate 12.

4 Vgl. zuletzt Y. Meshorer, *Festschrift L. Mildenberg* (1984), 172.

5 Auch unter den Einzelfunden der Zeit (datierte Gräber) sind voraugusteische Denare nach Y. Meshorers Beobachtungen ausserordentlich selten; vgl. auch sein Werk *Ancient Jewish Coinage I* (1982), 59. Entsprechend betont Crawford, *CMRR* 252 für die Zeit nach Caesars Tod die fehlende Zirkulation römischer Reichsmünzen in Syrien.

6 Vgl. Crawford, *CMRR* 201f.

7 Ein städteübergreifendes Nominalsystem ist beim *aes* schwer zu erkennen. Das Gewicht der gängigen Kleinbronze schwankt um 7g.

8 *Geschichte des römischen Münzwesens* (1860), 71f.

9 Zuletzt Meshorer, *Festschrift L. Mildenberg* (1984), 172, 175f. u. 178.

10 Dazu knapp: Crawford, *CMRR* 252f.

11 Zur syrischen Prägung unter Augustus vgl. S. Walker, A. Burnett, *Augustus* (BM Occas.Pap. XVI, 1981), 23.

12 Die Buchstaben etc. im Abschnitt sind keine Datierungen, *contra* Crawford, *CMRR* 203.

13 Vgl. die tarsischen Gegenstücke mit AP : *AMC* 1424 mit 1435.

14 Das 'Stuhl'bein hat ab jetzt unten eine dreieckige statt der bisherigen ovalen 'Schwellung', s. Taf. 12.

15 C.M. Kraay, *RN* 1965, 58.

16 So in letzter Zeit auch: M.J. Price, *SNG Fitzwilliam* VIII (1971), 5857; *AMC* 733; Walker-Burnett, *Augustus* Nr. 38; Crawford, *CMRR* 262.

17 Zuletzt Crawford, *CMRR* 266f. m. Abb.118 r.; C.J. Howgego, *NC* 1984, 1ff.

18 *RRC* 533.

19 *RRC* 545f.

20 Zu dem armenischen Fund *IGCH* 1746 vgl. auch *CH* 1 (1975), Nr.105.

21 *RRC* 543/1.

22 Einige Jahrgänge der 50er und 40er Jahre dieser städtischen (!) Bronzen erwähnt Crawford, *CMRR* 203.

23 Crawford, *CMRR* 266: bis 23/2 v.

24 Seyrig, *Syria* 27 (1950), 19: das *aes* 'Dionysoskopf/Thyrsos' erst ab 30/29 v. geprägt.

25 Daneben 9+ Tdr. Seleucia Pieria bis J.15 der Aera von 109 oder 108 v. und 10+ Tdr. Tyros bis J.64 der Stadt = 63/2 v.

26 Alter Name von Berytos: Laodikeia in Phoinikien.

27 Die Drachme mit dem Revers '*aplustre*, *La-The*' (Head 781) scheint ganz am Anfang der Tetradrachmen-Produktion zu stehen.

28 Der Darstellung von J. Kromayer (*Hermes* 29 (1894), 579f.) folgend, halte ich Josephus' Bemerkung, die Schenkung habe den Küstenstreifen vom Eleutheros bis Aegypten - Sidon und Tyros ausgenommen - umfasst (*Ant.Jud.* XV 4,1(95)), für zu salopp formuliert. Wörtlich genommen, impliziert sie Kleopatras Herrschaft auch über die Küstenstädte südlich von Tyros.

29 F. Imhoof-Blumer, *Choix de monnaies grecques du Cabinet de F.I.B.* (Winterthur, 1871).

30 G. Manganaros Darstellung, dass ein epigraphisch überlieferter Brief Oktavians dieser Zeit nach einer *caesarischen* Aera von Rhosos datiert ist (*Sicul. Gymn.* 11 (1958), 290f. Anm.6; Hinweis W. Leschhorn), braucht kein Grund für die Umdatierung genannter Prägung auf ca. 43 v. zu sein. Denn die Textredaktion der Seleukosinschrift erfolgte erst ab 30 v., und auch an anderer Stelle sind Retuschen zu Ungunsten der ehemaligen 'Kollegen' im Amt des Triumvirn nachweisbar. Offenbar hat man die Antoniusära von Rhosos in der ersten Zeit nach Oktavians Machtübernahme durch eine caesarische ersetzt, um später wieder zur Antoniusära zurückzukehren.

31 Statt eines (verschieden gedeuteten) Porträts vielleicht eine Göttin (Astarte ?), da derselbe Kopf schon früher begegnete: vgl. *BMC* CXX Taf.43,9.

32 Dazu 9+ Tdr. Seleukeia P. bis J.15 der Aera von 109 oder 108 v. und 34+ Tdr. Arados bis J.199 der Stadt = 61/60 v.

33 T.V. Buttrey, *Festschrift Ph. Grierson* (1983), 26ff. m. Abb.; zuletzt Crawford, *CMRR* 253f. m. Abb.108 unten.

Meine Karte (auf der Basis von A.H.M. Jones, *The Cities of the Eastern Roman Provinces* (1971), Karte 5 nach S.226; *CAH* IX, 1951, Karte 11 nach S.396 u. 12 nach S.436; E. Kornemann, *Weltgeschichte des Mittelmeerraumes* I (1948), Karte 12 nach S.416; Westermanns *Atlas zur Weltgeschichte* I (1956), 28 Mitte) zeichnete I. Bayer, München.

EGITTO

Alessandra Gara

La conquista augustea dell'Egitto e l'assetto provinciale che ne deriva rappresentano un evento di grande rilievo all'interno della storia di Roma, il cui significato e le cui conseguenze devono ancora essere letti nella globalità delle relazioni biunivoche tra impero e nuova provincia. La valenza dei rapporti creatisi con la conquista e la assimilazione politica dell'Egitto appare chiarita - e illuminante - negli aspetti più propriamente amministrativi della gestione imperiale[1], ma non sembra essere patrimonio comune della storiografia contemporanea, anche se recentemente sono apparsi segnali incoraggianti di una maggior integrazione tra i due ambiti di ricerca, principalemente ad opera degli studiosi del diritto (Modrzejewski) e dei papirologi (Lewis).

Questo problema mi sembra centrale per un'indagine sulle modalità e sugli effetti del mutamento constituzionale avviatosi a Roma dopo la battaglia di Azio. La conquista di Alessandria infatti non solo portava a naturale maturazione una sostanziale sudditanza politica dei Tolemei che si protraeva ormai da molti decenni, ma concludeva la formazione territoriale dell'impero entro un ambito geografico che fino a Traiano non subirà modifiche di rilievo[2].

E questo all'interno di un quadro istituzionale che proprio dopo la conquista dell'Egitto tende a fissare nei fatti e in nuove forme - non solo giuridiche - l'esito dei mutamenti avvenuti durante le guerre civili, in particolare durante lo scontro che aveva visto in posizione antitetica, anche culturalmente, Ottaviano e l'occidente da un lato, Antonio e l'oriente dall'altro.

Niente di meglio dunque par indagare l'impatto della monarchia romana[3] - e non soltanto dell'imperialismo di Roma - sulle strutture di una provincia di nuova formazione e sulla sua organizzazione monetaria, intendendo quest'ultima in una doppia accezione: come espressione della politica finanziaria del nuovo sovrano e come volontà di trasformazione piuttosto che di adesione a modelli preesistenti e di lunga durata.

I

Di che cosa è composta presumibilmente la circolazione monetaria egiziana negli anni immediatamente precedenti la conquista? Di tetradracmi tolemaici, sopratutto di Cleopatra VII ma anche di Tolemeo XII[4], e di monete di bronzo emesse forse in parte da Tolemeo IX[5], ma sopratutto da Cleopatra stessa che riprende, con l'emissione del bronzo, una tradizione poco seguita dai sovrani successivi a Tolemeo VIII.

Cleopatra emette tetradracmi d'argento (da 12,06 a 14,46 gr. circa[6]) in quasi tutti gli anni del suo regno, dal primo al ventiduesimo (51 - 30 a. C.), e in grande abbondanza[7], accompagnati da due emissioni di dracme nel sesto e nell'undicesimo anno[8].

Con un'importante innovazione pero, che consiste nell'abbassamento della lega: il tetradracmo contiene solo il 45,72% di argento, cioè circa gr. 5,76[9]. Il suo valore reale è quindi dimezzato rispetto a quello emesso dal sovrano precedente, Tolemeo XII[10].

Il tipo del tetradracmo è quello tradizionale:

D/testa di Tolemeo Soter, anepigrafa,

R/aquila su fulmine a sinistra, dietro ramo di palma, a sinistra la data (e.g. L A), a destra PA,[11] sopra l'acconciatura di Iside; la leggenda è in corona Ptolemaiou Basileos.

Diverse sono tipologia e titolatura della dracma[12]:

D/busto diademato di Cleopatra con diadema, anepigrafo,

R/come il tetradracmo, ma con la leggenda Kleopatras Basilisses, data (L IA) a sinistra, a destra PA.

Molto interessanti sono pure le emissioni di bronzo, anch'esse abbondantissime[13] ma purtroppo non datate - come avviene per tutto il bronzo tolemaico:

D/busto di Cleopatra, come sulla dracma,

R/aquila su fulmine a sinistra, davanti una cornucopia; la leggenda è ancora Kleopatras Basilisses; nel campo la lettera greca, pi o mu, a seconda dei pesi[14].

La presenza di queste due lettere sulle monete è stata interpretata convincentemente come segno del valore, rispettivamente 80 e 40.

Proprio questa reintroduzione della moneta di bronzo, col segno del valore - un unicum nella tradizione tolemaica, ma che trova significativi riscontri nell'area occidentale (Etruria, Campania e Sicilia, ancor prima che in Roma stessa) - rappresenta, assieme al debasement del tetradracmo, una sostanziale innovazione, se non addirittura una riforma monetaria introdotta dalla regina.

Non a caso, mi sembra, Cleopatra è ricordata come autrice di un trattato su pesi e misure (Hultsch, MSR I, 233 ss.). Se anche essa, come parrebbe accertato, non ne è l'autrice, è pero significativo che la tradizione antica abbia potuto procedere ad una simile attribuzione. Forse proprio nella sua iniziativa in ambito monetario è da ricercare l'origine di una rinomanza così peculiare quale è quella acquisita in campo metrologico.

Più difficile è pero comprendere in che cosa consistesse questa presunta riforma. L'ipotesi oggi accettata è che i segni del valore sui bronzi indichino la loro valutazione in dracme di bronzo (cioè secondo lo standard chalkou). Così i pezzi marcati con pi varrebbero 80 dracme di bronzo, quelli marcati con mu 40.

Nell'Egitto greco-macedone, fin dagli inizi del II secolo a.C., erano apparsi nei papiri due sistemi di computo: quello che definirei 'normale', cioè in tetradracmi, dracme e oboli argyriou (monete reali), e un altro, di origine probabilmente egiziana - lo standard chalkou, appunto che denuncia una *ratio* estremamente variabile con lo standard *argyriou*.

Le conversioni fra i due standards - effettuate prevalentemente per tetradracmi - sono espresse molto frequentemente nei testi, e la *ratio* fra le due dracme (*argyriou* e *chalkou*) che se ne desume, pur estremamente oscillante (da 1 : 200 a 1 : 600), tende ad addensarsi nei papiri del periodo fra la fine del secondo e il primo secolo sui valori di 1:480 - 1:500.[15]

Appare chiaro quindi che la dracma *chalkou* dei papiri è solo moneta di conto, *teorica*, che non ha alcun rapporto di peso o di valore metallico con quella *argyriou*.

Alla luce di questi dati la conclusione sembra obbligata : nella riforma di Cleopatra i pezzi di bronzo marcati *pi* o *mu* (80 o 40 dracme *chalkou*) rappresentano il tentativo di monetare, per la prima volta, una moneta che è il multiplo di una unità di conto, utilizzando la *ratio* più diffusa (1:480), stabilizzandone così il valore a 1 obolo (o mezzo obolo) sullo standard *argyriou*.

L'operazione effettuata sulla moneta di bronzo consisterebbe dunque nel fissare, in modo definitivo, la *ratio* fra i due standards, per impedire le oscillazioni dell'epoca precedente, permettendo in questo modo la circolazione reale del bronzo.

Il tentativo di stabilizzare il valore nominale della moneta divisionaria - sia in termini di valuta d'argento che in termini di unità di conto (le dracme *chalkou*) - ha avuto probabilmente anche l'effetto non secondario di rimonetizzare l'Egitto dopo decenni di emissione quasi esclusiva di tetradracmi, il cui elevato valore doveva aver grandemente ridotto la loro possibilità di circolazione nel paese.

In effetti i documenti dell'ultimo secolo dei Tolemei denunciano una tendenza alla smonetizzazione della *chora* e un ritorno, abbastanza generalizzato, all'antica economia naturale, ammesso che essa sia mai stata profondamente intaccata dall'introduzione della moneta portata e diffusa dai greco-macedoni dopo la conquista.

Di questa riforma dell'ultima Cleopatra non possiamo stabilire la cronologia né individuare gli effetti, ma vi sono due elementi che vanno evidenziati:

1) Non si tratta di una iniziativa transitoria, infatti le emissioni sono abbondantissime.[16]

2) Questi bronzi, nonostante il contemporaneo *debasement* del tetradracmo, constituiscono una monetazione fiduciaria, il che spiegherebbe almeno in parte la loro assenza dai ripostigli.[17]

Infatti la *ratio* metallica *teorica* fra argento e bronzo[18] nella monetazione di Cleopatra sarebbe di circa 1:75, ma il rapporto reale deve essere abbassato per tener conto del fatto che il 50% del tetradracmo (circa gr. 6,90) è formato di bronzo e piombo, ed equivale già di per sé a più di 1/3 del valore metallico del pezzo marcato *pi*. Tenuto conto di questo il rapporto reale si fissa perciò intorno a 1:50.

Elementi di raffronto li abbiamo solo per il terzo secolo a.C.: in P.

Cairo Zen. 59662 la *ratio* fra i due metalli non monetati sembra essere di 1:94 - comprensibile in base all'alto costo dell'argento in Egitto -, mentre, nello stesso periodo, per i metalli monetati è di 1:60.[19]

Molto probabilmente all'epoca di Cleopatra il tesoro avrà accettato il bronzo riformato in pagamento del debito fiscale, praticando un aggio (*allage*) qualora lo ritenesse necessario, come accadeva già nei *Revenue Laws* del Filadelfo. Ma non bisogna dimenticare che una quota sempre più elevata del reddito fiscale è percepita in natura.

II

Questo è il quadro monetario in cui si inserisce l'iniziativa augustea. Un quadro intricato cui fanno da cornice sistemi di computo, rapporti di valore fra i metalli non monetati (in particolare fra oro e argento), modelli di circolazione e un sistema fiscale del tutto peculiari, sostanzialmente estranei all'esperienza romana, anche nella sue gestione provinciale.

Inizialmente il nuovo sovrano segue i modelli instaurati da Cleopatra, ma solo per quanto riguarda il bronzo; infatti per tutta la durata del regno di Augusto (30 a.C.-14 d.C.) la zecca di Alessandria non emetterà una sola moneta d'argento.

La tipologia dei primi bronzi è modificata, rispetto a quella di Cleopatra, solo per il diritto, dove compare la testa di Ottaviano con la leggenda *Theou Yiou* nel campo;[20] a rovescio ancora l'aquila su fulmine, la cornucopia a sinistra, la leggenda in corona *Kaisaros Autokratoros*, a destra il segno del valore, *pi* o *mu*.

La pondometria, pur nell'estrema varietà degli esemplari, resta ancorata al sistema instaurato da Cleopatra.

Dopo il 27 a.C. viene emessa moneta anche a nome di Livia:

D/ busto di Livia, *Liouia Sebastou*.
R/ cornucopie legate da diadema,[21] segno del valore a destra.

Augusto intanto appare ancora sul diritto, ma ormai con l'appellativo *Sebastos*, mentre il rovescio dei suoi bronzi si modifica. Abbandona cioè l'aquila tolemaica per un vaso rituale, ornato da un uraeus e da altri particolari accessori; la leggenda è *Kaisar*.

Il segno del valore è scomparso e l'insieme dei pesi di questa che viene definita la II serie o gruppo da Milne è calante rispetto alla prima con segni del valore.[22]

In questa fase, cronologicamente non definibile, subentra un profondo mutamento sia nella tipologia delle emissioni che nella gamma dei nominali (fino ad allora solo due, marcati *pi* e *mu*).

Assistiamo cioè all'abbandono totale della tipologia tolemaica e all'adozione di tipi diversi, spesso coniugati variamente fra loro, che sembrano costituire un sistema articolato in 4 nominali per questa fase (II gruppo), tutti però senza segno del valore. L'elenco dei tipi del rovescio è dato da Milne nell'*Appendix* del Catalogo dell'Ashmolean Museum (p.

XLIX),[23] e che divide la monetazione in 5 serie complessive[24] che denunciano fin dalla 2ª serie una riduzione dei pesi all'interno del sistema dei nominali.

A partire anzi dal quarto gruppo vi sarebbe - sempre secondo Milne (1927) - un raddoppio del valore facciale delle monete, nel momento in cui i pesi, progressivamente calanti, avrebbero raggiunto la metà circa dei pesi iniziali, mentre i nominali si sareberro ridotti a 3.[25]

Un'ulteriore modifica viene introdotta nel 28° anno 28 del regno di Augusto (3-2 a.C.; Geissen 17): sul rovescio dei bronzi compare la data, allo stesso modo in cui compariva sulla moneta d'argento tolemaica.

Si tratta indubbiamente di una innovazione di rilievo, il cui significato non è però chiaro. Si voleva forse intendere, con la presenza della data sui bronzi augustei, che questa monetazione era considerata equivalente alla valuta d'argento tolemaica, e che non si trattava di pura moneta divisionale?

Questo sembrerebbe impossibile dato l'andamento dei pesi che, con i successivi abbassamenti, hanno decisamente accentuato il carattere fiduciario della moneta di bronzo.

Ma il problema più rilevante è un'altro, ed è quello della identificazione dei nominali.

La maggior parte degli studiosi ha accettato la struttura per nominali proposta da Milne, tranne Geissen che deve aver avvertito la precarietà di una simile classificazione di fronte ad un sistema che non solo denuncia progressivi abbassamenti del peso - e una grande irregolarità nei singoli pezzi -, ma soprattutto, iniziato con i segni del valore sulla moneta, abbandona presto questa pur recente tradizione.

In via del tutto ipotetica penso si possa soltanto proporre un confronto fra la struttura ponderale degli ultimi gruppi e quella del bronzo romano d'epoca augustea. L'ipotesi si basa su un duplice convincimento: 1) i bronzi augustei emessi a partire dal secondo gruppo Milne dalla zecca di Alessandria sono l'esito di una riforma monetaria,2) non conosciamo i criteri ispiratori - dal punto di vista tecnico, e soprattutto pondometrico - della riforma, ma abbiamo la testimonianza per i decenni immediatamente successivi dell'equivalenza <u>teorica</u> fra tetradracmo e denario. <u>Teorica</u> in quanto il denario (e la moneta romana in generale) non può circolare in Egitto.

Perchè non pensare allora ad una pondometria di origine romana per questi bronzi riformati? Una volta abbandonati tipologia e pesi tolemaici, quali modelli potevano essere immediatamente disponibili, culturalmente e politicamente accettabili, per reinventare una monetazione provinciale, se non quelli forniti dal <u>mainstream</u> imperiale?[26]

Ma un altro elemento mi sembra creare ancora difficoltà, ed è un problema per il quale non riesco a formulare nessuna ipotesi.

I tipi usati nella monetazione augustea che definirei post-tolemaica (o post-riforma), cioè a partire dal secondo gruppo Milne, e che si rifanno a motivi generalmente presenti anche nella monetazione romana o provinciale di altre aree, vengono comunemente usati per nominali, o meglio per pesi, totalmente diversi.[27]

Così il tipo Milne 18 (D/Augusto laureato, Pater Patridos; R/ spighe di grano, Sebastos) pesa gr. 5,32; ma in SNG Copenhagen abbiamo lo stesso tipo (nr. 21) battuto su un tondello di gr. 10,19. E ciò accade anche con le monete datate: il tipo Milne 24b (D/testa di Augusto laureata; R/ corona di quercia in cui sta la data 39) pesa gr. 4,39, mentre in SNG Copenhagen 30, pesa gr. 9,63. Così pure il tipo di Livia, con al rovescio l'Atena Nikephoros, dell'anno 42, pesa gr. 4,31 in AMC 824, e gr. 10,60 in Geissen (nr. 45).

La presenza della stessa data su questi ultimi due tipi sembra far escludere che si tratti di un raddoppio del valore facciale della moneta in corso d'anno. Oppure dovremmo pensare a due raddoppi nell'arco di quattro anni soltanto. Ora, come si sarà comportata l'utenza di fronte all'uso di una identica tipologia per nominali apparentemente diversi, distinguibili principalmente in base al peso e solo parzialmente per il modulo?

L'altro problema è quello della possibilità di valutare l'entità di queste emissioni. Non esistono dati quantitativi, e scarse mi sembrano le possibilità di identificare i conii, soprattutto per il cattivo stato di conservazione della maggior parte dei pezzi.

Ma si possono fare alcune considerazioni:

1) La gamma dei tipi utilizzati non è ricchissima, ma abbastanza considerevole. Milne (p. XLIX) elenca almeno 25 tipi principali di rovescio.

2) Gli stessi tipi vengono utilizzati talvolta per quelli che sembrano essere nominali diversi, l'uno doppio dell'altro.

3) Nelle collezioni in cui le monete sono pubblicate con documentazione iconografica si vede chiaramente come uno stesso tipo è spesso prodotto da conii diversi: diverse le dimensioni del tipo principale, diversi i dettagli accessori.

4) Dattari, nel suo catalogo, elenca 73 monete di Augusto, un numero molto elevato rispetto a quante ne attribuisce agli imperatori successivi, ma sappiamo anche che si tratta di una scelta rispetto al materiale da lui esaminato direttamente.

Né molti dati abbiamo sulla tesaurizzazione. Una lettera di Dattari a Milne parla di tre ripostigli di monete di bronzo, ora dispersi, uno dei quali conteneva 3.500 pezzi. Dattari ne avrebbe selezionati alcuni per la sua collezione (Christiansen A7, A8, A77). A lettere dello stesso tenore, conservate a Oxford, si rifanno i nrr. A4, A5, A6, 98, 100, 103, 104, 105 di Christiansen. I dati sicuri si limitano ad un ripostiglio acquistato nel 1935-37 (Christiansen A13)[28] da un commerciante che lo diceva proveniente da Abydos, e alle monete augustee provenienti dagli scavi di Karanis, 16 in tutto.[29]

Resta il fatto che molte collezioni nel mondo posseggono monete alessandrine di Augusto, ma che la maggior parte di esse sono inedite.[30]

Nell'assoluta carenza di dati quantitativi penso però che si possano avanzare alcune supposizioni sulla circolazione di epoca augustea.

Le emissioni di Augusto considerate nel loro complesso - cioè come prima fase di imitazione tolemaica e come fase successiva, riformata, con maggior spettro di nominali - dovettero avere un notevole impatto sulla circolazione.

Innanzi tutto modificarono i metodi di computo determinando la progressiva, ma rapida, scomparsa della contabilità sullo standard chalkou, scomparsa che avviene in modo definitivo entro il regno di Augusto. Nella stessa epoca assistiamo ad una riorganizzazione fiscale che porta ad un incremento delle imposte in denaro rispetto a quelle in natura, e che introduce il metodo dell'adaeratio degli arretrati, che sembra procedura ignota all'epoca tolemaica. C'è anche un abbassamento drastico del tasso di interesse massimo legale che proprio in epoca augustea passa dal 24 al 12%.

Mi sembrano questi indizi del fatto che l'operazione iniziata da Cleopatra col tentativo di ristabilire un bimetallismo valutario argento - bronzo è stata portata a termine da Augusto nella sua istanza fondamentale, quella cioè di arrivare ad una stabilizzazione del corso del rame.

Ma Augusto è andato ben oltre. Con una riforma monetaria di cui sfuggono i meccanismi ha senza dubbio rimonetizzato almeno in parte la chora, affiancando ai tetradracmi tolemaici sempre in corso un sistema articolato di monete divisionarie, totalmente fiduciarie, che potevano - probabilmente con un certo aggio - essere utilizzate nei pagamenti fiscali in luogo dell'argento.

In questa operazione di riforma il dato più significativo dal punto di vista sia finanziario che economico mi sembra la scelta attuata con l'emissione esclusiva del bronzo, che denota la consapevolezza dei problemi della circolazione del paese. Solo nel settimo anno di Tiberio, cioè nel 20-21 d.C., quindi almeno cinquanta anni dopo l'ultima emissione di tetradracmi tolemaici, la zecca di Alessandria riprenderà a coniare moneta d'argento.

Ma significative sono anche le scelte tipologiche attuate dall'amministrazione augustea dopo la riforma;[31] esse indicano il totale abbandono dei tipi tolemaici, e scarso interesse per quelli egiziani (solo Ibis, Euthenia e dettagli secondari), mentre riconducono la moneta alessandrina all'interno del grande mainstream della moneta imperiale romana. Nessuna continuità in questo senso, nessuna ambiguità in campo monetario: l'Egitto è provincia romana.

NOTE

Per la bibliografia generale papirologica, come per i rapporti fra circolazione monetaria e sistemi di computo, si veda A. Gara, 'Continuità e trasformazione nella politica monetaria di Augusto', Atti del XVII Congresso internazionale di Papirologia (Napoli, 1984), 1007 ss.

Nel testo ho usato le seguenti abbreviazioni (cf. anche la bibliografia generale, p. viii): BMC Ptol.: R.S. Poole, Catal. British Museum, Ptolemies, (London, 1882).

Boston: A.B. Brett, Museum of Fine Arts - Boston, Catal. of Greek Coins (New York, 1974).

Christiansen: E. Christiansen, The Roman Coins of Alexandria 30 B.C. to A.D.296: An Inventory of Hoards, CH VII, 77 ss.

Dattari: G. Dattari, Nummi Augusti Alexandrini (Cairo, 1901).

Geissen: A. Geissen, Katalog Alexandrinischer Kaisermünzen der Universität zu Köln, I (Opladen, 1974).

Milne: J.G. Milne, Catal. of Alexandrian Coins, Ashmolean Museum, (Oxford, 1933, reprint, 1971).

Milne 1927: J.G. Milne, 'The Alexandrian Coinage of Augustus', JEA XIII, (1927), 135-140.

1. P.A. Brunt, 'The Revenues of Rome', JRS LXXI (1981), 161-72; G. Urögdy, in Oikoumene (Budapest, 1976), 157-71.

2. Z. Yavetz, in Caesar Augustus, Seven Aspects, ed. F. Millar, E. Segal (Oxford, 1984), 9 ss.

3. F. Millar, in op. cit. (n. 2), 37 ss.

4. IGCH 1721 e ss.

5. Ma che sembrano essere tesaurizzate solo negli anni 80, v. IGCH 1715-1717.

6. SNG Copenhagen, Ptolemies.

7. A detta di Svoronos, col. 466; v. anche O. Morkholm, 'Ptolemaic coins and chronology', ANSMN 20 (1975), 7-24.

8. Svoronos, ibid.; Boston 2303, Morkholm, ibid.

9. Walker, Metrology 139 ss.; per R.A. Hazzard, I.D. Brown, 'The Silver Standard of the Ptolemaic Coinage', RN 1984, 234, i tetradracmi di Cleopatra contengono soltanto 1/3 di argento.

10. Che contiene una media di gr. 11,46 di argento (Walker, ibid.).

11. Per la sigla di Paphos su monete di produzione alessandrina si vedano I. Nicolau, O. Morkholm, Paphos I, A Ptolemaic Coin Hoard (Nicosia,

1976). Per trovare precedenti alla presenza della titolatura della regina sulla moneta tolemaica bisogna risalire ai bronzi di Cleopatra I (180-170 a.C., SNG Copenhagen 273, 277) o all'argento non datato e al bronzo di Berenice II (246-221 a.C.).

12. Per. es.: Boston 2303; il peso di questo esemplare è di gr. 3,23.

13. Svoronos, coll. 470-1; H.R. Baldus, 'Ein neues Spätporträt der Kleopatra aus Orthosia', JNG 1973, 24.

14. Questi pesi nella SNG Copenhagen vanno da 15,86 a 18,61 grammi per gli esemplari marcati pi, da 8,85 a 9,56 per quelli marcati mu.

15. A. Gara, Limiti strutturali dell'economia monetaria nell'Egitto tardo-tolemaico, Studi ellenistici (Pisa, 1984), I, 107 ss.

16. V. n. 13.

17. I ripostigli ritrovati sono pochi per questo periodo (4: IGCH 1722-1725), e in essi, ad eccezione di un caso (IGCH 1724), la moneta debased di Cleopatra si trova associata ai tetradracmi 'buoni' dei sovrani precedenti. E' forse questa presenza di una moneta debased di argento, apparentemente scambiabile alla pari con la moneta 'buona', a scoraggiare la tesaurizzazione del bronzo.

18. Difficile è definire gli standards teorici data la grande oscillazione nei pesi degli esemplari pubblicati e il loro cattivo stato di conservazione.

19. Cl. Préaux, L'Economie royale des Lagides (Bruxelles, 1939), 277. Nel mondo ellenistico in generale la ratio è di 1:120 (Crawford, RRC, 626, n.7); a Roma, sotto Augusto, la ratio AR:CU è 1:55 (M.H. Crawford, CMRR 59, n. 19).

20. Fino al 27 a.C., presumabilmente; poi viene sostituita da Sebastos.

21. La doppia cornucopia era già comparsa a R/ di una emissione cipriota di Cleopatra (Svoronos 1874; BMC Ptol., p. 122 nn. 2 e 3), in cui la regina è ritratta al D/ come Afrodite-Iside con Cesarione come Eros.

22. Riporto, per comodità, la distribuzione in gruppi di Milne 1927, 139 (cfr. anche Geissen):

	Size 1	Size 2	Size 3	Size 4
1st group	17,2	8,3		
2nd group	13,2	6,4	3,5	0,9
3rd group	8,3		2,5	
4th group	10,7	5,6	3,1	
6th group	9,0	4,2	1,9	

23. Sui nominali più piccoli la testa di Augusto al D/ è talvolta sostituita da tipi aniconici, utilizzati anche per il R/ di altre monete.

24. O piuttosto 6 (v. n. 22), ma con una 5ª serie non identificabile (Milne 1927, 139). A partire dalla 3ª serie la testa di Augusto è laureata. E. Christiansen (SNG Copenhagen, Alexandria) non sembra accettare questa divisione in serie, che è comunque insoddisfacente.

25. Per Milne 1927 diobolo, obolo e mezzo obolo. Fino a questo punto la cronologia delle emissioni appare molto incerta. Gli elementi utili come terminus post quem, adottati concordemente dagli studiosi, sono molto ridotti:

1) il tempio di Mars Ultor, post 20 a.C. (Milne secondo gruppo).
2) la testa di Gaio Cesare, che per Milne, 1927, non puo comparire prima dell'8 a.C. (Milne terzo gruppo).
3) il titolo Pater Patridos, post 2 a.C. (Milne quarto gruppo).
Gli strumenti sacerdotali (Milne secondo gruppo) potrebbero forse essere riferimento al pontificato massimo di Augusto (12 a.C.).

26. In base a queste considerazioni i gruppi 4 - 6 (Milne 1927) portrebbero essere cosi identificati:
il pezzo da gr. 10 = 1 obolo 1/2 Milne si riporterebbe al peso dell'asse;
il pezzo da gr. 5 = 3/4 obolo Milne (6 chalki) si riporterebbe al semisse;
il pezzo da gr. 2,5 = 3 chalki Milne si riporterebbe al quadrante.
Applicando a ritroso questo schema di valutazione ai bronzi emessi prima della riforma, il pezzo di tipo tolemaico con pi (circa gr. 18) sarebbe valutato a 3 oboli; quello con mu (circa gr. 10) a 1 obolo 1/2. Se, come ritiene Milne 1927, 139, a partire dal quarto gruppo si fosse verificato un raddoppio del valore nominale delle monete in circolazione, il risultato sarebbe stato il seguente:
pi = 6 oboli = 1 dracma,
mu e pezzo da gr. 10 = 3 oboli,
pezzo da gr. 5 = 1 obolo 1/2,
pezzo da gr. 2,5 = 3/4 obolo (6 chalki).
L'esistenza di una moneta da 6 oboli (dracma) potrebbe giustificare la menzione frequentissima di 'dracme d'argento' nei papiri di epoca augustea in quantità inferiore ad un tetradracmo. Spiegherebbe anche le dracmas augustas et ptolemaicas date in prestito alla pari in P. Vindob. Lat. 135 del 27 d.C. (D. Foraboschi, Minima Papyrologica, in P. Rainer Cent., Wien 1983, 101), se il termine augustas non si riferisce ai nuovi tetradracmi di Tiberio.

27. Molto più ridotta è la differenza dei moduli.

28. 16 bronzi di Cleopatra VII e 55 di Augusto.

29. R.R. Haatvedt, E.E. Peterson in Coins from Karanis, ed. E.M. Husselman, (Ann Arbor, 1964), nrr. 53-63, probabilmente dal ripostiglio 1 non descritto.

30. Devo queste informazioni, come molte anticipazioni sui ripostigli di epoca augustea, all'amico Christiansen.

31. Cioè a partire dal secondo gruppo Milne col tempio di Mars Ultor.

CRETE AND CYRENAICA

T.V. Buttrey

Roman coinage in Crete and Cyrenaica[1] during the first century BC must be viewed in the context of the already existing circulation. In addition there is the problem of political organisation: at what periods were Crete and Cyrenaica united to form a single Roman province; and to what extent was the organisation reflected in the coinage? To begin, the two areas were acquired by the Roman Republic at different times, and it is useful to take them in order.

CYRENAICA (1)

Cyrenaica came under Roman rule, technically, in 96 BC on the death of Ptolemy Apion, who bequeathed it to the Republic, but for the next twenty years the Romans gave little thought to claiming and organising it. The coinage in use at that time was simply the third and second century BC products of the mint of Cyrene. There are no hoards after the third century BC, but the excavation finds, admittedly almost entirely of bronze, indicate that local circulation included very little foreign material. As to the Cyrenaican coinages, no gold was struck after Ptolemy I, 305-285 BC, nor silver after the revolt of Magas, 277-261 BC. But such pieces must still have been in circulation in the first century BC, as is shown by the frequent discovery of third century silver in a very worn state. Bronze coinage, however, appears to have been issued in a regular stream to the end of Ptolemaic domination of the area in 96 BC.

The last Ptolemaic coinages struck in Cyrenaica were almost certainly struck at Cyrene alone, bronzes, mostly of small module (10-15mm), with reverses of Libya, eagle, or Isiac headdress, of ever more regrettable style and fabric. Their denomination is unknown. The Libya issues are obviously Cyrenaican, but the attribution of the others, and their extent, was for long not appreciated: the eagle and Isiac headdress issues were traditionally attributed to Egypt[2]. However, they are quite unlike the Egyptian issues in crudity of style and fabric, and they have been found in great abundance in Cyrenaica[3].

Unfortunately there is no possibility of establishing their date with any exactitude. Robinson applies a global date, 140-96 BC, from Ptolemy VII to the death of Ptolemy Apion. That these are the latest coinages of Ptolemaic type is certain: the continuous decline of style and weight, and the growing carelessness in the fabric, guarantee as much. These are the coins which the Romans would have found to be the small change in circulation at the time of their acquisition of Cyrenaica. So abundant were they that they continued to circulate into Imperial times, and in the Demeter Sanctuary excavation at Cyrene they occur in strata datable as late as the third century AD.

For the first twenty years after the death of Apion, until the province was finally organized in 75, no coinage was struck by the virtually autonomous cities of Cyrenaica which can be recognised today (although it is conceivable that the dreadful small Ptolemaic bronzes continued to be struck into the Roman period - there is no evidence one way or the other, only a natural disinclination to believe in such a possiblity). And even after the creation of the province, no coinage was struck immediately, for the earliest coinage for Roman Cyrenaica already recognises the Roman possession of Crete - i.e., it must fall after 67 BC.

CRETE (I)

The state of the currency in the first century BC is suggested by four hoards which date to the first two decades of the century.

IGCH 330 Axus early 1st cent. BC
small silver of the Greek mainland, especially Achaean League, and of Rhodes
bronze of Axus and six other Cretan cities

IGCH 331 Crete 90-80 BC
Athens, New Style tetradrachms

IGCH 332 Limani-Chersonisou 90-80 BC (Le Rider, Thompson) [75-70 BC (Lewis)]
Lysimachus, posthumous tetradrachms
Athens, New Style tetradrachms
Cretan civic tetradrachms
Mithradates VI, tetradrachm
Nicomedes IV, tetradrachms
Tenedos, tetradrachm

IGCH 338 Gortyna 87-85 BC?
Rhodian imitation drachms
Gortyna, drachms

The picture provided by the hoards does not change much after the conquest of 67 BC. Two are attributed to the remainder of the century:

IGCH 350 Crete 65-60 BC (Raven)
Cretan civic silver, from hemidrachms to tetradrachms

IGCH 352 Hierapytna 44-42 BC (Raven)
Athens, New Style tetradrachms, drachm
Achaean League, triobol
Cretan civic silver, from drachms to tetradrachms
Cistophori
Roman Republic, denarii

Thus silver circulated aplenty on the island in the first century, deriving from Athens, Asia Minor, and the Cretan mints themselves, but not from Rome. Even the apparent breakthrough in the second half of the century is misleading: what is striking in the Hierapytna deposit is the number and chronological extent of the denarii, 200+ pieces beginning as early as the anonymous issue with Victory in biga, 157-156 BC (RRC 197), and running down to Mn Cordius Rufus, 46 BC (RRC 463). This is in sharp contrast to the other first century BC Cretan hoards, which indeed contain not a single Republican denarius. Raven dated the burial of the Hierapytna hoard rather arbitrarily to 44-42 BC to accommodate it to the occasion of the island's capture for Brutus by Lepidus;[4] but he saw that the denarius of Cordius Rufus is actually adjunct to the main body of denarii which end c. 49 BC. He must be right in suggesting that these were coins brought to Crete by mercenaries after Pharsalus in 48 BC or by Pompey's veterans settled in Crete.[5] They do not then indicate denarius circulation in Crete at this time, or prior to this time. This suggestion is consonant with the complete absence of denarii in the earlier hoards, and with the results of the current excavations at Cnossos (see below).

Crete contrasts with Greece proper, where a number of hoards of the second and first centuries BC include Roman Republican denarii, and in sufficient quantity to make their circulation there very likely. A few sporadic finds of Roman coins can be dated to the first three-quarters of the second century BC. Then the great Agrinion hoard (IGCH 271 = RRCH 158) appears, already including 39 denarii, ending with Q Pilipus, 129 BC (RRC 259). Finally, the hoard from Naupactus (IGCH 317) ends with Mn Aemilius Lepidus, 114-113 BC (RRC 291).

In the first century BC IGCH 346 = RRCH 228 contains c. 50 denarii, along with Athenian New Style tetradrachms, the denarii running down to L Titurius Sabinus, 89 BC (RRC 344); RRCH 242 from Peiraeus, 42 denarii down to Gal, Ogul, Ver, 86 BC (RRC 350A); IGCH 653 = RRCH 283 from Kerassia, 47 denarii down to L Caesi Q f, 78 BC (RRC 386); IGCH 660 = RRCH 336 from Kavalla, 59 denarii down to M Scaur, P Hypsaeus, 58 BC (RRC 422) - and so on, with later substantial hoards from Delos and the mainland extending to Antony's legionary denarii (RRCH 465, 467, 473).

Thus on the mainland and the islands Roman denarii appear to have circulated in quantity during the first century BC, even as the Athenian New Style tetradrachms continued to be struck. The tetradrachms percolated into Crete (and must have circulated there vigorously, as their imitation by six different Cretan cities shows), but the denarii did not. Nor did Cretan silver penetrate the other circulation area; it is wanting in all the first century BC hoards from Greece and the islands (IGCH 319-353). In these regards the silver usage of the two areas was quite distinct.

But the lack of Roman coin in Crete does not mean that Rome had no impact on the Cretan coinage after the conquest by Metellus in 67 BC. The mint at Gortyna continued to strike, issuing a tetradrachm of New Style weight and fabric, but with types Roma/Artemis Ephesia and the elephant head symbol of Metellus. Roman domination did not put an end to local silver coinage in the traditional Greek denomination; but new types reflected the new political situation. And when the late cistophoric tetradrachm of Kydas was struck (for Kydas, see below), it was "in fact a Roman provincial issue"[6].

CRETE AND CYRENAICA

The earliest coinage by Romans assignable to either area implies their possession of the other. No silver or gold was struck in the name of Rome in the new double province. But there was a sporadic coinage of new issues in bronze, in addition to, rather than in lieu of, the already circulating medium. To retire the Ptolemaic or the Cretan small change would have required a massive recoinage, impractical even if desirable. Rather, the Romans added to these a coinage of their own. Two issues were struck in non-Roman modules which in their types or legends purported to serve both

Crete and Cyrenaica; two others initiated a sporadic series of bronzes struck to a Roman standard which thereafter were continued in Cyrenaica but not in Crete.

The first of these four issues bears the types Roma head/bee (BMCCyrenaica pp. ccii-cciii, 1b-f; p.113, 1), and apparently the legends ROMI [= ROME] or KRET/KYRA. In spite of the reverse legend, both types are characteristically Cretan. The Roma head appears on the Gortyna tetradrachm mentioned above; the bee is found as the reverse type of a number of coinages of small silver and bronze. Especially noticeable is the silver issue of Elyros (Svoronos, Crete 1-6), struck from dies smaller than the flans, so as to produce a raised edge around the reverse, just as on the bronzes of Crete and Cyrenaica. The Roma/bee bronze issue cannot be dated, except that it must fall after 67 BC and before the 40s, to which are attributed the coins of Lollius below.

The second Roman issue (if it is the second) is even more mysterious. A single issue of the first century BC reads fully KRETE and KYRENE, referring explicitly to the two areas together. On this rare bronze of small module the Roman magistrates P Licinius and a man whose name has been read as P Lepidius sign in Latin; they are unknown, and the piece cannot be dated.[7]

The third and fourth issues, signed by Lollius and Crassus respectively, were struck to a module new for Cyrenaica, and perhaps for Crete, fitting Roman weight standards and denominations even though the types were local. Each issue is double, in including separate Latin and Greek series. Robinson recognised that the discrete Latin and Greek issues must have been produced simultaneously for Crete and Cyrene respectively, though their legends do not say so. That of Lollius reveals central control in the co-ordination of balanced but distinct Cretan and Cyrenaican types and the use of a common engraver. Variation in fabric and die position show that actual production of the coins took place at two different loci, presumably Cnossos and Cyrene.

Lollius, like the other Roman magistrates holding office in Cyrenaica, is otherwise unknown, and no date can be put to him. Obviously he struck after the conquest of Crete in 67 BC. But his coinage is difficult to understand even so early, given its weight standard. I have argued that we should accept neither Müller's nor Robinson's view, who held, respectively, that Lollius's unit was a semuncial dupondius or a quartuncial sestertius. The former would accommodate it to the semuncial reform of c. 91 BC; the latter, to the 'Fleet coinage' of Antony. But no bronze was produced to the semuncial standard after c. 84 BC (RRC 355), and there is no evident connection of Lollius's issue nor of Cyrenaica with the Fleet bronze.[8] Rather, it can be shown from the persistence of denominational types that Lollius's unit makes a good as of the uncial standard, and its fractions correspond to the uncial semis and quadrans.[9] They would have circulated along with the abundant Ptolemaic bronzes, these perhaps valued as unciae or sextantes. Now uncial bronze had not been authorised at Rome after the late 90s BC, but there was a reversion to it c. 44-38 in the great numismatic war between Sextus Pompey and Octavian. Each struck large quantities of uncial asses, the former in Sicily with Janus head of Pompeius Magnus (RRC 479)[10], the latter probably in Italy with heads of himself and Caesar (RRC 535). It is now, in the late 40s and early 30s BC that this mass of uncial asses appears, to circulate not only in their area of issue but throughout the west. Lollius's issue might best be considered their contemporary - which is to say that the Romans provided no local coinage specifically for Cyrenaica for the first half-century after they took nominal control of the area.

Crassus, unlike Lollius, employed a persistent type on his asses in both areas, the crocodile. Yet on present evidence it appears that there was no attempt to produce parallel denominations in the two series. Both style and fabric suggest that Crassus's two issues were quite separately undertaken, and he used three mints, Knossos, Cyrene and Ptolemais, the last otherwise unattested in the history of Cyrenaican coinages.[11] But the common type, and the fact of there being simultaneous Latin and Greek series, again points to an overall command of both areas even though the coinages produced for them were distinct.

The identification of Crassus is quite uncertain. His coinage should be subsequent to Lollius's since it is struck to the semuncial standard, as is that of Pupius Rufus and of Antony and Cleopatra. If his crocodile type does in fact refer to Egyptian domination, then of course the coins must precede Cleopatra's loss of the province after Actium; more specifically, Grant has suggested that they could fall between the acquisition of the joint province by Cleopatra in 37 BC and the gift of Cyrenaica alone to Cleopatra Selene in 34.[12]

No other coins can surely be attributed to the united province of Crete-and-Cyrene; that is, none of the remaining issues was evidently struck for or used in both areas. Of course the coins need not reflect the political organisation, but it seems safest to consider the remaining issues separately.

CYRENAICA (II)

According to Robinson, the joint coinage ceased after Actium. In fact it stopped earlier than that. There is the Greek issue of semuncial asses and semisses of Antony and Cleopatra, 31 BC (Sv. 1899-1900), intended only for Cyrenaica; the coins of Pupius Rufus, which also occur in only a Greek series, are probably earlier still. After 31 BC there was a gap of a few years until three issues were struck in the name of Augustus, imitative of his reformed <u>aes</u> at Rome; then after a gap of several decades, one issue of Tiberius, post 19 AD.

None of these issues made a large impact. In the absence of hoards in Cyrenaica the best evidence for their general sparsity is provided by the excavations. At Apollonia, the port of Cyrene, the finds of the fifth century BC to the first century AD are nearly all Greek Cyrenaican:[13]

Sicily	1
Greece, Syria, Phoenicia, 5th cent. BC	3
Egypt, 3rd-1st cent. BC	2
Cyrene, 5th cent. BC-Ptolemy VII	37
Ptolemy VII-Ptolemy Apion	56
Roman Cyrenaica, Republic-Augustus	2
Tiberius	1
Roman Republican (halved as)	1

The late Ptolemaic coins heavily outnumber the Roman Cyrenaican. (As is characteristic of the several site finds, non-Cyrenaican coin is very uncommon). It might be objected that this is not a hoard, and that many of the Ptolemaic pieces could represent pre-Roman losses. But as indicated above, these issues flooded the local currency, continuing to circulate into Imperial times. At any given moment their numbers must have been much greater than those of the Roman Cyrenaican issues. Coins of the mint of Rome were also relatively uncommon at Apollonia in imperial times: from the first to the third century AD, 8 pieces. Yet the epigraphical evidence shows that the city was thriving under the Empire.

Similarly at Cyrene, the excavations in the Sanctuary of Demeter, currently in course of publication, have produced the following tentative results:

Egypt, Cleopatra VII	1
Augustus	3
Cyrene, 5th cent. - Ptolemy VII	c. 200
Cyrene, Ptolemy VII - Ptolemy Apion	354
Roman Cyrenaica	5
Roman Republican, plated denarius	1
Roman Imperial, 1st cent.	1
2nd cent.	6
3rd cent.	5

Finally, the coins brought back from Cyrenaica by Norton paint the same picture with regard to the relative scarcity of the Roman Cyrenaican issues:[14]

Egypt, 3rd-1st cent. BC	2
Cyrene, 4th cent. to Ptolemy VII	181
Ptolemy VII - Ptolemy Apion	176
Roman Cyrenaica, Republic - Augustus	4
Tiberius	1

With the bronzes in the name of Tiberius the Roman coinages of Cyrenaica stop completely until the 2nd century AD.

Add to the bronzes the denarii struck by Pinarius Scarpus in 31 BC in the name of Antony and Octavian (RRC 546). These come suddenly on the scene, and are plainly military issues struck for the occasion. For this reason they are included in Crawford as simply Roman Republican issues, and excluded from BMCCyrenaica as not germane. While their types are in part local, viz. the obverse head of Zeus Ammon, it is not unusual for Roman military issues to bear local types; and there is no reason to suppose that they played a regular role in local circulation. Admittedly there are no hoards as evidence one way or the other, and the excavation coins are almost entirely of bronze. But I am disinclined to take the issues of Scarpus as evidence that "the denarii had already become a staple currency in Cyrenaica" (Price, p. 121), especially in view of the likelihood that such was not the case in Crete.

CRETE (II)

The joint Cretan and Cyrenaican coinages of Lollius and Cassius were followed in Crete by the bronzes and rare cistophoric tetradrachms of Kydas the Cretarch (Sv. Cnossos 142-151, Province 1). Some have taken Kydas to be the friend of Antony whom we find in Cicero Phil. 5.5.13; though Perl doubts that the bronze and the silver were struck by the same official (pp. 346-349). In any case the period is right for the bronze since some examples are overstruck on the as of Crassus. And these are not the last such bronzes struck at Knossos. Chapman[15] identified two more issues of the same types but in the names of different moneyers, issues which must follow that of Kydas.

Thus Lollius, Crassus, and at least three Knossian officials all struck in fairly close succession during the period late-40s to (probably) late-30s BC. Three other Knossian officials also signed similar large bronze. While they cannot be precisely dated, Chapman has shown that two of them have a close stylistic connection with Lollius[16]. Perhaps therefore the civic issues, with some traditional types and Greek legends, and the provincial issues, with some new types and legends in Latin, were parallel rather than serial. The overstrike of Kydas on Crassus shows that his bronze, and therefore that of the other officials who produced the same modules and types, is equivalent to the Roman as and semis. Here again is accommodation to the Roman system of coinage without the imposition of Roman types, legends or stated denominations.

After these Roman or Roman-like issues come small bronzes of the Roman colony of Knossos (BMCCrete 72-77). Perl believes the colony to have been founded only after Actium; Sanders, only after 27 BC, taking the coin with plough and AVG as a deductio issue.[17] Therefore the unnamed portraits of BMCCrete 72-73 cannot be Antony and Octavian, or Lepidus and Octavian, as suggested by Svoronos (Sv. 180). They are possibly Augustus and Agrippa, as Robinson suggested[18].

The evidence of the finds in Crete is comparable to that from Cyrenaica. The excavations of the Sanctuary of Demeter in Knossos included[19]

Crete, 4th cent.- 68 BC	85
Roman Crete, Lollius	4
Knossos, asses of Kydas	8
municipal bronzes of [the triumvirate and] Augustus	9
Tiberius - Nero	6
Crete as Province, Claudius-Antoninus Pius	7
Roman Republican, as	1
Roman Imperial, 1st-3rd cent.	none

Here too there was no deliberate importation of Roman coin, but the bronzes of Kydas were equivalent to the Roman as, and the municipal bronzes were perhaps used as Roman semisses or quadrantes. Even in imperial times properly Roman coin was not imported. Coldstream speaks of "a remarkable revival of the [Demeter] cult during the first two centuries of the Roman Empire" and reports that the votive offerings from this period "include a large number of coins".[20] They were not Roman coins.

Most recently the excavations of the 'Unexplored Mansion' at Knossos have produced comparable figures, as Martin Price has kindly informed me:

Crete, 4th cent.- 68 BC	65
Roman Crete, Lollius	3
Crassus	1
Knossos, Kydas	9
other named issues	7
municipal bronzes of Augustus	9
Tiberius - Nero	18
Crete as Province, Claudius - Antoninus Pius	16
Roman Republican	2
Roman Imperial 1st cent AD	1
Hadrian to Gallienus	9

In the first century BC Crete is even less productive of Roman provincial coinage than Cyrenaica. Contrary to the Cyrenaican case, there was no overtly Roman coinage at all intended specifically for Crete after the double issues of Lollius and of Crassus. Rather, a number of bronzes were signed by Greek officials, then smaller module municipal issues began under Augustus at Cnossos (Sv. 180-195) and Cydonia (Sv. 94-108), and finally coinage of the Koinon was instituted from Caligula onwards.

Conclusion

The numismatic evidence for the chronology of the joint or separate provinces is indecisive.[21] The Roma/bee issue combines Cretan types with the legend ROMI or KRET/KYRA; the issue of Licinius/Lepidius bears the names of both areas; Lollius and Crassus strike parallel series for the two areas. But this is of little help in the absence of dates for any of the Cretan and Cyrenaican issues. And while no other joint coinage was produced, from which one might conclude that at no other time of striking was there a joint province, the very division between the Cretan and Cyrenaican varieties of Lollius and Crassus makes it conceivable that, e.g., Pupius Rufus coined for one area of the joint province and not the other. In short, the coins are not reliable evidence for the solution of the political problem.

The survey shows that in any case there was little Roman intervention in the coinages of Crete and Cyrenaica. In each area there must have been a full circulating medium already available on the occasion of Roman possession, to which nothing was added from Rome. In Cyrenaica Roman coins seem not to have been used; so too in Crete, in spite of the Hierapytna hoard, which cannot represent a general permeation of the currency with Roman denarii. Rather, the Romans used what was already available, struck in addition sporadic issues of bronze with types locally appropriate, and only occasionally and irregularly imported their own coin. None of the local issues was of spectacular size or importance in the general currency, although there is clear evidence of their adaptation to the Roman denominational system. To that extent the Roman could be confident that he was using the equivalent of Roman coin. But otherwise this survey supports the general thesis of Gruen's recent work, which argues that Roman intervention in the Greek world was largely unplanned and even diffident.[22]

NOTES

1. Two recent articles have discussed the development of coinage in Crete and Cyrenaica during the early Roman period. This survey draws extensively on them, and the reader should repair to them for the arguments whose results are simply asserted here: M. Price, 'Crete, Cyrene, and Dio LII.30.9', Israel Numismatic Journal 6-7 (1982-3), 118-127; T.V. Buttrey, 'The Roman coinage of the Cyrenaica, first century BC to the first century AD', Studies in Numismatic Method presented to Philip Grierson edd. C.N.L. Brooke et al. (Cambridge 1983), 23-42. On the history of Crete and Cyrenaica in the first century BC, see S.I.Oost, 'Cyrene, 96-74 BC', CPh 58 (1963), 11-25; G. Perl, 'Die römischen Provinzbeamten in Cyrenae und Creta zur Zeit der Republik', Klio 52 (1970), 319-354; 53 (1971), 369-379.

2. Svoronos, nos. 1646-1647, 1651-1652, 1655-1656, 1715-1716, 1717-1724, 1732-1733, 1845; and not included in E.S.G. Robinson, BMCCyrenaica.

3. T.V. Buttrey, 'The Coins', in Apollonia, The port of Cyrene. Excavations by the University of Michigan, 1965-1967 ed. J.H. Humphrey (Tripoli, 1976) 345-346, 31 pieces; excavated or purchased by Norton at Cyrene, reported in Apollonia 366-367, 125 pieces; excavated by the University of Pennsylvania in the Demeter Sanctuary at Cyrene, to be published, several hundred pieces; noted by E.S.G. Robinson, 'Greek coins found in the Cyrenaica', NC 1944, 105-113, over 40 pieces.

4. The latest study of the New Style component of the hoard places the last of these tetradrachms in the late 40s BC: M Caramessini-Oeconomides and F.S. Kleiner, 'The Hierapytna Hoard. A Supplement', RBN 121 (1975), 1-19.

5. E.J.P. Raven, 'The Hierapytna Hoard of Greek and Roman Coins', NC 1938, 133-158.

6. Metellus: J. Svoronos, Numismatique de la Crete ancienne (Macon, 1890), 190-191. For Kydas, see Price (n.1.) p. 120 and A.M. Rouanet-Liesenfelt in Mélanges H. van Effenterre (Paris, 1984), 343.

7. Price p. 119 and n. 5 corrects Grant's reading of LEPIDVS to LEPIDIVS, thus countering the proposed attribution of the issue to the Lepidus who conquered the island for Brutus, and so to 42 BC.

8. Robinson believed he could see Antony's features in the beardless head of Lollius's Latin unit (p.ccxv), a dubious notion. I doubted, op. cit. (n.1.), 33, that Antony's Fleet bronze were ever even found in Cyrenaica, but that is wrong: a deliberately cut quarter of a Fleet sestertius is in the ANS, from the collection of Richard Norton who brought back a large variety of numismatic material from Cyrene. Cf. the catalogue of Norton coins included in Apollonia (note 3 above), 361-370, which does not include this piece, then unknown to me. But it is still the case that the Fleet bronze is not assignable to Cyrenaica, and that Lollius's issues are quite unlike it in type, style and fabric.

9. Buttrey (see note 1 above), 33-36.

10. Crawford's division of good style and poor style between mints of Spain and Sicily (p. 94) is not supported by the extensive finds of this type at Morgantina, where the two styles occur in about equal number.

11. The one possible exception is Svoronos 859 = BMCCyrenaica p.cxlv, 47b, a Soter/Libya bronze which Robinson takes to carry the Ptolemais mintmark (p.clix).

12. Grant, FITA 55-56. Contra, A.E. Chapman, 'Some First Century BC Bronze Coins of Knossos', NC 1968, esp. p.14. This is all very uncertain.

13. Apollonia (see note 3 above), 342-346.

14. Apollonia (see note 3 above), 361-370.

15. Op. cit. (n.12), 23.

16. Op. cit. 18.

17. I.F.Sanders, Roman Crete (Warminster, 1982), 14.

18. BMC ccix, fn. 2, followed by Anne Jackson, 'The Coins', in J. N. Coldstream, Knossos. The Sanctuary of Demeter (= BSA Suppl. vol. 8, 1973), 102, nos. 94-99).

19. From Jackson (see note 16 above), 99-106.

20. Op. cit. (n.18), 10-11 and 186.

21. However Perl (353-354) is too strict in narrowing the evidence for the joint province to 40-34 BC and post-27. Whatever the date of the Roma/bee issue, its fabric is surely earlier than 40 BC.

22. E. Gruen, The Hellenistic World and the Coming of Rome (Berkeley, 1984).

AFRICA

Andrew Burnett

The defeat of Hannibal at the battle of Zama brought to an end the confusing variety of coinages minted by Carthage in the western Mediterranean. All the coinages of the Hannibalic War and earlier seem to have been demonetised, and were taken out of circulation and melted down. Thereafter Punic coinage was confined to the mint of Carthage, although there is some uncertainty about its chronology and extent.

The main reason for this uncertainty lies in the position of the so-called El Djem coinage of debased silver or billon coins, whose chronology has been confused by Robinson's view that one of the Punic coins of Spain was struck over an El Djem coin;[1] the consequence of this view was to put the El Djem coins, together with their associated gold and bronze issues, in the period between the First and Second Punic Wars.[2] Robinson's interpretation of the overstrike, however, does not seem to be accepted nowadays, and hence the El Djem coinage has been freed from an earlier date, and dated to the very end of the Second Punic War, or indeed later,[3] and a date of around 200 BC has been suggested for the corresponding bronze issues by Baldus,[4] who based his view on the very worn condition of the bronzes in the destruction layers of Carthage. On the basis of this chronology one can then associate the El Djem coinage with Livy's report that the Roman quaestors were dissatisfied with the quality of the silver being paid by Carthage as a war indemnity.[5] One can think either that the indemnity was paid in debased coin, of the El Djem type, or alternatively that the connection between Livy's report and the debased coinage is only indirect: the poor quality of the coinage and of the indemnity silver (perhaps paid in bullion) are independent reflections of Cathage's impoverished state, which can also be seen in the very small size of the corresponding gold issues (only four obverse dies)[6] and in the need to supplement the precious metal coins with extremely large bronze ones (averaging some 100 grams).[7]

The other main group of coinage minted by Carthage before her destruction in 146 consists of pure gold,[8] pure silver,[9] and bronze coins[10] of various denominations. Many of these have peculiar serrated edges, an artistic fashion which occurs also in Macedonia and Syria at about the same time.[11] Again, the questions of date and size of issue arise. Despite the numerous variety of control symbols and letters which occur on the reverses, each denomination was struck from only a single obverse die,[12] so that we can be fairly sure that the coinage was on a very small scale and minted for only a short period. Although Baldus has suggested a date early in the second century for the silver, the good condition of the pieces in the British Museum from the Cani Island hoard,[13] of 146 BC, makes it tempting to think that they were made just before or during the Third Punic War,[14] and this would provide an obvious occasion for the gold as well.[15]

The fall of Carthage in 146 brought a complete change in the precious metal currency of Africa. Gold coinage completely disappears, and Punic silver was replaced by Roman denarii, as a number of hoards show, the earliest of which dates to about 125 BC.

These hoards, with only one exception, consist exclusively of denarii. The exception is the Cani Island hoard, which has a mixture of Republican denarii, down to 146 BC, and Punic silver of the last group discussed above. Given the date of the latest denarius, the hoard should probably be regarded as plunder taken from the destruction of Carthage (it also included silver ornaments),[16] and so not typical of coinage in circulation (and hence not suggestive of a period, however short, of a mixed currency of Punic and Roman coins).

Apart from the Cani Island hoard, the hoards we know all contain only denarii. Unfortunately there seem to be very few reports of these hoards and even fewer details of their contents (see apendix), so it is not possible at the moment to see if there is any pattern in their geographical or chronological distribution.

Outside the Roman province, in Mauretania and Numidia (with its Tripolitanian addition) there is even less evidence. The only substantial coinage is of the Numidian king Massinissa, which may but probably did not continue after his death,[17] and which consisted of only base metal pieces. There is no Numidian silver, either of Massinissa or, as used to be thought, of Jugurtha and Hiempsal, and Massinissa's coins are either of bronze or lead, the latter apparently being intended for use in graves.[18] His coins are found widely around the western Mediterranean,[19] and presumably represent occasional losses, whether at first hand or subsequently, by travellers including traders (although this is not to imply that they were objects of trade). Similar explanations may well be valid for the foreign coins, of Athens, Cyrenaica, Rhodes, Massalia and Rome, which have been reported from Algeria;[20] the presence of Italian businessmen at Cirta (modern Constantine), the capital of Numidia, is notoriously well known for the time of the war against Jugurtha (112-106 BC),[21] as is that of the Greeks, whom, according to Strabo,[22] Micipsa encouraged to settle there. The peculiar silver hoard from Cirta, which apparently contained a mixture of silver coins of Iberia, Massalia, Athens and Rome, may also reflect the activities of traders; on the other hand, its probable date of deposition, about 105 BC,[23] invites some connection with the Jugurthine War, so perhaps we are dealing with a mercenary's various wages.

For the province of Africa, however, it is hard to see any numismatic sign of the Jugurthine War. Neither Jugurtha or Rome minted coins in Africa: according to Sallust,[24] Jugurtha made payments of silver bullion, while we hear, in 111 and 110 BC, of the Romans sending money, stipendium, with their armies to Africa.[25] The similar despatch of money is reported for Pompey's campaigns against Domitius and Hiarbas in 82 BC,[26] but neither this or Sertorius's brief crossing to Africa in 81/0 has left any clear material trace.

The next event to affect Africa was the civil war between Pompey and Caesar, when coins were struck by both sides in the area. Reasonable numbers of denarii (and some rare quinarii) were struck by Metellus Pius and Cato in 47/6 BC,[27] and perhaps also by the Caesarians.[28] This war too is surely the historical explanation for the silver coinage of Juba I, the partisan of Pompey who died in 46. His coinage first appears in hoards of 46,[29] and so was probably minted late in the reign (60-46). Some confirmation of the date can perhaps be seen in the smallest silver denominations he minted. As well as quinarii, he also produced silver sestertii,[30] a denomination which is not likely to have been minted before the revival of the silver sestertius at Rome in 48. There is then quite good evidence that Juba's silver was struck in 47/6 to aid the Pompeian cause.[31] We can also see that his contribution was of a fairly substantial size. Using hoards we can establish that the issue was larger than Cato's, but somewhat smaller than Metellus Pius's.[32]

The same explanation probably holds good for the rare silver coins of Bogud, king of Mauretania from 49 to 38 BC.[33] Because of their rarity, these coins do not appear in hoards, but it seems reasonable to regard them as minted in 47/6, although on a very small scale.

These coins of Juba and of Bogud also illustrate the complete integration of the coinage of Africa - not just the Roman province - with that of Rome, at least as far as precious metals go. The denarii of both were interchangeable, as can be seen from the widespread circulation of Juba's denarii in hoards of late Republican and early Imperial times together with Roman denarii.[34] There is even a quinarius of Juba in a find from France (of 31 BC), along with Roman denarii and quinarii.[35] All three denominations, denarii, quinarii and sestertii, were struck at Roman weight standards, and the interchangeability of the two currencies is neatly illustrated by one of the very few provenances for Roman silver sestertii of the Caesarian age, one of which was found in Tunis.[36] The coinage of Bogud, too, illustrates the integration of non-Roman with Roman, since his denarii were struck on the Roman standard, and in one case over a Roman denarius.[37] His coins are denarii in every sense.

Before considering the bronze coinage of Africa, mention must be made of a small issue of silver, made by the city of Lepcis Magna.[38] It is the only example of local silver from Africa (the other alleged issue, from Hadrumetum, is not authentic[39]), and is known from only a very few pieces[40] with the designs of the attributes of Heracles and Dionysus, the patron deities of Lepcis. When was it minted? It has been suggested that it too was struck during the Pompeian civil war;[41] another possibility, on Spanish and north Italian analogies, is early in the first century BC. Müller thought, on the contrary, tht it was made just before or during the reign of Augustus,[42] while Grant believed it marked a gift of freedom to the city in about 8 BC.[43] While the reasons advanced by Müller and Grant are not all very cogent, I think that they were probably right. An examination of the epigraphy of coins of Lepcis reveals that they use two forms of the neo-Punic letter Y in the ethnic LPQY.[44] The first form is used on all the apparently pre-Augustan issues and on several of the issues in Augustus's name, one of which can presumably be dated no earlier than about 15 BC since it copies the capricorn from Augustan denarii of early in the teens.[45] The second form is used only on one Augustan issue (with peacock) and on all the Tiberian issues (including some "autonomous" ones).[46] The silver coin has the second form of the letter, and so must be later than 15 BC, although how much later is impossible to say.

The coin looks as if it is supposed to be a denarius, although, as Müller observed, its weight is rather low (the one in the British Museum weighs 2.77, and Müller gives a weight of 2.85).[47] It is presumably supposed to be a denarius of the reduced weight standard used by Juba II, for Juba II and his successor Ptolemaeus did not continue the practice of Juba I, to mint coins on the exact model of Roman denarii. They, on the other hand, minted coins on a lower standard, presumably as one of the measures taken to establish their kingdom as a closed currency area on the Hellenistic model.[48]

The bronzes minted in Africa raise two questions. As with the silver, there is the question of when they were made, and there is also the problem of the denominations they use. For the reign of Augustus we are very fortunate in having coins from Leptis Minor, bearing as value marks the Greek letterrs delta, beta and alpha, that is 4, 1 and 1 as.[49] There are two series. One is dated by Tiberius's titles to the very end of Augustus's reign, but the other, struck with obverses of DIVOS IVLIVS and CAESAR DIVI F (the two obverses are die-linked, so form a single series), is much earlier; a date of about 30 BC has been suggested.[50] The 4 as coins have a characteristic flan, with a diameter of about 35mm. and a weight of about 30 grams, a flan which is recognisable on coins of Augustus and Tiberius from other African sities, such as Hadrumetum, Thapsus, Lepcis Magna, Achulla, and indeed coins of Juba II.[51] These coins seem clearly intended to pass as 4-as coins or sestertii, their weight being heavier than sestertii of Rome to compensate, as in Spain, for their lack of orichalcum. From this reasonably secure starting point, one can classify most of the imperial smaller bronzes as dupondii and asses, with weights and diameters of about 26mm/15g and 22mm/8g respectively.

When does this denominational structure appear? Not much, if at all, before the reign of Augustus, since the earliest coins with these characteristic flan shapes seem to be the coins from the first series of Leptis Minor. Their exact date is, however, slightly uncertain: against the appearance of Divos Iulius, which suggests an early date, must be set the consideration that the new broad flan shape seems most likely to be derived from or a reflection of the new Augustan sestertii, which would imply a date of about 20 BC.

Before this the picture is unclear. The coins of the various kings and cities have various weight standards, and we must ask, first, do they adhere to Roman denominations, and, secondly, if so, how? Neither question can be clearly answered. One might perhaps argue that the appearance of value marks at Leptis Minor implies a change from a different system of denominations; but this innovation might only indicate that new sorts of coin were being introduced for the same old, i.e. Roman, denominations. There is, moreover, a presumption that areas which embraced the Roman silver monetary system would also have adopted bronze denominations, although late Republican Sicily[52] shows that this is not necessarily compelling.

On the assumption that Roman denominations were used, one can perhaps look for coins which might be convincingly identified with them. There are, in fact, two good candidates for pre-Augustus asses which can be found in Mauretania.[53] These are the very rare bronzes of Bogud, which are some 25 mm. in diameter and 12g. in weight; on the obverse they have a head, possibly the king's portrait, and on the reverse a prow highly reminiscent of the prow on Republican bronzes. I tend to the view that these coins are asses, on the semuncial standard. This is, of course, lighter than the contemporary Pompeian asses, some of which are found in Africa, but the same as the slightly later asses of L Atratinus (minted in N W Asia Minor) or the coins inscribed REX BOCCHVS SOSI F in latin and 'Bocchus King' in neo-Punic.[54] These coins, with a head of Africa and a Janus head, were minted perhaps in Cherchel in the reign of Bocchus, and also seem clearly intended to be asses, to judge from the Janus head.

These coins support the idea that Roman bronze denominations were used in Africa before Augustus, but it seems to me quite pointless to try and apply Roman names to the other coins of this period, since we can never be sure exactly which coin was supposed to be which denomination, a situation familiar from other areas of Roman provincial numismatics.

A related question is of course the date of the civic coins of the Roman provinces of Africa, in the cases where there is no portrait of Augustus, Tiberius or a proconsul to help. Such issues occur at Lepcis, Oea, Sabrata, Alipota, Hadrumetum, Hippo and Utica. There is no good evidence, as far as I know, from hoards or excavations to help, and we must fall back on style and fabric. Few views seem to have ever been expressed on this question. Jenkins, in his Sylloge of the Copenhagen collection, assigned everything to the first century BC, with the single exception of the coins with the Dioscouri which he correctly assigned to Utica,[55] which he dated to the second century. This dating has been followed by Alexandropoulos, who pointed out the similarities of fabric with the second century coins of Carthage and Numidia.[56]

All the remaining issues are usually dated to the first century, but this is at least partially misleading, since it seems clear that a number of them are "autonomous" imperial issues. This can be seen, for example, from the copying of Augustan types at Oea[57] or Sabrata,[58] the presence of magistrates known on imperial coins (Sabrata)[59] or for stylistic and epigraphical reasons (Lepcis).[60] The remaining quantity of civic bronzes is very small indeed, and almost non-existent in the Roman provice. We may perhaps assume that most of it was made during the civil wars from 49, on the analogy of the function of the coins of Juba I[61] and Bogud, but this is not sure.

If, then, hardly any bronze was minted in the province of Africa during the first 100 years or so of its existence, the question arises as to what bronze coins were used there. The bulk of the bronze currency seems in fact to have consisted of the earlier coins of Carthage, which, unlike Punic silver and gold, remained in circulation until imperial times.[62] To these were added the small issues of Utica, and apparently a fairly small quantity of Roman Republican bronzes. Roman bronzes have been reported in small quantities from Africa,[63] and, while it seems likely enough that at least some of them reached the province in Republican times, their presence at the second century sites like Lambaesis (constructed under Hadrian)[64] raises the possibility that some of them may have been later imports.

We can then trace the rough outline of the history of African currency, but cannot fill in any of the details. It is not possible to identify different patterns of circulation, on a geographical or chronological basis. We might guess that there was a reduced function for coinage after the fall of Carthage, since Punic coinage seems to have been related mainly to expenditure on mercenaries. After 146, monetary activity would have been reduced to any remaining functions, no doubt stimulated from time to time by the arrival of various Roman armies with money to spend in the markets which grew up by their camps.[65] The Caesarian wars may also have stimulated indigenous civic issues, but the real increase seems to have come with the reign of Augustus.

Appendix: hoards of denarii from Africa (see Crawford, CMRR App. 42).

TUNISIA

1. Cani Island, 1926.
146 BC
18 Carthage (SNG Cop. 403-6)
132 denarii (to C Antesti, RRC 219)
silver bracelets
RRCH 132 = IGCH 2301

2. Henchir-Djebel-Dis, 1913.
about 125 BC
23 denarii to T Q (RRC 267)
RRCH 160

3. Hamman-Lif, near Tunis, 1903.
about 75 BC

The reports about the hoard's contents vary somewhat. Gauckler, Compte rendu de la marche du Service 1903 (Tunis, 1904) records that 200 pieces were acquired by the Bardo Museum, while Gsell (MEFR 1904, 339) talks of 'un millier'. A fuller record is given by de Bray, Bull. de la Soc. Arch. de Sousse 1907, 98-100: he gives the total as about 800; he gives a list of the gentes represented in the parcel of 140 pieces examined by him, but frustratingly does not give the detailed references to Babelon, which he says he used. He says that "les dernières, appartenant aux Gens Caecilia et Cornelia, sont de 74 av. J.-C." Babelon has no Caecilia for 74; he does have one for 79 (= RRC 374, 81BC). Babelon has two Cornelias for 74; one is now dated to 76/5 (RRC 393), the other to 74 (RRC 397).

4. Sminja, 1938.
45 BC
944 denarii and 5 quinarii to Sex Magnus Pius Imp (RRC 477)
RRCH 395

5. Mateur.
Uncertain date
The only reference to the hoard (MEFR 1904, 339) mentions "une centaine" of Republican denarii, but gives no details.

6. Fernana.
Uncertain date.
17 denarii.
The coins are described only as "de la République romaine" (Bull. Arch. de Com. des Trav. Hist, 1902, cxvii).

7. Uzita, 1971.
?AD 14
64 denarii to Augustus
JMP 1971-2, 144.

ALGERIA

8. Constantine, before 1912.
about 105 BC.
12 drachms of Massalia

75 Iberian denarii
14 Athenian new style tetradrachms
136 denarii: "les deniers les plus récents et les plus nombreux (16 ex.) appartenaient à L. Thorius Balbus" = RRC 316 (105 BC).
IGCH 2306.

9. Bettioua (ancient Portus Magnus), about 1940.
about 60 denarii ("de la Répbulique romaine")
P. Salama, Simposium Numimatico de Barcelona Vol. II (Barcelona, 1979), p. 126 no. 17.

10. Rasseremt, 1952.
after 2 BC
2 denarii (Caesar with elephant, and Augustus/C L Caesares)
RRCH 544.

MOROCCO

11. Casablanca, 1926 (from a wreck on the beach)
17 BC
168 + denarii to Augustus's "Spanish" issues.
The publication, which is detailed and well-illustrated, is obviously selective, since, e.g., it describes one coin of each of Antony's legionary denarii.
J.D. Brethes, Contribution a l'histoire du Maroc par les recherches numismatiques (Basablanca, 1937), 5-17.

There is also an Augustan gold hoard of about 20 coins from Tipasa (Salama (n. 22), p. 131 no. 71).

NOTES

1. E.S.G. Robinson, "Punic Coins of Spain and their bearings on the Roman Republican series", in Essays Presented to Harold Mattingly, ed. R.A.G. Carson and C.H.V. Sutherland (Oxford, 1956), 35-6.

2. G.K. Jenkins and R.B. Lewis, Carthaginian and Gold and Electrum Coins (London, 1963), p. 47 (group XIV).

3. See, for instance, the discussion by L. Villaronga, Las Monedas hispano-Cartaginesas (Barcelona, 1973), p. 159 no. 34: "Robinson la (the overstruck coin) compara con las procedentes de El Djem, y cree esta reacunada sobre de estas monedas. Consultando este problema al professor Jenkins, nos comunica que cree se trata de una reacunacion sobre otra moneda hispanica de la serie 2k de Robinson". Consequently the El Djem coinage was dated by Jenkins in SNG Copenhagen for Africa (1969) to "late CIII - early CII BC".

4. H.R. Baldus, 'Naravas und seine Reiter', Deutscher Numismatikertag Munchen 1981 (Bayer. Num. Gesellschaft, 1983), 15.

5. Livy xxxii, 2, 1-2.

6. Jenkins and Lewis (n. 2), group XVIII.

7. E.g. SNG Cop. 399-400.

8. Jenkins and Lewis group XVIII.

9. SNG Cop. 403-8.

10. SNG Cop. 409-13.

11. Cf. Jenkins and Lewis (n. 2), p. 53-4.

12. This remark is based on an examination of the 23 silver coins in the British Musuem; for the single obverse die for each of the two gold denominations, see Jenkins and Lewis (n. 2), group XVIII.

13. RRCH 132 = IGCH 2301; see appendix.

14. Baldus (no. 4), 15, however, dates the silver to the early second century.

15. The occasion also suggested by Baldus (no. 4), 15.

16. The hoard does not seem to have been used by Crawford in establishing his Republican chronology, and so provides good confirmation for his dating of this period.

17. Crawford CMRR 140-1.

18. J. Baradez Libyca 5 (1957), 226, Latomus 58 (1962), 216-7.

19. S. Gsell, Histoire ancienne de l'Afrique du Nord (Paris, 1913), VI. 80 gives references to finds in Spain, France and Yugoslavia (on the last, see Crawford, CMRR appendix 49); see also B. Fischer, Les monnaies antiques d'Afrique du Nord trouvées en Gaule (Paris, 1978), and P. Salama, "Huit siècles de circulation monétaire sur les sites cotiers de Mauretanie," Symposium Numismatico de Barcelona II (Barcelona, 1978), 113.

20. Gsell (n. 19) VI. 80, Salama (n. 19), 114.

21. Sallust Jugurtha XXI.2, XXVI.1-2 (Italici), XXVI. 3 (negotiatores), Diod. Sic. XXXIV-V. 31.

22. Strabo XVII. 3. 13 (832).

23. IGCH 2306; see appendix no. 9, for the correct date; cf. Crawford, CMRR 141.

24. Sallust Jugurtha XXIX. 6, LXII.5.

25. Sallust Jugurtha XXVII.5, XXXVI.1.

26. Plutarch Pompey II.

27. RRC 459-462.

28. RRC 458.

29. RRCH 383 and 384 (the latter from France).

30. SNG Cop. 526.

31. The same date was suggested by F. Bertrandy, 'Remarques sur l'origine romaine du monnayage en bronze et en argent de Juba Ier, roi de Numidie', Bull. Arch. du Com. des Trav. Hist. et Sci. 12-14 (1976-78) fasicule B (1980), 9-20, on the basis of the stylistic similarity of the denarii of Juba with those of Cato and Metellus Pius. For the same reason Bertrandy suggested that Juba's silver was minted at Utica; he also suggested that the coins were minted from bullion given to Juba by the Pompeians.

32. The same hoards as used by Crawford RRC II, table L include a total of 12 coins (RRCH 440: 4/1671; RRCH 475: 2/740; RRCH 488: 2/422; RRCH 493: 3/689; RRCH 506: 1/870). The same hoards included 8 coins of Cato and 39 of Metellus. For what it is worth, the 11 legible denarii in the British Museum were struck from 10 obverse dies. Crawford, CMRR 246-7 slightly overestimates the size of Juba's coinage.

33. J. Mazard Corpus Nummorum Numidiae Mauretaniaeque (Paris, 1955), nos. 103-5. I have noted weights of 2.90, 3.55, 3.76, 3.64, 3.50 and 3.55.

34. They occur in many of the hoards from RRCH 383 to 546, and, of course, in later imperial hoards until Flavian times.

35. RRCH 516.

36. A piece of C Considi (RRC 465/8) from Tunis is reported by F. Caronni, Ragguaglio del Viaggio Compendioso di un Dilettante Antiquario (Milan, 1805), plate V. 28 (a reference I owe to M.H. Crawford).

37. The piece in the British Museum is overstruck on a denarius with a turretted head, perhaps RRC 409, 419 or 431.

38. L. Müller, Numismatique de l'anciennne Afrique (Copenhagen, 1864-6), no. 13.

39. The coin which was still accepted by M. Grant, FITA 227 and 340 was discarded by H. Dressel, ZfN 1912, 109 n. 2 as being a bronze coin silvered in modern times. M. Amandry tells me that the coin has been recently relocated and is to be analysed.

40. Müller (n. 38) coites "Coll. de feu M. Tochon d'Annecy (2 ex., Cat. de Vente no. 986) et M. Judas". The Judas piece was acquired by the British Museum (1867-11-9-113, 2.77g); the whereabouts of the others is not known to me, although one of them may have weighed 2.85g, which Müller gives as a weight. The BM coin is illustrated by G.K. Jenkins, 'Some ancient coins of Libya', The Society for Libyan Studies. Fifth Annual Report, 1973-74, pl. XVIII.1-2.

41. Jenkins (n. 40) 33-34, Gsell (n. 19), VII. 42-3.

42. Müller (n. 38) p. 14 "...se rapproche le plus au regne d'Auguste, ou parait meme frappe sous celui-ci". His view was based on the low weight, the types, which he compared with ones used by Juba II, and the guess that the letter A on the coins stood for Augustus.

43. FITA 340.

44. The first form is used on SNG Cop. 1.-4, 6-8 and 10-15, as well as another type (Müller 16); the second on SNG Cop. 5, 9, 16-19.

45. SNG Cop. 15. Müller 16 is described as "Tiberius", but could as well be Augustus.

46. SNG Cop. 16 (peacock); for the Tiberian "autonomous" coins, see n. 60.

47. See note 40.

48. Hoards of the period contain only Mauretanian silver (e.g. IGCH 2307-09). Crawford, CMRR 249 thinks that Mauretania was probably fully integrated into the Roman monetary system. The evidence to which he alludes is presumably the Rasseremt "hoard" (RRCH 544, appendix no. 10). As this contained only two denarii it could be rather later, and its apparent implication, that Roman denarii entered Mauretania in large numbers, seems refuted by the other hoards.

49. M. Amandry, 'Le Monnayage Augustéen de Leptis Minor' SM 33 (1983), 11-14.

50. Amandry, (n. 49).

51. J. Alexandropoulos, 'La circulation monétaire en Afrique Proconsulaire de 146 avant J.-C. à la fin du règne de Tibére', REA LXXXIV (1982), 96-103, at 98-101.

52. M.H. Crawford, CMRR 114, and App. L.

53. There are, apparently, only four specimens: one in Copenhagen (SNG 537, 12.41g.), one found at Thamusida (J.-P. Callu, J.-P. Morel, R. Rebuffat and G. Hallier, Thamusida I (Paris, 1965), p. 76 and pl. LIV. 4 (10.8g.), and 2 from Banasa in Rabat (J. Marion, 'Notes sur quelques monnaies maurétaniennes inédites', Bull. Arch. Maroc. IV (1960), p. 62 no. 106: 11.05 and 9.1g, both in poor condition).

54. Attributed to Tingi by Grant FITA 175; see Mazard (n. 33) nos. 118-121. The only provenances seems to be Gunugu (Salama (n. 19) no. 37) and Caesarea (Libyca 1956, 59), perhaps suggesting Cherchel as the mint.

55. Specimens have been found at Tunis (F. Caronni (n. 36), pl. V. 23, and Carthage (in the recent British excavations), which obviously support the attribution.

56. Alexandropoulos (n. 51), 96-8.

57. The type with two or one shields and spears are copies or adaptations of the C L Caesares gold and silver type of Augustus (SNG Cop. 23-4 and 26).

58. The capricorn and globe (SNG Cop. 43-46) copied from Augustan denarii of the teens BC (cf. no. 45).

59. SNG Cop. 43-6.

60. See note 44. This consideration makes it clear that SNG Cop. 5 and 9 are the two smallest denominations of the Tiberian issue (SNG Cop. 17, and 18-19).

61. Bertrandy (n. 31) suggests that Juba's bronzes were minted at the beginning of the reign, but his reasons do not seem compelling.

62. Alexandropoulos (n. 51), 97. R. Cagnat, 'Remarques sur les monnaies usitées dans l'Afrique romaine à l'époque du Haut-empire', Klio 9 (1909), 194-205 gives instances of Punic and Numidian coins from imperial contexts, for instance the 11 Punic and 24 Numidian pieces found at Lambaesis (founded under Hadrian). Salama (n. 22)[113] regards these survivals as of negligible importance.

63. Alexandropoulos (n. 51), 97 "...l'expérience des nombreuses petites collections privées que nous avons vues semble montrer que si l'on trouve des bronzes républicains en Afrique proconsulaire, ils ne constituent qu'un modeste apport a la circulation monétaire". H.R. Baldus has kindly told me of Republican bronzes from the excavations at Bulla Regia and Chemtou, both in the interior) and from the excavations at Carthage (including a quadrans): another as was found at Thamusida in Morocco (n. 53), 77, and a second in a second century BC tomb at Las Andalouses, Algeria (Salama (n. 22) p. 125 no. 7a). None of the British, American or Canadian reports on the recent Carthage excavations includes any Republican bronzes.

64. Cagnat (n. 62).

65. Vividly described by Sallust Jugurtha XLIV. 5.

www.ingramcontent.com/pod-product-compliance
Lightning Source LLC
LaVergne TN
LVHW071209210926
848482LV00015B/763